GUIDE to the coast of VICTORIA, TASMANIA and SOUTH AUSTRALIA

Reader's Digest Guide to the coast of Victoria, Tasmania and South Australia was edited and designed by Reader's Digest Services Pty Limited, Sydney

Contributing editor: Robert Pullan

Contributors
Elizabeth Denley, PhD, Hopkins Marine Station, California
Robert Duffield
Jenny Flute
Edgar Frankel, PhD, Lecturer in Sedimentology, Department of Geology
  and Mineralogy, University of Queensland
Carol Frith, BSc(Hons), Coastal Studies Unit, University of Sydney
Pat Hatchings, PhD, Curator of Marine Invertebrates, The Australian Museum, Sydney
Brian Lees, BA(Hons), Coastal Studies Unit, University of Sydney
Dick Lewers
Dr Ian Mackie, Honorary Education Officer, The Surf Life Saving Association of Australia
Gia Metherell
Jo Moss BSc
David Pollard, PhD, Senior Research Scientist, New South Wales State Fisheries
Jeff Toghill
Lyle Vail, Technical Officer, The Australian Museum, Sydney
Alan Yuille, BArch

Aerial Photography
Qasco Pty Limited, Sydney.
Additional aerial photography by Stereomatic
Services, Melbourne

Illustrators
Sheila Hadley
David Horne
Sue Oakes
Margaret Senior
Robyn Single

Maps by Reader's Digest

First edition
Published by Reader's Digest Services Pty Limited (Inc. in NSW)
26-32 Waterloo Street, Surry Hills NSW 2010
Part of the material in this book first appeared in Reader's Digest Guide
to the Australian Coast, first published by Reader's Digest in 1983.

© 1986 Reader's Digest Services Pty Ltd
© 1986 Reader's Digest Association Far East Limited
Philippines copyright 1986 Reader's Digest Association Far East Limited

National Library of Australia cataloguing-in-publication data:
Reader's Digest Guide to the coast of Victoria, Tasmania and South
Australia
 Includes index
 ISBN 0 86438 010 0
 1. Coasts – Australia, Southeastern – Guide-books.
 2. Australia, Southeastern – Description and travel –
 Guide-books. I. Reader's Digest Services.
 II. Title: Guide to the coast of Victoria, Tasmania and South Australia.
919.4'0463

Typeset by Adtype Photocomposition, Sydney
Printed and bound by Dai Nippon Printing Co. Ltd., Hong Kong

Reader's Digest

GUIDE to the coast of VICTORIA, TASMANIA and SOUTH AUSTRALIA

Contents

Introduction

THE coasts of Victoria, South Australia and Tasmania, forming the greater part of Australia's magnificent underside, offer the traveller a refreshing diversity. In contrast to the country's more commercially developed east coast, here dramatic natural scenery and the subtleties of wildlife are emphasized. Varying influences are brought to bear by the bodies of water associated with this coast—the Tasman Sea, the Bass Strait, the Great Australian Bight and so on. The notoriously stormy Southern Ocean reveals markedly different characteristics as it washes the Victorian and South Australian coasts.

Whether their preference is for the peaceful Gippsland Lakes or the spectacle of the sea's fury around Mornington Peninsula, the safe shallow suburban beaches of Adelaide or the extraordinary limestone formations at Port Campbell National Park, the residents of the south's great population centres can find scope for every type of seaside recreation. Conservation deserves special mention, because this sector of Australia has distinguished itself with the creation of numerous refuges for rare or threatened wildlife species.

Traces of history abound, from the penal colonies of Tasmania to the remains of formerly great trading ports for wool and grain (superseded by the railways) to the Great Ocean Road, heroically hewn by returned World War I servicemen. In some areas, concentrations of wrecks—victims of the Southern Ocean's treachery—remain to fascinate today's divers.

Here, as elsewhere around Australia's shores, all water sports are enthusiastically pursued. Almost all Australians can swim; they surf in their hundreds of thousands and boat in their millions. By far the predominant water activity, however, is fishing. An estimated 30 per cent of all Australians go fishing, and this proportion rises to 60 per cent among boys aged between 13 and 17.

Guide to the Coast of Victoria, Tasmania and South Australia is for all those who visit the seashore—whatever their special interests. The core of the book, Discovering the Coast, is a guide for travellers and coast users. Scores of aerial photographs, many of them joined together in a unique series of panoramas, show the most attractive and easily accessible parts of the coast in unsurpassed detail. The photographs are supported by a thorough and up-to-date description of the places depicted and their attractions. We have divided these coasts into six regions, each of which is introduced with notes on its general nature and climate, and a map.

Three additional parts of the book provide important information for those who visit the coast. Part one—Understanding the Coast—describes the range of plants and animals that live around the shore. The aim is to help visitors identify some of the things they see, and also to understand how plants and animals interact with one another in a range of habitats. Drawings of birds, shells and marine creatures make identification of common species easy.

Part two—The Ocean and the Weather—will be particularly useful for swimmers, surfers and boat owners. A basic understanding of winds, tides, waves and currents will help readers to avoid some of the dangers of nearshore waters, and also to make the best use of conditions they encounter.

Part three—Advice for Holidaymakers—is addressed to particular groups of coast users. There is information for fishermen, boat owners, swimmers and surfers as well as general advice on first aid, access and hazards.

Two indexes, one listing all the places mentioned in the book and the other the subjects, make it easy to find any information quickly.

THE EDITORS

PART 1

Understanding the coast

Nature's ingenuity meets no sterner test than on the seashore. Life forms have to contend with changeable environments—neither wholly marine nor wholly terrestrial—and on much of the coast they must withstand the violent assault of waves.

In the face of such adversity, shore zones could be assumed to be biologically impoverished.

On the contrary, they are the special domains of a diverse range of animals and plants, intriguing in their ways of adaptation and often astonishing in their profusion.

Many of the most interesting creatures go unnoticed. And such is their degree of specialisation that they are restricted to particular habitats.

The curious need to know not only what to look for, but also where to look.

A grasp of geological and geographical factors brings a fuller appreciation of the richness of coastal life.

With it comes awareness of how delicately this life is balanced—and of the dangers posed by unwise human pressure.

A group of sea lions basking among seaweed on a Kangaroo Island beach

What makes a coast   Natural forms that change with time

A coast is a battlefront—a line where land, sea and air meet that changes from second to second, season to season, decade to decade and millennium to millennium. Short term changes, over a range of metres, occur as waves break and move sediments on or off shore and as tide-waves cause the local sea level to rise and fall. In the longer term erosion and accretion change the coastline, sometimes on a scale of kilometres a century. Over tens of thousands of years sea levels rise and fall by hundreds of metres as ice ages come and go. Coasts are always changing—they can never be regarded as permanent. It is only because the large scale changes seem to occur so slowly, in terms of human lifetimes, that people come to regard the shoreline as fixed.

Ancient coastlines can be found scores of kilometres inland. Others are far out to sea. The earliest fluctuations were associated with the evolution of land masses over hundreds of millions of years: their emergence and erosion, their repeated submergences and reappearances, the transformation of their material under pressure, their distortion by twisting, folding and fracturing, and their disruption by volcanic activity. The coast near Mount Gambier in South Australia has risen in the last few thousand years, while the Murray River mouth region has subsided; Melbourne's shores on Port Phillip Bay surround an area of recent sinking. Nevertheless the Australian land mass is now relatively stable. Unlike New Zealand or New Guinea, it is far from any point where the earth's mobile crustal plates collide. So throughout the time of human occupation, the most striking shifts of the Australian coastline have been caused by changes in the sea level.

The planet's total store of moisture has probably remained much the same since its crust solidified. But the distribution of that moisture—in the oceans, on or under the land, in the atmosphere or locked in ice—has varied vastly. Even a small change in temperature affects the density of water, causing it to expand or contract signifi-

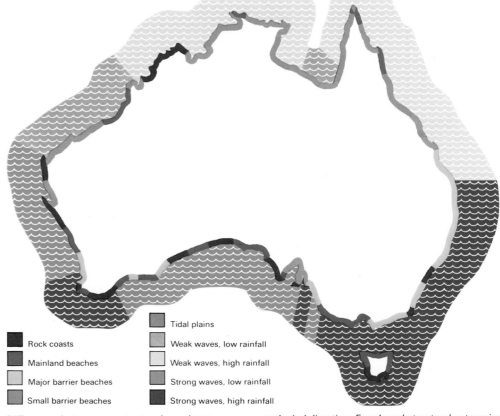

Rock coasts
Mainland beaches
Major barrier beaches
Small barrier beaches
Tidal plains
Weak waves, low rainfall
Weak waves, high rainfall
Strong waves, low rainfall
Strong waves, high rainfall

Differences between coasts at various places around the continent are the result of a combination of factors, such as rock type, the power of local waves, the width of the continental shelf, rainfall and wind direction. Four broad structural categories describe the physical appearance of any particular coast, and four climatic categories encompass the important forces that helped to shape the shoreline

cantly. A fall of just 1°C in the overall average temperature of the oceans would lower sea levels by about 2 metres. And that is only a minor effect of climatic change. Prolonged reduction of average atmospheric temperatures actually robs the oceans of water. Evaporated moisture, instead of returning in the usual cycle of conden-sation, precipitation and run-off, stays frozen on the land. During the most recent ice age, which had its maximum effect between 50 000 and 10 000 years ago, so much moisture accumulated in icecaps that the sea level receded more than 100 metres. Its ascent when melting set in was an uneven process over thousands of years,

The evolution of Botany Bay

ANCIENT estuaries all around the coast were 'drowned' when the sea returned to its present level after the last ice age. It was a gradual process, with marine sand being pushed up to form barriers in places where there was a large enough supply of sand, and then driven ashore to form beach ridges and dunes, and also into estuaries. Here is a geologist's reconstruction of what happened in Botany Bay, Sydney.

Vegetated land
Cliffs, rock platforms
Mobile sand
Water
Vegetated sand

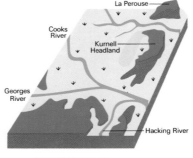

Before 9000 years ago

With the sea more than 20 metres below today's level, Botany Bay was a swampy plain, interrupted by occasional rocky outcrops. Many of the sediments were left over from the last period of high sea levels

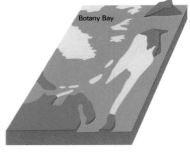

9000-7000 years ago

Seas rising to 9 metres below their present level moved a sand barrier onshore to enclose a shallow estuary: longshore drift swept sand north past the headland and around into the newly formed bay

interrupted by spells of renewed glaciation.

Sea levels regarded as normal today were attained about 6000 years ago. There are signs, however, that the oceans came even higher during some more recent periods. At no time may constancy be taken for granted.

Scientists may classify coasts of various kinds in a dozen or more categories, related mainly to their origins. In terms of natural life and the human use of Australia's shores, climatic conditions are more important and only four broad structural distinctions are needed: rock, mainland beach, barrier beach and tidal plain. **Rock coasts,** all cliffed to some degree, occur largely in the south and the north-west. If beaches occur at all, they are pockets of minor significance. **Mainland beach coasts** (the term applies also to Tasmania and other major islands) may have some rocky sections, accompanied by shore platforms, but extensive open beaches are predominant. On **barrier beach coasts,** beaches have formed offshore in the vicinity of rocky promontories, enclosing or nearly enclosing lagoons and estuaries between themselves and the old shore. Where wave action is consistently powerful the barrier is the dominant feature, containing a massive accumulation of sand. Otherwise it is the lagoon or estuary margins that give the coast its character. Major barriers are commonest on the east coast between the Tropic of Capricorn and Bass Strait, and in eastern South Australia and south of Perth. Small barriers are mostly found on the tropical Queensland and Northern Territory coasts. **Tidal plain coasts** are usually marked by the growth of salt-marsh plants or mangroves, and sometimes in the tropical zone by fringing coral. They are extensive between North-West Cape and Port Hedland, and occur elsewhere in gulfs.

On a coastline as extensive as Australia's, location and climate play significant roles in determining what kind of structure evolves. Deep ocean waves are generally bigger and more powerful in the southern latitudes, and day-to-day local winds are usually stronger. The offshore slope of the sea floor is also steeper towards

Measuring Australia's shores

THE MORE precisely a coast is measured, the longer it becomes. Tracing a simplified outline of Australia, for example, makes the mainland coast seem to be about 15 000 km long. Measurements from detailed sectional maps would produce a total twice as great. And taking the argument to absurdity, it is estimated that if the slighter twists and turns of the coast were charted millimetre by millimetre, the length would be more than 130 000 km. Precision is a matter of what is practical. Geographers have a choice of measuring methods, and a choice of rules as to what should be included—literally, where to draw the line.

Australia's officially recognised measurement was made by government cartographers in 1973. High-water lines were chosen, so mangrove flats and coral reefs were excluded. Open estuaries were cut off where they appeared to take the shape of rivers. On maps of 1:250 000 scale, points about 500 metres apart were plotted. Then it became a theoretical exercise: the straight-line distances between those points were computed and totalled. By that method, the shores of the mainland, Tasmania and the continental shelf islands were taken to be about 36 735 km long.

In 1980, a CSIRO geographer, Dr Robert Galloway, directed a manual measurement of greater precision. Maps of the same scale were used, but this time the entire line of coasts was followed with fine wire. A mid-tide level was taken; mangroves were included but coral reefs were still left out. Islands less than 12 hectares in area were ignored, as were straits less than 1 km wide. Estuaries were cut off where they narrowed to less than 1 km. The total length of the mainland and Tasmanian coasts came to about 30 270 km. Coastline lengths of islands, computed from their areas after one-sixth of them had been measured in detail, came to a further 16 800 km. So by Dr Galloway's method the total is 47 070 km—rather more than the circumference of the earth.

the south and the continental shelf is narrower, permitting more wave energy to be transmitted ashore. This north-south difference in wave energy levels is accentuated by the shape of the continent: its bulges at each side mean that the sections running south from North-West Cape and Fraser Island tend to confront the normal approach of waves, while the receding northern sections do not. Much of the Queensland east coast is further shielded from the full impact of waves by the Great Barrier Reef system.

Another major geographical distinction, in this case roughly between east and west, is created by unevenness of rainfall. Where there is a substantial run-off of rain, at least seasonally, material washed from inland formations contributes to the building of beaches, river mouth bars and nearshore barriers. It also hastens the infilling of enclosed waters, producing new land. But its long-term effects are not so constructive. Sand from inland rocks is rich in silica, which keeps it loose. Water soaks through easily, leaching out minerals that are redeposited on the grain surfaces of underlying material as a skin—this red skin gives silica sand its typical colour, as silica sand without such a skin is white. The layers of heavy 'black sand' sought by mining companies are a result of the different densities of mineral sand and silica sand, and the sorting effect of waves and swash. The sorting effect is similar to that used by prospectors in separating gold from gravel in a pan. Meanwhile the loose, light material above, whether in beaches or dunes, remains prone to destruction by high winds and storm waves.

On arid coasts, however, the major chemical component of beach material is often calcium. Where winds drive the sand inland, piling it up in dune ridges out of the reach of sea water, it is eventually calcified and forms a solid mass of new rock. Many of today's limestone cliffs, islands, offshore stacks and reefs originated as high dune ridges, formed when the sea level was lower and the climate of their hinterland was arid. In the scale of coastal evolution, eons long, such a transformation is merely a passing phase.

7000-4000 years ago

Seas reaching today's levels pushed barrier sand shoreward to form beach ridges along Bate Bay. Wind-waves transported sand from the bed of Botany Bay north and west to the shores of the bay

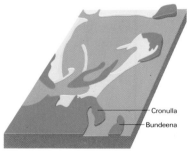

4000-1000 years ago

With the sea close to its present level, there were two phases of parabolic dune emplacement and stabilisation by plants; a long period of coastal stability seems to have followed

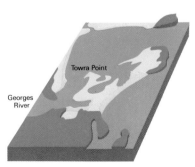

Last 1000 years

The tidal delta of the Georges River took shape, forming Towra Point from a complex of levees, spits and bars; renewed erosion of the barrier beach fed a dune sheet that continues to move today

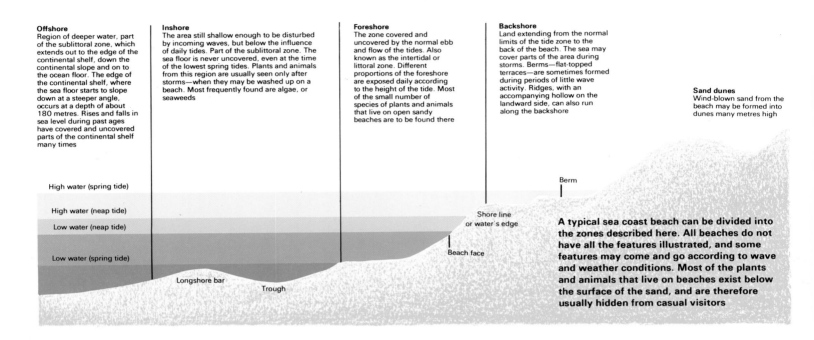

Offshore
Region of deeper water, part of the sublittoral zone, which extends out to the edge of the continental shelf, down the continental slope and on to the ocean floor. The edge of the continental shelf, where the sea floor starts to slope down at a steeper angle, occurs at a depth of about 180 metres. Rises and falls in sea level during past ages have covered and uncovered parts of the continental shelf many times

Inshore
The area still shallow enough to be disturbed by incoming waves, but below the influence of daily tides. Part of the sublittoral zone. The sea floor is never uncovered, even at the time of the lowest spring tides. Plants and animals from this region are usually seen only after storms—when they may be washed up on a beach. Most frequently found are algae, or seaweeds

Foreshore
The zone covered and uncovered by the normal ebb and flow of the tides. Also known as the intertidal or littoral zone. Different proportions of the foreshore are exposed daily according to the height of the tide. Most of the small number of species of plants and animals that live on open sandy beaches are to be found there

Backshore
Land extending from the normal limits of the tide zone to the back of the beach. The sea may cover parts of the area during storms. Berms—flat-topped terraces—are sometimes formed during periods of little wave activity. Ridges, with an accompanying hollow on the landward side, can also run along the backshore

Sand dunes
Wind-blown sand from the beach may be formed into dunes many metres high

High water (spring tide)

High water (neap tide)

Low water (neap tide)

Low water (spring tide)

Longshore bar

Trough

Shore line or water's edge

Beach face

Berm

A typical sea coast beach can be divided into the zones described here. All beaches do not have all the features illustrated, and some features may come and go according to wave and weather conditions. Most of the plants and animals that live on beaches exist below the surface of the sand, and are therefore usually hidden from casual visitors

Sandy shores Beaches and the life they support

What lives on and under beaches, between the high and low tide limits, depends on how the beaches are composed. Beaches of coarse sand usually slope more sharply than those of fine sand, and are more exposed to wave action. They support the lowest number of organisms. Protected beaches with fine sand have many more creatures—provided that the sand is of the right consistency for them to burrow. Plenty of water must be held between the particles. Few animals will be found in the sort of sand that whitens around an area that is trodden. Such sand gives up its moisture too readily under pressure: deeper down, it is too tightly packed to allow

much movement. Some fine sands, however, react to pressure in the opposite way. They become softer and easier to penetrate, and remain moist below the surface.

Sands behave differently because they are made differently—from rocks of varying structure and mineral content. That affects the size, smoothness and slipperiness of particles, as well as the colour of beaches. By no means all beach sand comes from coastal rock in the immediate vicinity. Much may be carried from inland by rivers, by rain run-off or by wind. In some places sand from other coasts is pushed onshore from the sea floor by waves. Tropical mainland

beaches are often composed mostly of coral fragments from reefs. And sands nearly always contain worn-down shell from a multitude of marine organisms, in concentrations that vary locally. On Australia's most frequented non-tropical coasts, however, the mixture is usually dominated by silica in the form of quartz. Its glassy quality keeps the sand loose. Bigger particles and heavier minerals slip down easily, leaving the sands near the surface fine and light. They are prone to erosion and other damage, but in protected conditions they support a fairly large range of animals. Plants in the tide zone are almost non-existent, except for microscopic algae. Bigger seaweeds may inhabit the nearshore if they find purchase on pebbles or heavy shell fragments, and stable backshore and foredune areas are frequently vegetated by banksias, casuarinas and acacias among spinifex grasses and a few flowering plants.

Tiny organisms abound in the spaces between particles of subsurface sand, but special laboratory procedures are required to isolate and study them. In Australia almost nothing is known about such creatures. Only animals more than 3 mm long have been the subject of detailed study, and that has been concentrated on New South Wales beaches. The most obvious of beach-dwellers are ghost crabs, *Ocypode*, distinguished by their paleness and long eye-stalks. Their burrows are well above high water but they forage in the tide zone at night, scampering ahead of human intruders. Also common high on the shore are various species of isopods—little crustaceans that are sometimes called sea-slaters or marine lice. Nearer the water are their

When sand turns back into rock

SAND collecting at great depths in the ocean is converted by pressure into sandstone rock. On arid coasts, dunes rich in calcium solidify as limestone if left undisturbed. Both processes are very slow. But beach sands sometimes cement themselves together as if of their own accord, and with surprising speed. Recent artefacts such as coins and war relics are found in shelves of Australian beach rock.

Scientists are unable to agree on the binding agent in beach rock. Some believe it is calcium carbonate, precipitated during the repeated risings and fallings of the water table under the sand. Others think it is salts deposited when sea water evaporates. Micro-organisms deep in the sand and warm temperatures may aid the process.

The rock is tough enough to resist erosion, so that sheets of it are sometimes left jutting out as the only evidence of a vanished beach.

Beach rock with aircraft wreckage from 1945

Giant beach worms can exceed 2 metres in length. Fishermen use the worms for bait and lure them from their holes with rotten fish. Once the worm's head (below) emerges it can be grasped and the worm pulled from the sand

relatives the amphipods, often known as sand-hoppers or sea-fleas. Sand bubbler crabs, *Scopimera*, are prominent in the intertidal zone. They burrow to the water table, leaving blobs of sand in radiating lines on the surface. Battalions of little pink-and-blue soldier crabs, *Mictyris longicarpus*, frequently emerge from sandy tidal flats, but seldom from beaches where waves break. Of bivalve molluscs buried in the sand, by far the most common is the pipi, *Plebidonax deltoides*. Wedge pipis, cockles and dog cockles are found in deeper water. Smaller bivalves are the principal prey of the giant beach-worm, *Onuphis teres*, which grows to more than 2 metres in length. It is prolific, but seldom seen unless a lure of smelly fish is trailed in the backwash of waves. A smaller worm, *Diopatra dentata*, is best known by the tube that it builds to live in, consisting of shell fragments, small stones and other debris embedded in a fibrous substance. The worm can move freely in and out, so if a tube is pulled from the sand there is rarely an animal inside it.

Small holes seen in a beach surface behind a retreating wave are often assumed to be signs of animals below. If the wave was unusually strong, a few holes or depressions may have been left by pipis or crabs which were uncovered by it and had to burrow deeper. But most holes are formed by the escape of air bubbles, trapped among sediments washed onto the beach. Another false indicator of animal movement is a sharply etched, branched mark at the flattened 'toe' of a sloping beach. Such patterns, called rill marks, are made by runnels of water escaping from higher sand after the tide has ebbed. Other marks, more regularly formed, are clearly the result of water action. Swash marks—sand ridges about 1 mm high, overlapping like curved roof tiles—indicate the farthest points reached by waves. Sand ripples—ridges and troughs in roughly parallel rows—are formed by the churning action of waves running up a beach. If wave motion alone was responsible, the ridges are evenly curved. But if a current was present as well, each ridge is steeper on the side towards which the current was running.

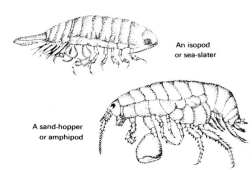

An isopod or sea-slater

A sand-hopper or amphipod

Amphipods and isopods are common on beaches

What the colour of a beach reveals

ALL BEACH sands are mixtures. They include shell and other marine material as well as grains from various types of rock. Nearly all Australian beaches are essentially light-coloured, being dominated either by silica from quartz and feldspar rock or by calcium carbonate of marine origin. Other minerals can produce different hues—some by coating the sands. Colour can be an indicator of many of the principal materials:

Sparkling white	Quartz grains coated with extra silica deposit
Dull white (non-tropical)	Worn quartz on rainy coasts; limestone on arid coasts
Dull white (tropical)	Coral, perhaps with pumice
Creamy/pinkish white	More than 90 per cent quartz
Yellow/gold/light brown	Impure quartz, feldspar, coloured shell
Darker brown	Compounds of iron, etc., coating sand grains
Silver/gold sheen when wet	Surface mica
Grey	Higher concentrations of volcanic or darker sedimentary rock—e.g., basalt or shale
Dark olive	Iron-magnesium-silica compound (eastern Torres Strait)
Black	Basalt dominant; surface iron ore
Dark flecks on pale beach	Fragments of compound granitic rock
Red flecks on tropical beach	'Organ pipe' coral debris
Brown/black lower band	Rutile, ilmenite, iron
Red/brown lower band	Garnet, rutile
Brown/black beach streaks	Organic acid staining
Red/brown/green dune layers	Oxides, etc., of iron or other minerals coating quartz (Queensland 'coloured sands')
Brown/black 'coffee rock'	Sand coated and cemented by iron or manganese compounds

Elusive inhabitants of sandy beaches

The most obvious things on sandy beaches are usually dead plants and animals washed up by the waves. But there are also many things that live in the sand, although they are often difficult to find because they spend most of their lives below the surface, or are too small to see. Many migrate vertically underneath the sand—such as the tiny, shrimp-like amphipods and isopods—while others migrate up and down the beach, towards and away from the water. Very little plant life is found on beaches because there is nothing for the plants to hold on to. There is a greater variety of creatures to be found in fine sand than there is in coarse sand—not so much because of the size of the particles, but rather because fine sand is found where the beach is not being churned up. In particularly calm areas there are lugworms—burrowing worms that leave a coiled cast. Giant beach worms, some longer than 2 metres, abound in some places, but nearly all the bubbling that you see and hear at the water's edge is caused not by worms but by air.

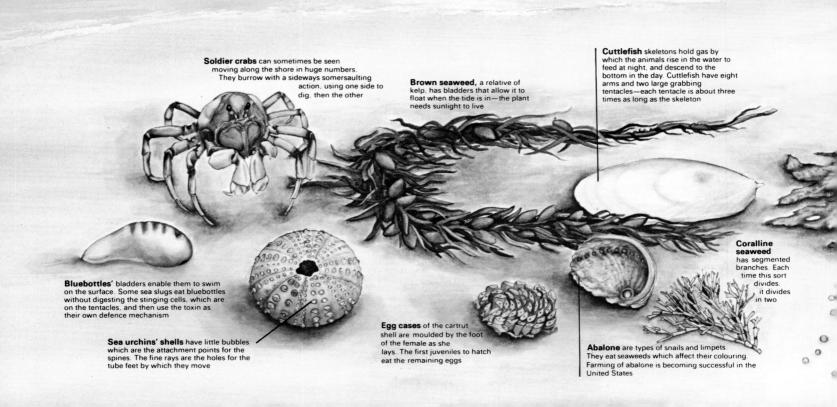

Soldier crabs can sometimes be seen moving along the shore in huge numbers. They burrow with a sideways somersaulting action, using one side to dig, then the other

Brown seaweed, a relative of kelp, has bladders that allow it to float when the tide is in—the plant needs sunlight to live

Cuttlefish skeletons hold gas by which the animals rise in the water to feed at night, and descend to the bottom in the day. Cuttlefish have eight arms and two large grabbing tentacles—each tentacle is about three times as long as the skeleton

Coralline seaweed has segmented branches. Each time this sort divides, it divides in two

Bluebottles' bladders enable them to swim on the surface. Some sea slugs eat bluebottles without digesting the stinging cells, which are on the tentacles, and then use the toxin as their own defence mechanism

Sea urchins' shells have little bubbles which are the attachment points for the spines. The fine rays are the holes for the tube feet by which they move

Egg cases of the cartrut shell are moulded by the foot of the female as she lays. The first juveniles to hatch eat the remaining eggs

Abalone are types of snails and limpets. They eat seaweeds which affect their colouring. Farming of abalone is becoming successful in the United States

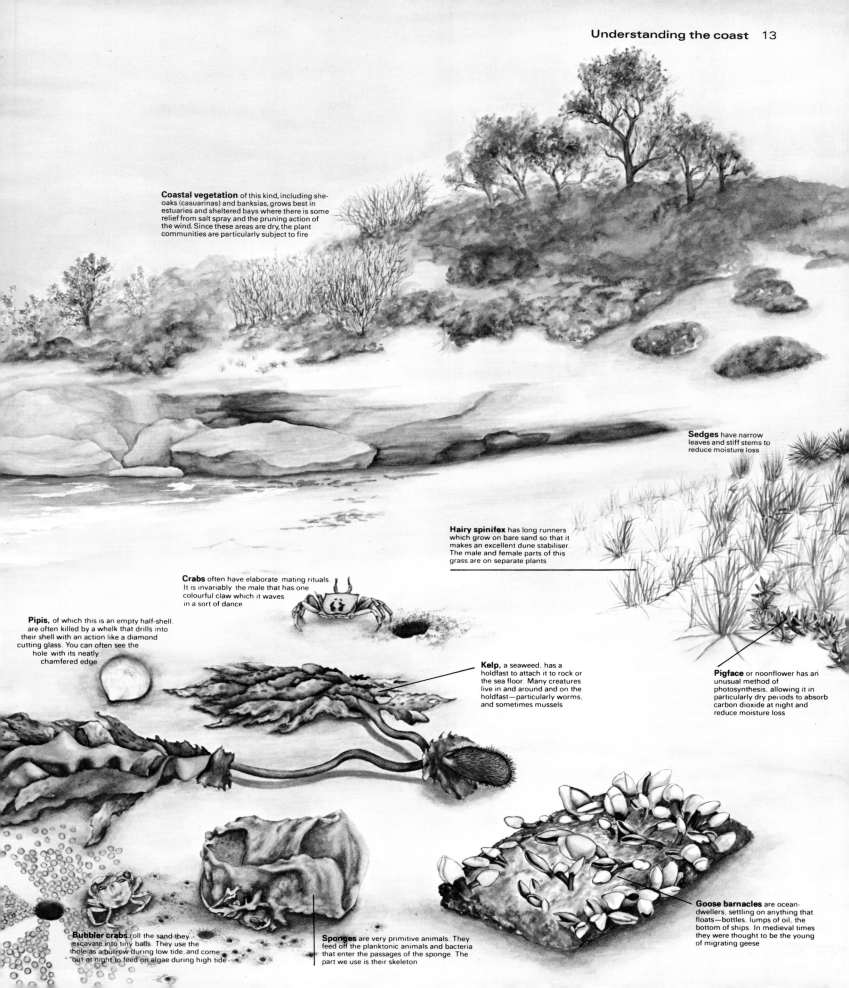

Coastal vegetation of this kind, including she-oaks (casuarinas) and banksias, grows best in estuaries and sheltered bays where there is some relief from salt spray and the pruning action of the wind. Since these areas are dry, the plant communities are particularly subject to fire

Sedges have narrow leaves and stiff stems to reduce moisture loss

Hairy spinifex has long runners which grow on bare sand so that it makes an excellent dune stabiliser. The male and female parts of this grass are on separate plants

Crabs often have elaborate mating rituals. It is invariably the male that has one colourful claw which it waves in a sort of dance

Pipis, of which this is an empty half-shell, are often killed by a whelk that drills into their shell with an action like a diamond cutting glass. You can often see the hole with its neatly chamfered edge

Kelp, a seaweed, has a holdfast to attach it to rock or the sea floor. Many creatures live in and around and on the holdfast—particularly worms, and sometimes mussels

Pigface or noonflower has an unusual method of photosynthesis, allowing it in particularly dry periods to absorb carbon dioxide at night and reduce moisture loss

Bubbler crabs roll the sand they excavate into tiny balls. They use the hole as a burrow during low tide, and come out at night to feed on algae during high tide

Sponges are very primitive animals. They feed off the planktonic animals and bacteria that enter the passages of the sponge. The part we use is their skeleton

Goose barnacles are ocean-dwellers, settling on anything that floats—bottles, lumps of oil, the bottom of ships. In medieval times they were thought to be the young of migrating geese

Common Australian sea shells

The tightly packed shelves and display boards in seaside museums exhibit the shells of only some of over 10 000 species of molluscs so far discovered in Australia. An estimated 80 000 species exist in the world, and new ones are constantly being found. Some large, brightly coloured and intricately patterned shells are much sought after by collectors and command high prices because of their rarity. The shells illustrated here are those commonly seen on beaches or in rock pools by casual visitors to the coast. Do not collect shells containing live animals. Sizes of average specimens are given.

Orange cockle
Acrosterigma reeveanum
Length 60 mm

Combed auger
Hastula strigilata
Length 30 mm

Orange jingle shell
Anomia descripta
Diameter 55 mm

Bubble shell
Bulla quoyii
Length 50 mm

Venus shell
Katelysia rhytiphora
Width 45 mm

Common southern bean cowrie
Trivia merces
Length 10 mm

Banded or silver kelp shell
Bankivia fasciata
Length 15 mm

Arrowed sand snail
Tanea sagittata
Diameter 10 mm

Leafy chama
Chama pulchella
Diameter 40 mm

Erroneous cowrie
Cypraea errones
Length 30 mm

Pretty trough shell
Mactra eximia
Width 60 mm

Dog whelk
Nassarius pyrrhus
Length 15 mm

Melon or baler shell
Melo amphora
Length 70-220 mm

Doughboy scallop
Mimachlamys asperrimus
Width 65 mm

Sand snail
Natica gualtieriana
Length 30 mm

Southern olive shell
Oliva australis
Length 30 mm

Olive shell
Oliva oliva
Length 30 mm

Orange sand snail
Polinices tumidus
Length 35 mm

Dove shell
Pyrene scripta
Length 10 mm

Angas's murex
Pterynotus angasi
Length 20 mm

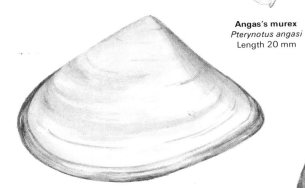

Pipi
Plebidonax deltoides
Width 60 mm

Pheasant shell
Phasianella australis
Length 55 mm

Creeper shell
Rhinoclavis sinensis
Length 50 mm

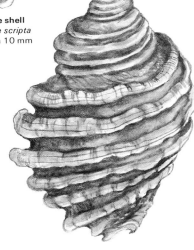

Dog winkle
Thais orbita
Length 70 mm

Turban shell
Turbo undulata
Length 65 mm

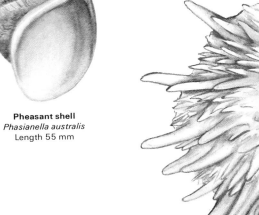

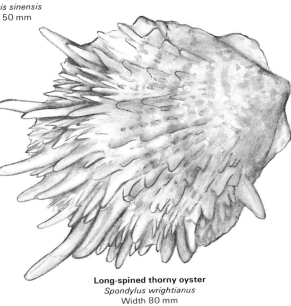

Long-spined thorny oyster
Spondylus wrightianus
Width 80 mm

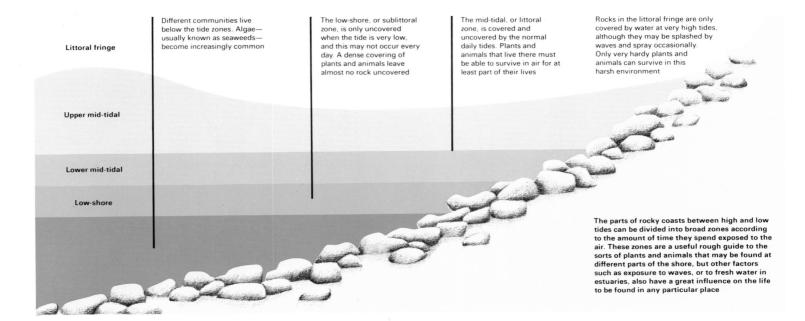

Littoral fringe

Upper mid-tidal

Lower mid-tidal

Low-shore

Different communities live below the tide zones. Algae—usually known as seaweeds—become increasingly common

The low-shore, or sublittoral zone, is only uncovered when the tide is very low, and this may not occur every day. A dense covering of plants and animals leave almost no rock uncovered

The mid-tidal, or littoral zone, is covered and uncovered by the normal daily tides. Plants and animals that live there must be able to survive in air for at least part of their lives

Rocks in the littoral fringe are only covered by water at very high tides, although they may be splashed by waves and spray occasionally. Only very hardy plants and animals can survive in this harsh environment

The parts of rocky coasts between high and low tides can be divided into broad zones according to the amount of time they spend exposed to the air. These zones are a useful rough guide to the sorts of plants and animals that may be found at different parts of the shore, but other factors such as exposure to waves, or to fresh water in estuaries, also have a great influence on the life to be found in any particular place

Rocky shores Where marine life takes a hold on the land

Shore platforms of rock, accommodating a rich diversity of marine animals and plants, are common in eastern and south-eastern Australia. They are formed by waves and rain eating at outcrops at and above the intertidal level. So they occur where wave energy is high and where the rock is only moderately durable. The sandstones of New South Wales, exposed to strong ocean swells and high rainfall, are ideal. Nearly every headland has its platform, to the delight of amateur fishermen. Platforms differ widely in character, however. Some are submerged at all but the lowest tides, while others are formed at or above the mean high tide level, and exposed to the air nearly all the time. Most are more or less flat but many have a slope, usually because a tilted block of more resistant rock has been uncovered. Some platforms have smooth surfaces; others are deeply fissured, pitted with pools, studded with pinnacles, raised with tiered benches, or strewn with boulders.

All those local differences have some bearing on the distribution of marine life. The degree of protection from heavy breakers is also important. So is the range between low and high tides: where it is greatest, marine communities are spread over the widest area. On many coasts the rock platforms are made up of discernible bands of height inhabited by different species. Many are fixed to the rock—for example, barnacles, oysters, tubeworms, sea-squirts, sponges and seaweeds. Some can move, but spend most of their time in one spot—anemones and mussels, for instance. Even the most mobile animals, such as gastropod shellfish, crabs and starfish, have habitual feeding areas. People who have learnt to distinguish a dozen or so dominant species of

animals, and a few seaweeds and grasses, can identify tide zones on different platforms. And they can tell where the tide is at a glance.

Many areas in the highest tide zone, the littoral fringe, are under water for only a tiny part of the tidal cycle. Some receive only the twice-monthly spring tides and a varying amount of spray. Marine organisms living here have to be hardy, and adaptable not only to fluctuating air temperatures but also to drastic changes in salinity—from salt water at high tide to fresh water if it rains while the tide is out. Littorinid snails of several species cope well with such conditions. The most common, throughout Australia

except in northern Queensland, is the periwinkle, *Littorina unifasciata*.

The mid-tidal area is often called the barnacle zone. At its higher levels barnacles are common except in Western Australia and so are gastropods such as sea snails and limpets. New South Wales has the six-plated grey barnacle, *Chthamalus antennatus*, and the small honeycomb barnacle, *Chamaesipho columna*. A limpet, *Notoacmea petterdi*, is widespread on vertical surfaces, and other gastropods occurring in some upper mid-tidal areas include a bigger limpet, *Cellana tramoserica*, and the black snail, *Nerita atramentosa*. Lower in the mid-tidal area,

Tools of the waves

CIRCULAR pools with smooth, vertical walls, often seen on wave-washed shore platforms, seem too perfectly formed to be natural. But at the bottom will be found at least one stray stone. It is these stones, of harder material than the platform rock, that make the pools. Lodging at first in shallow depressions, they are repeatedly spun about in swirling water. They become the tools of the waves, scouring the platform until they have drilled it to such a depth—sometimes more than 1 metre—that they are out of reach of disturbance by water movements and no longer move.

Pools still being scoured hold little marine life, though small fish are occasionally trapped in them. But when the drilling stones cease to move, the pools are soon colonised by seaweeds, anemones, gastropods and sometimes starfish—content to live in a sheltered environment.

A circular pool on a Sydney rock platform

barnacles continue in company with mussels, gastropods and sometimes oysters. On the most protected NSW shores, gastropods such as the mulberry whelk, *Morula*, limpets and three common grazing snails are dominant along with starfish, chitons, often called coat-of-mail shells because of their eight armour-like plates, and anemones. In slightly less protected areas, dense beds of honeycomb barnacles are often found with the limpet *Cellana* grazing over them. Plants are seldom obvious. An encrusting alga on many Sydney shores blends with the colour of sandstone and is only noticeable at close quarters. Pools often contain the brown seaweed *Hormosira banksii*, commonly called Neptune's beads, along with gastropods, anemones, starfish and sometimes the hairy mussel, *Trichomya hirsuta*. Areas exposed to stronger waves are usually dominated by one or both species of surf barnacles, *Catomerus polymerus* and the pink *Tesseropora rosea*. In South Australia, Victoria and Tasmania, mussels occupy a lot of space in many mid-tidal areas, while in parts of northern Queensland oysters are much more common.

Moving into low-shore areas, the covering of plants and animals becomes so dense that often no bare rock can be seen. Organisms may be exposed to the air only at low tide, or in some places not at all. Algae, particularly brown seaweeds, increase markedly. A fixed tube-worm, *Galeolaria caespitosa*, is found just above the seaweed or on patches among it. In Victoria, NSW and southern Queensland the sea-squirt or cunjevoi is so prolific on some platforms that the low-shore area is often referred to as the cunjevoi zone. Many other organisms live where they can find room among the dominant groups. Along with some that are more characteristic of higher shore levels, such as barnacles and whelks, are found turban shells, starfish, sea-urchins, sponges, octopuses and crabs.

Marine life distribution is consistent in its general patterns, but from time to time and place to place there can be significant changes. The most obvious causes of such changes are storm damage, human interference and water pollution. Shore communities are variable anyway, because of breeding and feeding behaviour. Most species spend a juvenile stage at sea. Larvae or spores drift for days, weeks or months at the whim of ocean currents. Many may be eaten by predators, or die before reaching a platform. Those that survive the seaborne phase do not necessarily find the same area or even the same shore as their parent colonies, and new-found homes may be less suitable. Barnacle larvae, for example, can fix themselves only to bare rock or to the hard shells of older barnacles and other gastropods. If other species already cover the rock, there will be no barnacles. Among the adult animals, many species prey on others, compete with each other for food or space, or interfere with the settlement of the tiny larvae. Some are even more variable because they are short-lived and seasonal, or because their young do not settle every year. The distribution of species on a rocky shore is continually changing.

Getting to grips with the cunjevoi

CRUSTY yet spongy, like a vegetable outside yet meaty inside, the sea-squirt or cunjevoi is a puzzle even to the rock fishermen who cut it up for bait. Just for fun a leading marine biologist, the late William Dakin, wrote to the Sydney *Sun* in 1945 inviting theories about the nature of this organism. A Dr Archibald Grubb replied:

'My observations of and on cunjevoi have been frequent, long, and even lurid, and its facility in depriving me of hooks and sinkers has always suggested that it is an animal, and a very low and objectionable animal at that. And when you walk over it gingerly to recover your hook, it looks up malignantly and spits sea-water into your eye; and when, in rage, you slash off the top of its crust, withdraw the animal or vegetable and place it upon a hook, all the other lowest animals in the water rush to the feast—woorrahs, or old boots, fortescues, weedies, muddies, sweep, toebiters, crabs, onkterspronks, mugfrubs, etc, and so forth, and you lose the an. or veg. off the hook and get snagged on its contemporaries and lose half your line. Yes, if the cungevoi isn't a lower form of animal life, the barnacle is a melon-plant, or I'm an onion.'

Dr Grubb was right. The cunjevoi is an animal. It belongs to the same division of the animal kingdom as some free-swimming, sac-bodied creatures, some beach worms and all the vertebrates.

Hundreds of cunjevoi form a lumpy brown covering over rocks exposed only at very low tide

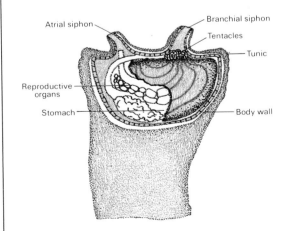

The most commonly encountered cunjevoi on Australia's rocky shores, Pyura praeputialis, is only one of some 250 known species. Inside the animal's leathery outer coat is the tough, muscular tissue sought after by anglers as bait. The tissue forms a body wall to protect the branchial sac, the main food collecting and respiratory organ. Food-laden water is sucked down the branchial siphon, filtered by the tentacles and trapped in the sac. Waste water is released in a stream through the atrial siphon. The cunjevoi is hermaphroditic, with both male and female cells

Miniature worlds along rocky shores

Rocky shores, and the pools along them, accommodate myriad fascinating animals and plants. Explore them in the early morning at low tide, before the animals have sheltered from the heat and glare. Cause as little interference as possible—even apparently bare rocks may be covered with microscopic life. If you turn over any rocks, replace them exactly as they were, otherwise you will kill the plants and animals living on both sides.

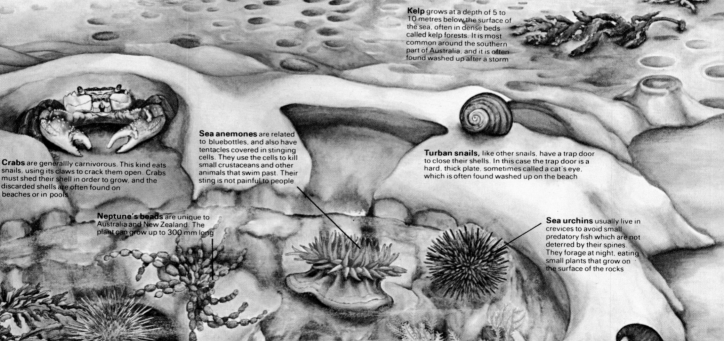

Kelp grows at a depth of 5 to 10 metres below the surface of the sea, often in dense beds called kelp forests. It is most common around the southern part of Australia, and it is often found washed up after a storm

Crabs are generallly carnivorous. This kind eats snails, using its claws to crack them open. Crabs must shed their shell in order to grow, and the discarded shells are often found on beaches or in pools

Sea anemones are related to bluebottles, and also have tentacles covered in stinging cells. They use the cells to kill small crustaceans and other animals that swim past. Their sting is not painful to people

Turban snails, like other snails, have a trap door to close their shells. In this case the trap door is a hard, thick plate, sometimes called a cat's eye, which is often found washed up on the beach

Neptune's beads are unique to Australia and New Zealand. The plant can grow up to 300 mm long

Sea urchins usually live in crevices to avoid small predatory fish which are not deterred by their spines. They forage at night, eating small plants that grow on the surface of the rocks

Coralline seaweeds are often mistakenly thought to be animals. They form a thick bed on the lower parts of many rock platforms, serving as a habitat for small animals including whelks, sponges and small snails

Seaweeds (algae) occur in a very large number of types. They mostly grow at low levels, in deeper water

Starfish are generally carnivorous, but this one eats plants: Starfish feed by extruding their stomachs through their mouths and digesting what they find

Sea lettuce is found in most places around the coast. It has translucent, flat blades that are a source of food for many snails and fish

Snails of many species occur in this zone of the shore

Brittle stars are related to sea urchins. They prefer pools with a sandy bottom because they filter food from fine sediment

Do not take anything home. Even empty shells are used by
creatures such as hermit crabs. Never reach into a crevice—there is
the risk of encountering a blue-ringed octopus, a dangerous species
of cone shell or a moray eel that could crush a finger badly.

Alga found at high
levels usually occurs
where it receives some
rainwater. Lower down it
is eaten by grazing
animals

Mussels are nearly always
found in clumps. They are
filter feeders and pump
seawater through their
bodies, extracting all the
minute animals from it

Lichens are a mixture of a
fungus and an alga

**Chiton or coat-of-
mail shells** live on
algae. Some grow to
130 mm long

Barnacles are cemented to the rock
and do not move. They often form
dense clumps. There are very many
species of these animals, which are
related to shrimps

Mulberry whelks eat shelled
animals, particularly
barnacles, by softening the
shell with a secretion and then
drilling a hole in it with their
proboscis. The process can
take four days

Erosion holes in soft
rocks often contain patches
of salt formed when
seawater has evaporated in
the sun

Hermit crabs have soft shells so
they have to live in the shells of
other, dead, animals. They try to
dislodge other hermit crabs from
larger shells as they grow

Limpets are usually
slightly raised from
the rock, but they
clamp themselves
down if threatened

Estuarine waters Fish habitats under human threat

Estuaries are principally the tidal parts of river mouths. Biologists also class some bay areas and lagoons as estuarine because they support similar marine life and fringing vegetation. Australia has few estuaries, considering the extent of its coastline. Where their shores were firm they made ideal Aboriginal campsites, offering fresh water close to an abundance of seafood and waterfowl. European explorers made for the same spots, not only for sustenance but also for protected anchorages. With colonisation the landing places became ports for access to the hinterlands, and many grew to be cities and sites of industry. Estuary beds have been raised for reclamations, or dredged to provide land-fill elsewhere. Other estuarine waters serve as fishing grounds and ever-busier holiday playgrounds—and some even as waste dumps.

These relatively rare waters are crucial to the existence of many fish, including some that are normally associated with deeper seas offshore. Snapper, for example, spend a juvenile stage in estuaries, where they may be known as cockney or red bream. In New South Wales, 31 of the 43 most important commercial species are caught in estuaries. Half of the total inshore and offshore catch, in tonnage and value, comprises species that depend on estuaries for at least a part of their lives. Including other seafoods such as prawns and oysters, the NSW fishing industry is about 70 per cent reliant on estuaries. The availability of smaller organisms for these fish to eat varies greatly in nature. Now it is increasingly threatened by human activities.

Seagrasses probably hold the key to marine animal life in estuaries. They are not important

as a direct source of food for commercial fish species, but they shield the youngest fish from predators and they generate the organic material on which a whole web of food supply is based. Dead or broken parts of eelgrass, *Zostera*, strapweed, *Posidonia*, or some other flowering plants and associated algae are grazed and further broken down by crustaceans and worms. The smaller particles are attacked by bacteria and fungi and eaten by other tiny organisms, which are in turn eaten. Reduced to its finest form—detritus—after repeated digestions and excretions, the organic matter readily yields up its mineral components to nourish more seagrass. Fringing mangroves and swamp plants contribute detritus in a similar way.

While the cycle continues, all marine animals have food—plant matter, micro-organisms, or

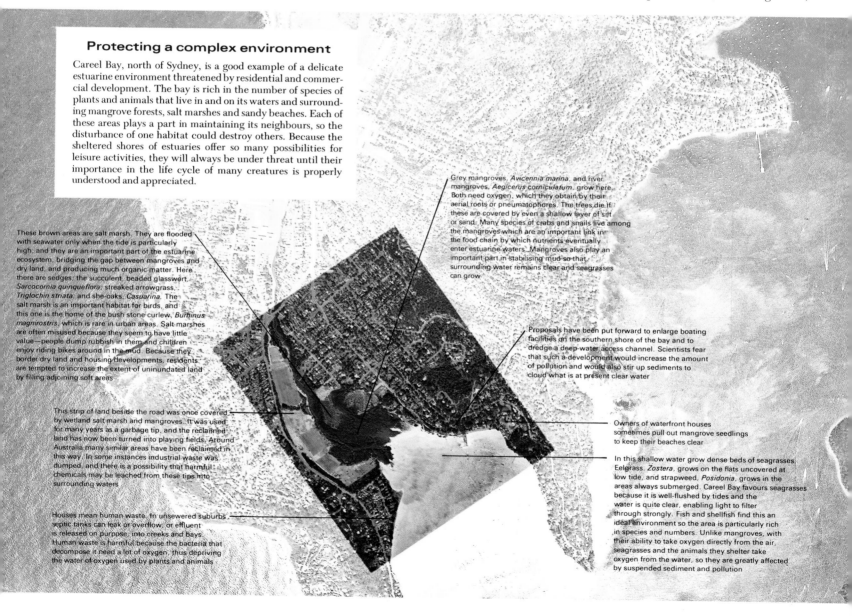

Protecting a complex environment

Careel Bay, north of Sydney, is a good example of a delicate estuarine environment threatened by residential and commercial development. The bay is rich in the number of species of plants and animals that live in and on its waters and surrounding mangrove forests, salt marshes and sandy beaches. Each of these areas plays a part in maintaining its neighbours, so the disturbance of one habitat could destroy others. Because the sheltered shores of estuaries offer so many possibilities for leisure activities, they will always be under threat until their importance in the life cycle of many creatures is properly understood and appreciated.

Grey mangroves, *Avicennia marina*, and river mangroves, *Aegicerus corniculatum*, grow here. Both need oxygen, which they obtain by their aerial roots or pneumatophores. The trees die if these are covered by even a shallow layer of silt or sand. Many species of crabs and snails live among the mangroves which are an important link in the food chain by which nutrients eventually enter estuarine waters. Mangroves also play an important part in stabilising mud so that surrounding water remains clear and seagrasses can grow

These brown areas are salt marsh. They are flooded with seawater only when the tide is particularly high, and they are an important part of the estuarine ecosystem, bridging the gap between mangroves and dry land, and producing much organic matter. Here there are sedges; the succulent, beaded glasswort, *Sarcocornia quinqueflora*; streaked arrowgrass, *Triglochin striata*; and she-oaks, *Casuarina*. The salt marsh is an important habitat for birds, and this one is the home of the bush stone curlew, *Burhinus magnirostris*, which is rare in urban areas. Salt marshes are often misused because they seem to have little value—people dump rubbish in them and children enjoy riding bikes around in the mud. Because they border dry land and housing developments, residents are tempted to increase the extent of uninundated land by filling adjoining soft areas

Proposals have been put forward to enlarge boating facilities on the southern shore of the bay and to dredge a deep-water access channel. Scientists fear that such a development would increase the amount of pollution and would also stir up sediments to cloud what is at present clear water

This strip of land beside the road was once covered by wetland salt marsh and mangroves. It was used for many years as a garbage tip, and the reclaimed land has now been turned into playing fields. Around Australia many similar areas have been reclaimed in this way. In some instances industrial waste was dumped, and there is a possibility that harmful chemicals may be leached from these tips into surrounding waters

Owners of waterfront houses sometimes pull out mangrove seedlings to keep their beaches clear

In this shallow water grow dense beds of seagrasses. Eelgrass, *Zostera*, grows on the flats uncovered at low tide, and strapweed, *Posidonia*, grows in the areas always submerged. Careel Bay favours seagrasses because it is well-flushed by tides and the water is quite clear, enabling light to filter through strongly. Fish and shellfish find this an ideal environment so the area is particularly rich in species and numbers. Unlike mangroves, with their ability to take oxygen directly from the air, seagrasses and the animals they shelter take oxygen from the water, so they are greatly affected by suspended sediment and pollution

Houses mean human waste. In unsewered suburbs septic tanks can leak or overflow, or effluent is released on purpose, into creeks and bays. Human waste is harmful because the bacteria that decompose it need a lot of oxygen, thus depriving the water of oxygen used by plants and animals

one another. But entire meadows of seagrass can be destroyed by massive movements of silt or sand, especially in floods or after storms. Even a milder disturbance making the water murky can stop their growth by cutting out sunlight. And human interference is not limited to the obvious effects of large-scale engineering. Seagrass beds are frequently damaged by water pollution, by high-speed boating over shallows, by bottom-trawling and by the dumping of junk.

Estuary beds are the world's most productive areas. Seagrasses alone generate as much as 4 kg of organic matter per square metre per year. The average is 2 kg in dry weight—equalled only by tropical forests. Temperate grasslands yield only 0.5 kg on average, and total land areas 0.75 kg. Ocean beds produce a mere 0.15 kg.

In addition, staggering quantities of animal tissue are produced in estuaries. Sampling of seagrass meadows in the United States indicated that every square kilometre harboured 90 million prawns, including larvae, and 36 000 million molluscs. And cultivated mussel beds in Lancashire, England, were found to produce 80 times more weight of flesh than cattle could gain by grazing on an equivalent area of pasture.

Sea water is heavier than fresh water, so an estuary fed by a big river—the Derwent passing through Hobart, for example—may be split into two levels with a wedge of sea water flowing upstream under river water flowing downstream. But Australia's generally low rainfall means that many estuaries are totally marine environments for most of the time. Their salt content is not much lower than the ocean's, except after heavy rain. Periods of reduced salinity are spasmodic and seldom long-lasting. In the far north, however, where rainfall is extremely seasonal, estuaries are virtually fresh for months during the 'Wet'. And over-saltiness, through evaporation, can occur in a lagoon when drought cuts its freshwater flow and waves build a sand bar blocking the entrance. That is common in the south-east and in parts of South Australia, and leads to the death of many animals and plants.

Most estuarine animals are sea creatures: their body fluids are in balance with sea water because the salt concentrations are similar. If floods overwhelm their habitat and drastically lower its salinity, they start absorbing extra water. For some species this is fatal. Fish can quickly retreat to more suitable waters. Molluscs and crustaceans have shells and regulatory mechanisms to delay water absorption. They may also be able to close their shells or burrow into the estuary bed—at the risk of starvation—until the crisis is over. The chief sufferers are soft-bodied animals such as worms. Some can stand a limited intake of water, slightly inflating their bodies, for a short time. But if low salinity continues, they die. After heavy floods, entire populations are wiped out. Other worms, especially those adapted to upstream areas, have organs that act like primitive kidneys and pump out water. But their young lack these organs, so reproduction has to be geared to periods of higher salinity.

Fish and other marine animals are renewable

Seagrass meadows, found in many bays and estuaries around the Australian coast, are among the most productive areas in the world

resources, provided that their habitats are preserved. But the estuarine plant life on which they depend can be destroyed forever by human actions, whether deliberate or unthinking. Not only are many uses of estuaries in conflict with nature—they are also often in conflict with one another. Port development, commercial fishing, sand mining, sewage disposal, oyster cultivation and recreation, for example, simply do not mix. Scientists are urging governments to consider all estuaries that are subject to human pressure and to allocate specific uses to each of them, taking into account their different physical characteristics, their type of vegetation, and their nearness to population centres. A major problem in planning their conservation, however, is the multiplicity of authorities in control of the wetland fringes (see overleaf).

The saving of Jervis Bay

SEAGRASS meadows in the sheltered northern reaches of Jervis Bay are probably the most extensive in NSW, reaching to depths of more than 10 metres. As well as being nurseries for commercially valuable fish and crustaceans, they are important feeding grounds for vast flocks of black swans. Yet in 1972 the shores behind were proposed as the site of a gigantic industrial complex. The north-western corner was earmarked for a steelworks bigger than Port Kembla's. To its east were to be engineering plants, metal refineries, a woodchip mill, a petrochemical plant, an oil refinery and a power station. Separate port facilities for the steelworks, for bulk products, for general cargo and for oil products were to be strung along Callala Beach. Urban zones, at first on the coast to the north but later on the western shore of the bay, were to house 300 000 people. But evidence of the ecological impact was so damning that a government inquiry threw out the whole scheme, recommending that the bay shores be preserved for nature conservation and recreation.

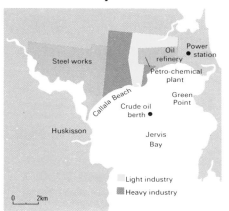
The plan of the 1972 development proposal gives some idea of the scope of the scheme

The shores of Jervis Bay remain unspoiled, despite attempts to establish heavy industry in the area

Wetland margins Where plants belong to both worlds

Mangrove swamps and salt marshes are customarily seen as nuisances. They are foul-smelling breeding grounds of mosquitoes and midges. They clog boating and fishing waters and impede land access to them. They collect floating rubbish. In the tropics, they harbour dangerous crocodiles. The eagerness of property developers to dredge out mangroves and wall the shoreline, or to refashion marshlands as canal estates, is understandable. But mangroves and marsh plants are vital, along with seagrasses, to estuary life. Where water, sunlight and nutrients are plentiful, each square metre of mangrove forest contributes an average 1 kg a year of organic matter to the food chain that supports most of the species sought-after by commercial fishermen.

The biological importance of mangroves was recognised only in the late 1960s, after pioneering research in southern Florida, USA. Only four species grow there, but Australia has more than 30, related to at least 15 different families of land-based trees. Mangroves were just as varied in South-east Asia, but their habitats are in heavily populated, underdeveloped tropical regions. Asian mangroves have been traditionally cut for firewood and for building jetties and fish traps. Now international companies in some places are mowing them down for woodchip production. They are being depleted so rapidly that by the

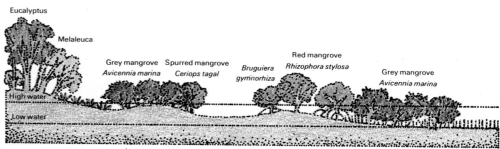

Different species of mangroves form distinct zones in tropical estuaries, partly as a result of the amount of time that the land spends under water. The landward zone is generally the richest in species

1990s Australia may have the world's last mature stands of highly diverse mangrove forest.

Mangroves are trees and shrubs with many different and unrelated characteristics. What they have in common is a unique tolerance of high concentrations of salt in their soil moisture. Some species discharge salt through glands on their leaves; others are able to restrict its entry through their roots. They have various ways of drawing air into oxygen-starved soil. All have adapted to daily flooding by sea water—in fact they rely on it. They use the tides to disperse their seeds, so that new areas can be colonised away from the shade of older trees.

Australia has the southernmost distribution of mangroves in the world. The common grey mangrove, *Avicennia marina*, is found in Corner Inlet, just north of Wilsons Promontory, and in other shallow, protected Victorian bays such as Western Port. Isolated *Avicennia* swamps also occur in the gulfs of South Australia and on the west coast, south of Perth. Mangroves are widespread in estuaries and sheltered bays on the east coast, with the number of species increasing northward. Two occur at Merimbula, NSW, and seven near Brisbane, while communities of more than 20 species are found in northern Queensland and north-western Australia. The breadth of swamps increases with the number of species, as does the height of plants. Southern mangroves are stunted and sparse; around Sydney they form open parklands and grow 10-20 metres tall; mangroves in the far north comprise broad,

Red mangroves, Rhyzophora stylosa, *with their tangled roots are the classic mangroves of tropical shores*

Fish that climb trees

MUDSKIPPERS, the oddest creatures in tropical mangrove swamps, are fish that prefer the open air and hot sun, as long as their skins are moist. They emerge from the water at low tide and walk over the mud on fins that are modified for use as limbs. Through stalked, swivelling eyes on top of their heads, these fish of the *Periophthalmus* genus watch for the small crabs and insects on which they feed. If alarmed they do not retreat into the water but skip across it to a safer mudbank. And if still hungry when the tide is rising, many species use their fins to elbow their way up mangrove trees. Queensland's commonest species grow to 100 mm in length, but others reach 250 mm.

A mudskipper, Periophthalmus koelreuteri

Altogether, over 30 species of mangroves live around the Australian coast, but all are only found north of 12°S. Only one species—the grey mangrove, Avicennia marina *(far left)*—grows in Victoria, South Australia and south-western Western Australia. Spurred mangroves, Ceriops tagal *(left)*, and milky mangroves, Exoecaria agallocha *(above)*, illustrate the diverse forms that these plants take

dense forest climbing to a height of 30 metres.

Because they grow in tidal mud, mangroves need extensive root systems to hold them in place. As well as subterranean systems, many species have branching aerial roots. The prop-roots of *Rhizophora* descend from higher on the trunk as the tree grows. *Bruguiera*, the tallest mangroves, send out low-level roots that travel horizontally and bend upwards before anchoring in the mud. Some other species have wide, flat aerial roots resembling planks wandering far from the tree. The tangle of roots put out by a community of mangroves traps fine silt carried down by any creeks draining into the swamp. Sediments brought in on the high tide also tend to settle out and remain among the mangroves. In this way the trees stabilise shorelines, and in the absence of floods or storm waves they can add to the land area.

Avicennia, *Bruguiera* and some other mangrove species send pegs into the air for metres around each tree. Called pneumatophores, these are root extensions with lip-like cracks through which the tree can draw oxygen while its lower levels are in poorly aerated mud. Other species have similar breathing openings in their aerial roots. Another peculiarity of many mangroves is that their seeds germinate before they leave the tree. In *Rhizophora* species, the seedling may protrude more than 300 mm from the fruit. When it falls into the water the fruit floats with the seedling shoot pointing down, ready to catch in shallows and quickly take root. *Avicennia* seeds, however, need long soaking in sea water before they will germinate.

Most land animals found in mangroves are casual visitors such as mice, canefield rats, flying foxes, snakes, goannas, crocodiles and many species of birds. Some come seasonally for protection while breeding, or because the trees are flowering or fruiting. A diverse community of insects includes some species found only in mangroves. Fish and prawns come in with the tide to feed. Mud crabs breed among the mangroves, but spend most of their lives in deeper water.

The permanent marine population is dominated by worms, molluscs and crustaceans. Some—especially molluscs with shells that resist dehydration—live on the surface. Fiddler and semaphore crabs, needing constant access to water, live in burrows, but feed on the surface and sometimes in the trees. Oysters encrust the tree bases on the seaward margins, along with limpets, small shrimps and worms. Other worms inhabit tubes in the mud or in pockets of water under fallen logs. Small crabs and snails also live under dead wood, while other creatures bore into it and gradually break it down. The 'ship worm', *Teredo*—really a tiny bivalve mollusc—is the dominant borer, though louse-like isopods such as the gribble may be locally common. Once such animals have made holes, other small creatures may move in.

Salt marshes, often found on the landward margins of mangrove swamps, present conditions so variable that few kinds of animals or plants can survive. Inundation by the sea normally occurs only during fortnightly spring tides. At other times, especially in dry summer weather, evaporation causes a build-up of salt concentrations. In the tropics and in arid regions there may by salt pans—areas where the soil is covered in salt crystals and devoid of vegetation. On the other hand fresh water may flood a salt marsh during heavy rain. Burrowing crabs and some small snails can cope with this range of conditions. Of the shrubby succulent plants that may grow, the dominant species is marsh samphire or glasswort, *Salicornia*. The shores of a marsh are often marked by a band of rushes and casuarinas.

How the law sees mangroves

Laws protecting mangroves were passed in all mainland states in the 1970s, after the importance of the trees was recognised. But biologists are far from satisfied with the effectiveness of such measures. In NSW, for example, the Fisheries Act was amended in 1979 so that any cutting of mangroves without a permit could incur a $500 fine. But three years later the amendent was still not in force: there was no machinery for apprehending and prosecuting offenders.

The effects of proposed coastal developments on mangroves can now be taken into account if environmental impact assessments are called for. The authority controlling a particular area of wetlands, however, need not call for such a study unless it already believes that the impact is likely to be significant. And that authority may have little ecological interest; its official concern could be port administration or shipping, or public works. Control of wetlands may be in the hands of as many as seven or eight different state government departments or statutory authorities, or it may be vested in local government councils.

Singling out certain mangrove areas for complete protection offers no permanent solution because they are changing environments. Through the gain or loss of soil, mangroves create their own fluctuations in sea levels and growth limits. And wildlife, especially migratory birdlife, is unpredictable. A mangrove swamp of no apparent interest in one season may become all-important breeding ground the following year.

Mangroves, an unattractive but vital nursery

Mangrove swamps have clearly zoned regions. In the waterfront mudflats exposed at low tide, the air-breathing roots of some mangrove species and sapling trees sprout through the oozing surface. Adult trees from over 30 kinds of mangroves found around the Australian coast form dense thickets of branches and ground and aerial roots further inland, but still on the tidal mudflats. As the swamp merges into firm land, mangroves intermingle with land plants.

Mud is trapped by the mangrove's tangled roots and, because the waters are unusually calm, algae, bacteria and fungi are held there. These organisms are what makes the swamps such smelly places, but they are also the basis of a food chain which supports a great diversity of molluscs, crustaceans and fish that are sought

Pulmonate slugs—like all slugs—are shell-less snails. They are air-breathers and feed on algae. The most common in mangrove swamps grow to about 70 mm long. They are very hard to see as they are usually covered in mud, but they can be traced by the trail they leave

Shipworms are misleadingly named—they are actually bivalves, relatives of oysters, mussels and cockles. They have a long siphon that they extend to the surface to breathe and eat. There are several species of shipworm; they used to be relished as food by Aborigines, but now they are only considered as pests, being responsible for much of the destruction of wooden pilings and other timber in water

Oysters occur in huge numbers around mangrove pneumatophores—many mangrove swamps in New South Wales are leased as nursery areas for the spats (young oysters). Sydney rock oysters change sex during their lifetime—they spawn as males but become females later. The females produce about 1 500 000 eggs every few weeks in the breeding season (mostly in summer); the eggs develop into larvae that can swim in a few hours. After two or three weeks they settle, and are collected from their first sites to be farmed in batteries. They take about three and a half years to grow to table size

Oysters are stationary, with one side of their shell cemented to a surface. They are filter feeders, using their gills—the gill forms a sieve and when taking in oxygen the creature also collects food particles

Snapping shrimps can often be heard in mangrove swamps, making a crack like glass breaking—it is not known why. Saltwater yabbies (which can be eaten but are generally used for bait) look somewhat similar, but snapping shrimps are quickly recognised by their single large-clawed leg—this has a peg on one finger which fits into a socket on the other. The feathered end sections are used as rudders

Hermit crabs are soft-bodied, with an abdomen that can be coiled to fit into their borrowed homes. As they grow they need to move into larger shells

after by commercial and amateur fishermen.
Waterfowl find the swamps ideal feeding
grounds. Worms live in both the mud and the
tree roots, and the air is often thick with insects
and the webs of spiders which prey on them.

Mangroves are not all coastal—
grey mangroves occur in the Great
Sandy Desert, about 40 km from the
coast. There are about 30 kinds of
mangroves in Australia, but they
have different ways of dealing with
the salt in their environment. One is
to prevent salt from entering in the
first place, by chemical activity in the
root system. Mangroves in tropical
areas store salt in succulent leaves,
and when they are too full they
become fleshy and drop off. The
third method is to excrete salt
through the leaves

Pneumatophores are parts of the root of certain kinds of
mangroves, including two of the most common ones—*Avicennia*
and *Brughuiera*. They function as gas exhangers, taking in oxygen
at high tide and giving out carbon dioxide at low tide. They provide
the tree with an increased surface over which to gather oxygen, and
they also help to cement together the mud in which the tree grows

Grey mangroves (*Avicennia*) and the
short black mangroves (*Aegiceras*) are
the most common kinds in the south-
eastern corner of Australia. At this stage of
their development they can only be
distinguished from one another by tasting
the surface of a leaf—*Avicennia* excretes
salt from the back of its leaf; *Aegiceras*
does not. *Aegiceras* sometimes grows in
very dense thickets

Small mangrove crabs have eyes
on stalks which can fold down
sideways into the small cavities
visible in their shells. This one is a
male with a highly coloured claw.
These crabs feed by shovelling
through the mud and extracting
organisms—the shells outside the
hole were probably cracked up by
blue swimmer crabs that are also
mangrove swamp dwellers, and
were merely dug up by this crab
when it excavated its burrow

Burrows of the small mangrove
crab extend for several metres under
the layer of mangrove tree roots,
dug out sideways and downwards,
housing several crabs. Sometimes
they contain more than one
nesting centre

Barnacles of this kind are more common
low down on the sides of trees facing the
water, since they depend on the tidal rise
of the water to find their sites. Although at
first glance barnacles may resemble
shellfish such as mussels, they differ
greatly, having many feathery limbs with
which they sweep for food

Snails can have lungs and
breathe air, like this kind and
most others found in mangrove
swamps, or have gills and breathe
underwater, like the majority
found on rocky shores

Snails of this sort generally live and graze
on mangrove leaves. They retain their
larvae, numbered in scores of eggs and
developing young, inside the shell until
they are strong enough to descend
into the water

Rough periwinkles have
a feather-like gill to
increase the surface over
which they draw in water
for oxygen. They feed on
the green algae which live
on the mud and tree trunks

Coral reefs
Marine builders reaching for the light

Coral reefs are complex associations of marine animals and plants, living on and in a framework built primarily of the skeletons of corals. When coral polyps die their cups of calcium carbonate fill with the skeletal debris of other creatures such as molluscs and sea-urchins, and with limy material from seaweed. The skeletons and their contents are bound by encrusting red algae and cemented by carbonic acid salts to form reef rock. It is porous, but rigid and tough enough to resist waves and provide a platform on which more corals can build.

Water warmth is the paramount factor in reef-building. Average minimum temperatures must not be less than 18°C. Reefs are largely confined to the tropics, but consistent warm currents foster their growth far to the south at Lord Howe Island, off NSW, and at the Houtman Abrolhos Islands, opposite Geraldton, WA. Great Barrier Reef formations could perhaps have extended much farther, well to the south-east of Fraser Island, but for the masses of shifting sand north of the island. Loose sediments smother corals, or prevent them from gaining a hold on the rock. And they cloud the water, cutting out sunlight—the other major factor in reef-building. Plant organisms that stimulate coral tissue growth and bind the coral together are so restricted by poor light that reef corals do not flourish below about 50 metres. Drilling has shown that reef structures go much deeper under the sea

Limpid water covers Wistari Reef—a reef flat near Heron Island, which can be seen on the horizon

than that—they are many hundreds of metres thick—but the lower levels were built when the sea itself was lower, during the last ice age, or even earlier when the continental shelf stood higher. Reefs as they are known today are veneers, no more than about 8000 years old, overlaying the earlier structures.

When a reef reaches sea level, exposing its top surface at low tide, upward growth stops. Corals reaching any higher would be starved of their plankton food and dehydrated. But sideways growth takes over, principally in the direction from which ocean swells normally come. Incoming waves have more plankton, and the sluggish waters on the sheltered side of a reef may be muddy. The further development of

reef surfaces, once they are at sea level, is largely a matter of wave and wind action.

A *barrier* reef in the strict sense is a long, almost continuous chain of ribbon reefs roughly parallel to a mainland shore, at a considerable distance from it. It screens the coast from ocean movement and creates an offshore lagoon. The Great Barrier Reef is not one in that sense, though it contains some barriers among its complex mixture of formations. Matthew Flinders named it simply because of the difficulties it presented for sailing ships. Scientists prefer to call the Great Barrier region a 'reef province'.

Platform reefs rise from the shallower parts of continental shelves in the shelter of barrier reefs. They are flat-topped and commonly oval in

The animals that start it all

Coral polyps, some with their tentacles extended

CORALS are closely related to sea anemones. They can reproduce sexually, in which case the young have a free-swimming larval stage. Once a coral polyp has developed its tentacle-fringed mouth and gut, to catch and digest its diet of floating plankton, it settles on a firm support and secretes a limestone base. Then it starts building up a skeleton. In soft corals this is a set of splinters or ridges embedded in the body, or a horny or chalky central rod. But in true corals the skeleton forms a stone casing around the polyp, which can draw itself inside for protection. Corals of many kinds may be found on submerged rocks in most parts of the world—sometimes solitary, sometimes in clusters. But only in warm waters will they be reef-builders.

Reef corals, whose vast communities could in theory have been founded by just one polyp of each species, reproduce asexually by budding. They keep on building upwards, then outwards, basing themselves on the skeletons of their dead predecessors. They are linked with membranes of living tissue overlapping their inorganic casings. Each species has its own colour and each is genetically programmed to follow a particular growth pattern. Some are branch-like, others form clumps, layers, fans and so on, giving a diverse reef its extraordinary variety of hues and shapes.

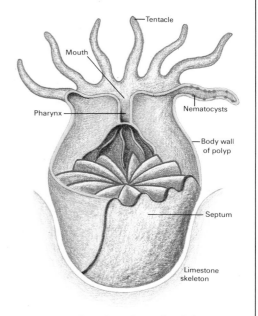

Cross-section through a polyp and its skeleton

Tentacle

Mouth

Pharynx

Nematocysts

Body wall of polyp

Septum

Limestone skeleton

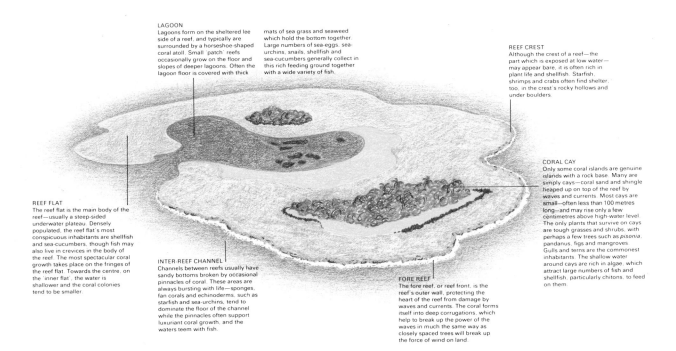

LAGOON
Lagoons form on the sheltered lee side of a reef, and typically are surrounded by a horseshoe-shaped coral atoll. Small 'patch' reefs occasionally grow on the floor and slopes of deeper lagoons. Often the lagoon floor is covered with thick mats of sea grass and seaweed which hold the bottom together. Large numbers of sea-eggs, sea-urchins, snails, shellfish and sea-cucumbers generally collect in this rich feeding ground together with a wide variety of fish.

REEF CREST
Although the crest of a reef—the part which is exposed at low water—may appear bare, it is often rich in plant life and shellfish. Starfish, shrimps and crabs often find shelter, too, in the crest's rocky hollows and under boulders.

REEF FLAT
The reef flat is the main body of the reef—usually a steep-sided underwater plateau. Densely populated, the reef flat's most conspicuous inhabitants are shellfish and sea-cucumbers, though fish may also live in crevices in the body of the reef. The most spectacular coral growth takes place on the fringes of the reef flat. Towards the centre, on the 'inner flat', the water is shallower and the coral colonies tend to be smaller.

CORAL CAY
Only some coral islands are genuine islands with a rock base. Many are simply cays—coral sand and shingle heaped up on top of the reef by waves and currents. Most cays are small—often less than 100 metres long—and may rise only a few centimetres above high-water level. The only plants that survive on cays are tough grasses and shrubs, with perhaps a few trees such as pisonia, pandanus, figs and mangroves. Gulls and terns are the commonest inhabitants. The shallow water around cays are rich in algae, which attract large numbers of fish and shellfish, particularly chitons, to feed on them.

INTER-REEF CHANNEL
Channels between reefs usually have sandy bottoms broken by occasional pinnacles of coral. These areas are always bursting with life—sponges, fan corals and echinoderms, such as starfish and sea-urchins, tend to dominate the floor of the channel while the pinnacles often support luxuriant coral growth, and the waters teem with fish.

FORE REEF
The fore reef, or reef front, is the reef's outer wall, protecting the heart of the reef from damage by waves and currents. The coral forms itself into deep corrugations, which help to break up the power of the waves in much the same way as closely spaced trees will break up the force of wind on land.

shape, with their longer axis aligned parallel to the prevailing wind direction. Smaller platform reefs may be called patch, shelf, bank, table or hummock reefs.

Fringing reefs grow outwards from continental or rocky island coasts. Because sedimentation and freshwater run-off are more pronounced on mainland shores, these reefs are more richly developed in the clear waters round islands.

An *atoll* is a ring of reefs, some surmounted by low cays of sand or shingle, enclosing a lagoon. Australia has none of the atolls common in the central Pacific—they usually occur in open oceanic waters, and are associated with volcanic activity. But some *lagoonal reefs* in Queensland waters, rising above the lagoon floors of bigger structures, may be ring-shaped.

All types of coral reefs have similar zones, running in bands that usually parallel their outer edges. Each zone is a distinct environment for characteristic forms of natural life. The *fore reef* extends from the lower limit of coral growth, up through the tide zone to the windward crest of the reef. The top edge often has closely spaced grooves running between ridges of coral. The grooves are pathways for tidal waves moving on to the reef, and for sediments to be removed. The *reef flat* extends to the back slope of the reef, or to a lagoon if there is one. The inner flats of some reefs may collect so much sediment that they are termed sand flats. Occasionally waves and currents push sand or shingle to a point towards the back of the reef where it forms a *cay*, permanently above the high-water mark. Cays, generally low-lying but up to 1 km long, are often colonised by vegetation and stabilised by the formation of beach rock around their rims. Green Island and Heron Island, well known to holidaymakers, are cays based on much more extensive reef platforms.

Subtidal fore reefs, with their profusion of

Enemies of coral

STARFISH are the leading predators of living corals, but few species do much harm. Since the 1960s, however, swarms of the huge, fast-breeding crown-of-thorns starfish, *Acanthaster planci*, have done immense damage to Great Barrier Reef structures. Adults may measure more than 500 mm across, and each may be capable of eating the polyps from a square metre of coral every week. In one survey at Green Island, off Cairns, nearly 6000 of them were found in 100 minutes. The crown-of-thorns seems to thrive on pollution that kills its own natural predators, such as the big triton shellfish. That may be the reason for the present population explosion, although there appear to have been others in the past.

Some coral is killed accidentally during the attacks of big marauding fish on other species. The swallowing of smaller invertebrates by predators such as crabs and octopuses depletes the supply of skeletal material that goes into reef rock. Burrowers and borers, including sponges, molluscs, algae and bacteria, penetrate the rock at all levels. Algae-grazing fish, sea-urchins and molluscs further erode the rock in their quest for food. Browsing animals break down the sediment to extract nutrients.

A crown-of-thorns starfish eating polyps

living corals, seaweeds and colourful fish, can be adequately examined only by snorkelling or scuba diving. The outer reef flat, also with living corals as well as an abundance of sea-urchins, starfish and molluscs, can be viewed in a glass-bottom boat or on foot at the lowest tide. Walkers must exercise great caution, however, to avoid unintentional damage to reef life. The reef crest is usually swept clear by waves, and supports only an algal mat. But big blocks of reef rock, broken from the mass below and cast up in storms, are often found just inside the crest. Many small animals shelter beneath them.

Sandy inner zones of reef flats have occasional clumps of living corals interspersed with patches of dead coral supporting heavy algal growths. Sausage-like sea-cucumbers are the most obvious animal inhabitants, but the sands hide a variety of burrowing molluscs. Some reef flats have mangrove swamps, with features generally similar to those of coastal wetlands. Reef lagoons, if they have internal reefs of their own reaching to low-water level, may provide the best viewing of all with a variety of true corals and soft corals and a multitude of small mobile fauna. The sheets of fine sediment of lagoon floors are constantly reworked by molluscs, shrimps and worms.

Vegetated cays are commonly dominated by dense stands of *Pisonia grandis*—sometimes called 'the bird killing tree'. Its seeds have a sticky coating which can trap nesting sea birds. The central forest is surrounded by a bank of small salt-tolerant trees and shrubs, with grasses on the seaward side. Along with a wide variety of birds, the inner parts of cays are inhabited by reptiles—mainly lizards—and numerous insects. Ghost crabs are the most prominent occupants of cay beaches, although big turtles are nocturnal visitors during their breeding season. If beach rock has formed, it will be encrusted with limpets and 'coat-of-mail' chitons.

Builders and inhabitants of coral reefs

The Great Barrier Reef's massive coral ramparts and maze of island-fringing reefs stretch for 2000 km along the Queensland coast and support an amazing range of marine plants and animals. The reefs, and especially the 1400 species of fish that live around them, are best seen with the help of a mask and snorkel. But even walkers on the upper surface, when it is exposed or awash at low tide, can discover the great variety of coral shapes and the brilliant colours of the reef's other inhabitants, just some of which are illustrated here.

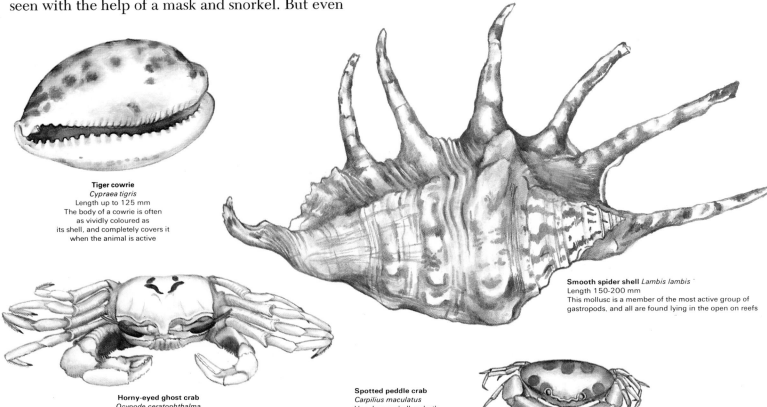

Tiger cowrie
Cypraea tigris
Length up to 125 mm
The body of a cowrie is often
as vividly coloured as
its shell, and completely covers it
when the animal is active

Smooth spider shell *Lambis lambis*
Length 150-200 mm
This mollusc is a member of the most active group of
gastropods, and all are found lying in the open on reefs

Horny-eyed ghost crab
Ocypode ceratophthalma
Width, 50 mm across carapace.
On sandy beaches above the waterline, conical piles
of sand beside a small hole betray the ghost
crab's spiral burrow

Spotted peddle crab
Carpilius maculatus
Very heavy shell on both
body and legs, and 11 large round
spots, distinguish this slow-moving crab which is
found from the shallows down to a depth of over 30 metres

Crenate swimming crab
Thalamita crenata
Width 100 mm across carapace
Five sharp spines behind the eyes on
each side clearly identify this crab.
It is caught in large numbers
for commercial markets

Double-lined sand crab
Matuta planipes
Width, 40 mm across carapace
This crab has wide, flattened claws,
well adapted for digging and swimming.
Matuta are common all around the continent

Leopard-spotted sea-cucumber
Bohadschia argus Length 250 mm
Sea cucumbers are animals, related to starfish
and sea urchins. They live among
coral debris on reef flats

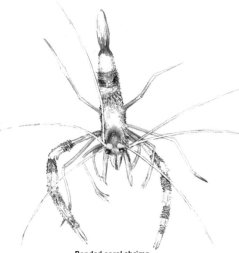

Banded coral shrimp
Stenopus hispidus
Length 50 mm. From crevices in coral, *Stenopus*
picks parasites and fungus growths from reef fish which
remain still while being cleaned

Staghorn coral *Acropora*
Forests of staghorn can
be up to 1.5 metres high and often cover
75 per cent of the reef area

Turban shell
Turbo perspeciosus
Length 50 mm
A hard, round plate on the
foot of the animal that inhabits
this shell allows it to withdraw
into complete protection

Orange-spotted mitre *Mitra mitra*
Length up to 150 mm
Also known as the giant mitre.
When alive, the shell of this
mollusc is covered with a thin skin
which partly hides the pattern

Cloth-of-gold cone shell
Conus textile
Length up to 100 mm. The timid *Conus* will
shrink into its shell at the least disturbance, but
it has a deadly venom, and a live one
should never be handled

Round-head coral *Porites*
Some species of *Porites* form micro-atolls,
over 2 metres in diameter, which are
common on many reef flats

Soft coral *Xenia*
Soft corals do not make hard skeletons, and are
therefore not reef builders. When exposed at low tide
they look tough and leathery

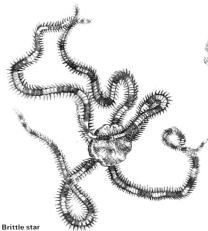

Brittle star
Ophiocoma scolopendrina
Diameter 200 mm
Brittle stars move much faster than starfish and have a more
clearly defined central disc. They inhabit rubble areas of
coral reefs and lie with only part of their bodies exposed

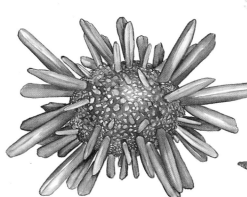

Slate-pencil urchin
Heterocentrotus mammillatus
Diameter 250 mm
The heavy, blunt spines of this sea
urchin may be up to 10 mm thick and
125 mm in length

Blue starfish *Linckia laevigata*
Diameter 250 mm
Great powers of regeneration allow
Linckia to grow a whole new disc and set
of arms on any severed arm

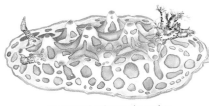

Sea slug *Halgerda aurantiomaculata*
Length 40-50 mm
Colourful sea slugs carry their gills
on the outside of their bodies

Giant clam *Tridacna*
Width up to 350 mm. A pair of shells from
the largest of all giant clams, *Tridacna gigas*,
exhibited at the Australian Museum
in Sydney, weighs over 220 kg

Honeycomb coral *Favites*
Colonies of honeycomb coral, up to 300 mm across,
grow on reef fronts and flats. Individual corallites
are about 15 mm wide

Birds of ocean and shore

Australia's extensive coastline is made up of many natural habitats—from rocky cliffs to tropical forests. Each habitat is the home of a great variety of birds. The 75 species illustrated on the following pages are the ones most commonly seen near the coast, although there are also occasional casual visitors and rarer species. The birds are all illustrated in their usual adult plumage, but there are sometimes slight differences between the sexes, and between adult and immature birds. The drawings are not all in proportion to one another, but an average length is given for each bird.

Sooty tern
Sterna fuscata
Length 460 mm,
wing-span 920 mm

Common tern
Sterna hirundo
Length 305-380 mm

Crested tern
Sterna bergii
Length 460 mm,
wing-span 1020 mm

Caspian tern
Hydroprogne caspia
Length 560 mm,
wing-span 1400 mm

Fairy tern
Sterna nereis
Length 215-265 mm,
wing-span 455-510 mm

Little tern
Sterna albifrons
Length 205-255 mm,
wing-span 445-495 mm

Roseate tern
Sterna dougallii
Length 360 mm,
wing-span 630 mm

White-fronted tern
Sterna striata
Length 420 mm,
wing-span 760 mm

Gull-billed tern
Gelochelidon nilotica
Length 355-430 mm

Pacific gull
Larus pacificus
Length 635 mm

Silver gull
Larus novaehollandiae
Length 400-425 mm

**Southern
black-backed gull**
Larus dominicanus
Length 570 mm

Sacred kingfisher
Halcyon sancta
Length 190-230 mm

Grey-tailed tattler
Tringa brevipes
Length 270 mm

Ruddy turnstone
Arenaria interpres
Length 230 mm

White-capped noddy
Anous minutus
Length 360 mm,
wing-span 650 mm

Mangrove kingfisher
Halcyon chloris
Length 250-280 mm

Banded stilt
Cladorhynchus leucocephalus
Length 380-410 mm

Common noddy
Anous stolidus
Length 400 mm,
wing-span 800 mm

Pied stilt
Himantopus himantopus
Length 385 mm

Beach stone curlew
Burhinus neglectus
Length 530-570 mm

Whimbrel
Numenius phaeopus
Length 400-460 mm

White-necked heron
Ardea pacifica
Length 910 mm

White-faced heron
Ardea novaehollandiae
Length 670 mm

Royal spoonbill
Platalea regia
Length 750 mm

White ibis
Threskiornis molucca
Length 700 mm

Little black cormorant
Phalacrocorax sulcirostris
Length 610 mm

Black cormorant
Phalacrocorax carbo
Length 800 mm

Mangrove heron
Butorides striatus
Length 480 mm

Pied cormorant
Phalacrocorax varius
Length 760 mm

Little pied cormorant
Phalacrocorax melanoleucos
Length 610 mm

Darter
Anhinga melanogaster
Length 900 mm

Black-faced cormorant
Phalacrocorax fuscescens
Length 650 mm

Wandering albatross
Diomedea exulans
Length up to 1350 mm,
wing-span to 3250 mm

Black-browed albatross
Diomedea melanophrys
Length 880 mm,
wing-span 2200 mm

Little egret
Egretta garzetta
Length 560 mm

Brown booby
Sula leucogaster
Length 740 mm

Large egret
Egretta alba
Length 830 mm

Sooty oystercatcher
Haematopus fuliginosus
Length 480 mm,
female usually larger
than male

Australian pelican
Pelecanus conspicillatus
Length 1600-1800 mm

Pied oystercatcher
Haematopus ostralegus
Length 480 mm,
female usually
larger than male

Swamp hen
Porphyrio porphyrio
Length 440-480 mm

Southern giant petrel
Macronectes giganteus
Length 900 mm, male
larger than female

Australasian gannet
Morus serrator
Length 875 mm

Great skua
Stercorarius skua
Length up to 630 mm,
wing-span up to 900 mm.
Female larger than male

Northern giant petrel
Macronectes halli
Length 900 mm,
male larger than female

Black swan
Cygnus atratus
Length 1200-1300 mm,
male larger than female

Bar-tailed godwit
Limosa lapponica
Length 380-430 mm,
female larger than male

Eastern curlew
Numenius madagascariensis
Length 650 mm

Reef heron
Egretta sacra
Length 600-750 mm

Black-tailed godwit
Limosa limosa
Length 380 mm,
female larger than male

Red-necked avocet
*Recurvirostra
novaehollandiae*
Length 440 mm

Greenshank
Tringa nebularia
Length 340-360 mm

Knot
Calidris canutus
Length 250 mm

**Sharp-tailed
sandpiper**
Calidris acuminata
Length 215 mm,
female smaller
than male

Curlew sandpiper
Calidris ferruginea
Length 210 mm

Large-billed dotterel
Charadrius leschenaultii
Length 225 mm

Hooded dotterel
Charadrius rubricollis
Length 205 mm

Terek sandpiper
Tringa terek
Length 240-290 mm

Mongolian dotterel
Charadrius mongolus
Length 200 mm

Double-banded dotterel
Charadrius bicinctus
Length 180 mm

Red-capped dotterel
Charadrius ruficapillus
Length 150 mm

Brahminy kite
Haliastur indus
Length 450-510 mm

White-breasted sea eagle
Haliaeetus leucogaster
Length of female 840 mm,
male 760 mm

Osprey
Pandion haliaetus
Length 500-630 mm

Grey plover
Pluvialis squatarola
Length 290 mm

Red-necked stint
Calidris ruficollis
Length 150 mm

Eastern golden plover
Pluvialis dominica
Length 250 mm

Black duck
Anas superciliosa
Length 470-610 mm,
male larger than female

Little penguin
Eudyptula minor
Length 330 mm
standing

Short-tailed shearwater
Puffinus tenuirostris
Length 400 mm

Fluttering shearwater
Puffinus gavia
Length 330 mm

Fairy prion
Pachyptila turtur
Length 230 mm

Flesh-footed shearwater
Puffinus carneipes
Length 450 mm

Wedge-tailed shearwater
Puffinus pacificus
Length 430 mm

PART 2

The ocean and the weather

The sea, even at its most placid, is the ruler of coasts. It draws its own boundaries. It determines the nature and extent of shoreline life.

Often its action moulds land margins and nearshore contours, prescribing what human activities a coast will support. Yet the sea is never its own master.

Global forces direct its movements, and atmospheric conditions dictate its moods. The ocean must do the bidding of winds.

And it can be made an agent of awesome destructiveness.

Science has achieved a broad understanding of weather systems and the sea's responses to them.

Vast current circulations can be charted and surface disturbances tracked.

But the complexity of coastal effects, in fair weather or foul, remains endlessly fascinating. Waves and shore formations, interacting, give each locality its own rules of water and sand movement.

Those rules can change—sometimes forever. People are learning, usually from costly errors, that coasts are dynamic environments.

They cannot conform with human notions of stability.

Winter winds whip spray from the crests of a choppy sea

Ocean currents How warm water can flow on a cold coast

Gentle currents in the world's great oceans represent massive movements of water. They carry chilled polar seas towards the equator, and they shift warm water far from the tropics. Near a coast, they are more important than the local climate in determining water temperature and the range of marine life.

Major currents have their origins in the push of prevailing winds. The steadiest winds—from the east near the equator and from the west in high latitudes—are deflected by the earth's rotation so that they circulate. Currents follow the same pattern of circulation—counter-clockwise in the Southern Hemisphere and clockwise in the Northern Hemisphere. Incidental winds may produce surface flows in other directions, but the basic pattern is constant.

Only northern Australia, shielded by islands, is not subject to currents flowing on an oceanic scale. The rest of the coast lies between the vast circulation systems of the South Indian, Southern and South Pacific Oceans.

Australia differs from all other continents in having no cold surface current on its west coast. A cold current does run consistently northward in the depths, but the central-west coast has two warm currents on the surface at different times of the year. Between October and April, anti-cyclones passing to the south push warm surface water up the coast from the Great Australian Bight at 1-2 km/h. From May to September, when anti-cyclones cross farther to the north, they push warm water from the Timor Sea to the Bight, usually at less than 1 km/h.

In the Southern Ocean the currents, forced by westerly winds, move generally eastward along the South Australian and Tasmanian coasts, but they are not constant. The water at any point may flow in any direction, usually at less than 1 km/h but often more rapidly in Bass Strait.

The East Australian current is really a series of eddies from a westward tropical flow which

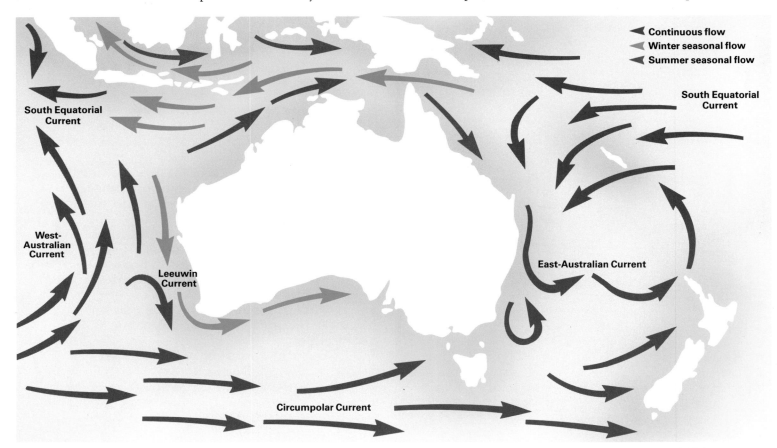

Continuous flow
Winter seasonal flow
Summer seasonal flow

South Equatorial Current

South Equatorial Current

West-Australian Current

Leeuwin Current

East-Australian Current

Circumpolar Current

Australia is bounded on three sides by large oceans; as a result much of the coast is affected by large, oceanic scale movements of water. In northern Australia, currents change direction in response to the annual monsoon winds.

Different fish for different water

FISH are called 'cold-blooded' but their body heat closely matches that of the surrounding water and varies with it. Each species has its own range of tolerance; at too high or too low a temperature, it may stop breeding or eating.

Fish and other creatures capable of moving can stay within their safe temperature range by travelling as seasons change. Many species, for example sharks and squid, migrate to warmer waters, and others simply change depth. Within the survival range of temperatures, fish have a narrower range at which they exhibit certain patterns of behaviour. Southern bluefin tuna, for example, feed alone in water below 16.7°C. Above 20° they move in schools but do not bite well. Only between these two temperatures are large quantities caught.

Under 16.7°C	16.7 to 20°C	Over 20°C

Exploring the currents from space

Buoys fitted with radio beacons have been set adrift off eastern Australia since the early 1970s. Their movements have been monitored by space satellites and charted by the Commonwealth Scientific and Industrial Research Organisation.

In 1979, as part of a much bigger international global atmosphere research programme, nearly 300 buoys carrying instrument packages were released in Southern Hemisphere oceans. Three satellites, Tiros-N and NOAA from the USA, and Argos from France, pick up transmissions. Their information, along with shipboard measurements, is expected to add much to the understanding of Australia's ocean currents, water temperatures and coastal weather. Other satellites, such as the US Seasat, continue and expand radar and microwave experiments that were begun with the Landsat and Skylab satellites. Seasat is presently testing an all-weather system of monitoring major currents, ice movements, sea conditions and fish productivity.

Satellite scanning of surface heat radiation can produce images, similar to photographs, known as thermal maps. Around the Australian coast they show the persistent but seasonally shifting fronts between bodies of water of different temperature, where fish congregate to feed.

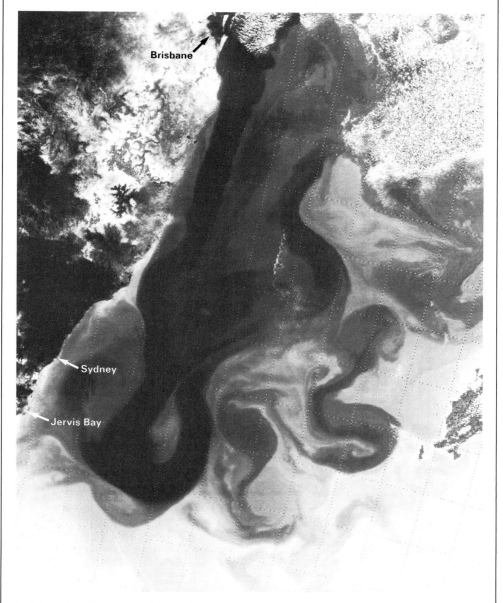

An infra-red satellite picture of the north Tasman and south Coral Seas in early December. Warm areas appear dark and cool areas light. The broad, warm East-Australian Current, flowing down the coast past Brisbane and Sydney and looping around off Jervis Bay, is very prominent

splits north-west towards Torres Strait and southward along the Great Barrier Reef. Inside the reef, circulation patterns are confused. The southward flow is strongest and most constant from outside the reef opposite Townsville, Qld, to Coffs Harbour, NSW. There it forms a belt 30-100 km wide and reaches speeds of 2-4 km/h in summer. Farther south the flow is less consistent and normal speeds are about 1.5 km/h in summer and 1 km/h in winter.

In northern Australia, currents are slow-moving and they change direction in response to the annual monsoon winds. Close to the north-west coast, the current flows predominantly north-east to east in winter, and north in summer. In Torres Strait the current flows eastward from December to March—when it is driven by the monsoons blowing from the north-west, and westward for the rest of the year.

The greatest temperature variation in Australian waters occurs off the mid-latitude Pacific coast, from central Queensland to central New South Wales. There the ocean currents shift most, and the origins of water masses change with the seasons. The temperature in a current can quite often vary as much as 3°C from that of the surrounding seas.

The surface of the sea also warms and cools with changes in air temperature, but not nearly as much as land surfaces. The sea is scarcely affected by day-and-night contrasts, and lags in its response to summer or winter extremes. It is usually warmest in February and coldest in August, with a year-round range in one place of only about 10°C.

Deeper in the ocean, temperatures vary little and the water is always cold. Shifts of current or strong winds blowing persistently from the shore can drive warm surface water out to sea, to be replaced by an upwelling of cold water. Upwelling from the continental shelf occurs within 15 km of the central east coast between July and December. It increases the concentration of dissolved nitrates and phosphates that nourish marine organisms. In extreme cases, the surface bloom of algae can be so profuse that the sea takes on a red tinge.

The richest concentrations of nutrients occur at the boundaries between bodies of water of different temperature. So fish—whether their diet is marine organisms or other species of fish—head for the margins of currents. They find them by aligning themselves to the flow of the current and adapting to its speed, or even by using visual markers such as the sun. Eggs and larvae drift passively with a current until they reach its edge.

Fishermen can sometimes spot a front of contrasting temperature as choppy water—caused by conflicting currents—or as a line of litter or scum. Often a change of colour can be seen. Another clue may be sea birds flocking to feed. But commercial fishing boats are increasingly equipped with instruments to detect changes in water temperature at a distance. Others follow courses plotted from thermal maps—aerial or satellite 'pictures' of the heat radiated from different bodies of water.

The tides Intricate rhythms of ocean advance and retreat

High tide comes twice a day to some parts of the Australian coast and only once to others. Even where two tides a day are usual, they may arrive at uneven intervals and reach markedly different levels. The height of the tide also differs widely on different parts of the coast. In the north-west the water level sometimes rises and falls by as much as 12 metres, changing the look of the coast beyond recognition in an hour or two. Yet along the coast south of Perth the tidal range is sometimes negligible.

The diversity of Australian tides is partly accounted for by the fact that each of the oceans and semi-enclosed seas around the continent has its own tidal system. Where systems meet, the tidal forces combine in some places and cancel each other out in others.

All the tidal systems have their origins in the gravitational pulls of the Moon and the Sun. The waters of the oceans are drawn towards the point of the Earth's surface nearest the Sun or the Moon so that they bulge outwards. This ocean bulging is slight, but if the world were a smooth sphere and covered to an even depth by water the bulges could be depicted as low waves, half as long as the world's circumference, moving continuously round the globe in company with the Moon and the Sun.

In practice, tides do not cross entire oceans but are trapped in ocean basins of irregular shape and depth, and they rock around one or more points in mid-ocean. Because the Earth is rotating beneath them, they take apparently curving courses, rebounding from coasts sideways so that they progress around the rims of ocean basins. They cannot match the speed at which the Moon orbits around the Earth. That is why the highest tides come just after new or full Moon.

Tidal waves rebounding from land masses run

Narrow range
Medium range
Wide range

The range of the tide—the difference between high water and low water—around the Australian coast varies from 600 mm in the south-west to more than 12 metres in the north-west of the continent

into one another. If they meet head-on and their wave motions match, they form 'standing waves' of constantly high water. Those waves are extremely long and low compared with the waves kicked up by winds at sea.

When a tidal wave travels in over a continental shelf, it shoals—slows and steepens—in much the same way as an ordinary wind-wave reaching a beach. The more extensive the shelf, the

steeper the tidal wave when it reaches the coast. But even after steepening, tidal waves are low in relation to the slope of most beaches. So they usually rebound without breaking.

If a tidal wave carries on into an estuary or a river mouth, it continues to shoal. In extreme cases it may oversteepen and break, picking up speed and moving up the river as a wall of surf called a tidal bore. Bores have been reported

---

How the oceans are pulled out of shape

THE MOON'S gravitational pull reduces the weight of anything on the part of the Earth's surface facing it by a mere 0.0000001 per cent, or 1 gram in 10 tonnes. The Sun, because it is so far away, exerts only about half that

pull. But each of these gravitational forces causes the oceans to bulge slightly towards it. The Earth's rotation produces a balancing force and on the opposite side of the planet the oceans bulge away from the direction of

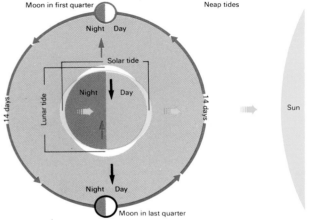

Tides are formed as ocean waters bulge towards the gravitational pulls of the Sun and the Moon. The Earth's rotation causes a balancing bulge on the opposite side. When Moon and Sun are in line their pulls combine to produce the greatest tidal bulge and spring tides result. The lowest tides, neap tides, occur when Moon and Sun are at right angles to each other

Two tides a day
Two different tides a day
One or two tides a day
One tide a day

There is wide variation in the type of tide around Australia. Little of the coast receives two equal tides daily. The part of the south-west that has only one tide a day is also a region of low tide range

Why tides bend

ANYTHING moving on the Earth or in its atmosphere, except along the Equator, is subject to a constant force, called Coriolus deflection, which pulls the moving body off a straight path. Caused by the earth's spinning, the pull is always to the left in the Southern Hemisphere and to the right in the Northern Hemisphere.

Friction is usually too great for the deflection to have any effect on movement over land. But if there is little or no friction, as with air and water movements, the moving body goes on a curving course. Free of any interference, it will travel in circles. If there were no coast, tides would swing in the direction of Coriolus deflection, as do all winds, except cyclones. Southern Hemisphere tides, continually bent leftward, would circulate anticlockwise, like bath water spiralling toward a plug hole. But interference by the coast is great. The tide rebounds from a shore and the leftward deflection sends it farther along the same coast, so that its progress is to the right of its original direction—clockwise in the Southern Hemisphere.

---

more than 80 km upstream in the Victoria River, 300 km south of Darwin.

Shoaling over a broad continental shelf causes a tide to rise quickly but ebb more slowly. It also increases the difference between high and low water levels. This tidal range is generally greatest on a broad continental shelf or in a wide-mouthed bay or gulf where the inner shores confine the rising tide and amplify it. In a wide bay with a narrow entrance, such as Port Phillip Bay in Victoria, the tidal range is reduced because the flow in and out is restricted.

Only one high tide a day reaches the shore on the Western Australian coast from Geraldton south, and in corners of the Gulf of Carpentaria. Many other parts of coastal Australia, including the stretch between Melbourne and Adelaide, receive a mixture of daily and twice-daily tides.

The times and levels of tides are predicted in the national tide tables, which are drawn up by the Royal Australian Navy's hydrographic office. They predict low and high water for each day of the year at 66 primary ports.

The tables also list variations for 352 secondary ports which have tidal characteristics related to a primary port. There are additional data from which to calculate levels at times between high and low water, and information on tidal currents.

The tide at any particular time and place may, however, be markedly different from the prediction in the tables. The calculations cannot allow for short-term local weather forces such as wind or atmospheric pressure.

---

the gravitational force. The oceans bulge most when the Sun, Moon and Earth are in line, at new Moon and full Moon. Then the gravitational effects of Sun and Moon are combined in the same direction. Soon afterwards, coasts receive spring tides—so called not because of the time of year but because of the way they jump up. The range between low and high water levels is up to 20 per cent greater than average.

When the Moon and Sun are at right-angles in relation to the Earth, at the first and third quarters of the Moon, each counteracts the other's effect. Ocean bulging is spread around the globe instead of being concentrated on two sides. The tides that result have a range of about 20 per cent less than average. They are called neap tides, from an Old English word which probably meant 'weak'.

The Moon exerts its strongest pull at any point every 24 hours 50.5 minutes, and its tidal effects on the open ocean occur twice in this period—when the point is nearest the Moon, and when the two are on opposite sides of the Earth.

Meanwhile, the Sun exerts its pull every 24 hours at any point, and its tidal effects at sea occur every 12 hours. Therefore after the Moon's and Sun's effects have

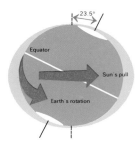

Tidal bulges of southern winter

The height of successive tides varies as the year progresses, because tidal bulges caused by the Sun's pull and the Earth's rotation change position on the Earth's surface. Like the seasons, the bulges move north and south, because the Earth's axis is tilted at 23.5° to its plane of orbit

coincided, at new and full Moon, there is a delay between solar and lunar influences, increasing by 25.25 minutes each time they occur.

The gap widens for seven days, with tides becoming correspondingly weaker, then starts to close again because the Moon's twice-daily effects catch up with those of the Sun. Tide heights go through a 14-day cycle of increase and decrease, twice every lunar month.

Heights of tides are further varied day by day because

the Moon's plane of orbit is tilted in relation to the Earth's axis of rotation, and because the Earth's axis is tilted in relation to the plane of its orbit around the Sun. A point on the Earth's surface passes through slightly different parts of the lunar and solar bulges in the oceans each time the Earth revolves. The Sun's maximum influence occurs when it is overhead at the Equator, so the highest tides of all come at the equinoxes, in late March and September.

Other slight variations in tide height occur because the Moon's orbit wavers, and because both it and the Earth's orbit are not circular but elliptical. The Moon repeats exactly the same orbit only every 18.6 years, although it swings in from farthest to its nearest point—a difference of 24 000 km—and out again every 27.55 days. The Sun is closest, exerting its greatest pull, in early January. Early in July it is about 5.5 million km farther away.

Friction is generated between the tides and the ocean beds and it is slowing the Earth's rotation by about a second every 120 000 years. Before land masses and oceans formed, the world probably rotated quickly so that days may have been less than 10 hours long and there may have been 1000 to the year.

Waves and their patterns
How the ocean carries wind energy to the coast

Ocean waves, arriving in never-ending procession, suggest to the eye that the sea is travelling with them. It seldom is. Apart from the slow movement of currents, the water beyond a coastal shelf virtually stays in the same place, rotating under the waves and rising and falling with them.

Some wave energy comes from tidal movement, and occasionally from disturbances such as coastal landslides or undersea earthquakes. But nearly all waves seen around the coast have been generated by winds transferring energy to the water surface.

The highest waves normally seen approaching a coast are driven by local storms. Sailors and weather forecasters call them 'seas'. Beneath them there is a smoother, more regular 'swell', born of faraway, long-ago gales. Their energy may have crossed an entire ocean.

Because winds seldom maintain exactly the same direction and strength for more than a few seconds, the waves they generate are confused and choppy at first. They have sharp individual peaks, and the intervals between successive peaks vary. Once waves move away from the influence of the wind, however, they settle into the regular patterns of ocean swell. They fan out about 35° on each side of the direction of the wind and take curving courses across the sea.

Eventually they form groups of long, low waves travelling at matching speeds. The group's width is that of the storm front generating the waves, and its length is determined by the location and duration of the storm.

Wave groups tend to generate long period waves. At the coast this long wave is often reflected seawards, and waves are higher or lower in relation to the shoreline depending on whether they arrive on the crest or in the trough of the long wave. Waves at the crest of groups are larger than those between groups, and the length of the group determines the number of waves between crests. The myth of the 7th or 9th wave being larger arises from local observation and may be correct for many days of the year—but it is only relevant to fully developed seas; developing seas are almost random.

Each wave in a swell pattern is evenly shaped. Smoothly curved crests are centred between troughs, with each crest as high above normal sea level as the following trough is below it. Water particles rotate under each wind-generated wave to a depth equal to about half the distance between successive crests. As the water shallows, the waves slow and bunch up. They steepen at the front and their crests mount to a peak.

Whether a wave breaks or not depends on its steepness in relation to the shore slope. Ocean swell waves and wind-driven local seas generally break if the slope is no steeper than 1:10. A gradual run-in gives them the distance needed to increase their height and angle of tilt. Where the sea meets a smooth cliff face, unstable local storm waves explode against it in showers of spray, but swell waves do not—unless they have already shoaled on a shelf at the cliff base.

The most consistent and easily observable result of wave action is beach drift. Waves rarely come in at right-angles to the shoreline: usually they carry sand, shingle and other debris obliquely up a beach. But when the water runs back, it takes the shortest way down. So successive waves shunt sand along in a series of zigzags.

More debris is drawn along, below the water-line, in a current set up by the thrust of the angled waves after they break. The combined effect is a gradual, massive shift of sediment. If, over the years, waves arrive predominantly from the same direction, sand accumulates at one end of the beach, and may form a spit jutting out into the sea, or a tombolo linking the mainland shore with a nearby island.

Waves generally break when their height is slightly less than the depth of water under them, and isolated early breakers indicate a submerged reef. A line of breakers curving in towards both ends of a beach shows that the sea bed is raised in the middle; if the breaker line fans the other way, there is shallower water at the ends. Interrupted lines indicate variations in depth.

In general, the greater the distance over which waves are affected by a shallowing sea bed, the more they slow and bunch up and the higher they

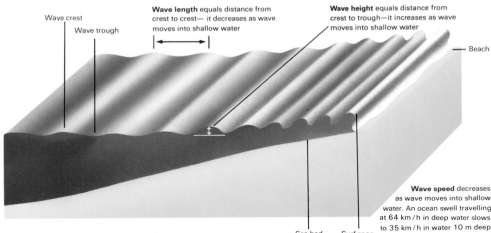

Wave crest

Wave trough

Wave length equals distance from crest to crest— it decreases as wave moves into shallow water

Wave height equals distance from crest to trough—it increases as wave moves into shallow water

— Beach

Wave speed decreases as wave moves into shallow water. An ocean swell travelling at 64 km/h in deep water slows to 35 km/h in water 10 m deep

Sea bed   Surf zone

A wave breaks when the water depth is slightly less than its height. When waves enter shallow water successive crests catch up with one another, they slow down and grow taller until eventually they become unstable, topple over, and break

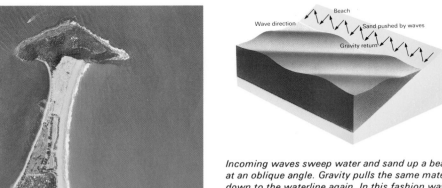

Beach

Wave direction   Sand pushed by waves

Gravity return

Incoming waves sweep water and sand up a beach at an oblique angle. Gravity pulls the same material down to the waterline again. In this fashion waves transport sand along beaches. This movement may be reversed when waves come from another direction, but over many years waves arriving from one principal direction can shift millions of tonnes of sand along an entire coast

Constant movement of sand in one direction can form a barrier that turns an inlet into a lagoon, or build a tombolo like that at Sydney's Palm Beach

How waves are bent

A WAVE slows only where the water particles rotating under it encounter friction with the sea floor. Elsewhere along the wave, in deeper water, its forward momentum is unchanged. So the wave bends around the point of interference—it is refracted. By the time all parts of a wave have reached shoaling depth, it may have been shaped into a curve almost matching that of the shoreline.

If a wave has no time to adapt fully and comes in at an angle, and if the beach is steep, it may rebound without breaking. Then it will be refracted further on its way out. It may even loop back, and in this fashion progress along the shore.

The refraction of waves around headlands into bays has a particularly noticeable effect on beaches. The bunching of waves just inside a headland concentrates their energy there. The surf is not high but the volume of water is. Farther up the bay, the waves are stretched—their energy and water volume are dispersed. The inequality creates a strong longshore flow, keeping sand out of the corner of the bay and depositing it in increasing amounts towards the other end.

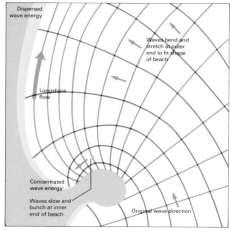

Above: A simplified headland refraction pattern, with red lines showing how wave energy is diverted to generate a longshore flow of water and sand. Left: Intricate refractions around a headland and islands at Batehaven, NSW

---

rise. Once this starts, all waves travel at the same speed over the same depth of water—regardless of their earlier velocity.

The tallest waves ordinarily seen on a coast, driven by gales in the immediate area, may break from heights of 20 metres or more. They may arrive twice as frequently as ocean swell waves, and be immensely destructive. But they travel no faster. And the harder a wind blows, the higher they mount. A wind averaging 37 km/h, blowing in a consistent direction for 10 hours, could be expected to produce waves about 2.44 metres high.

Even in violent and far-reaching gales, waves rarely exceed 25 metres on the deep ocean. If they are pushed to a height of more than one-seventh of their length, their surface tension is destroyed and they disintegrate in spray. There are exceptions, and the tallest ocean wave for which there is good evidence was observed from a US Navy tanker in the North Pacific in 1933, during a 125 km/h gale. It was judged to be 34 metres from trough to crest.

The length of a wave moving in a group does not have to be measured: it can be calculated from the time between the passage of one wave and the next. If a wave is followed 10 seconds later by another, it is about 157 metres long.

In ocean swell waves, the time interval can also be used to calculate velocity. So waves 10 seconds apart are travelling at about 16 metres per second, or 57 km/h. Wind-driven waves may hold together at more than 80 km/h, but do not normally exceed 60 km/h.

When any wave is crossing water of a depth less than half of the wave length, its speed is governed by water depth alone: a depth of 3 metres permits a speed of 20 km/h, but at six times the depth—18 metres—a wave cannot travel much more than twice as fast.

Mysterious patterns on the beach

No complete explanation for beach cusps has yet been found. They are probably the result of complex wave motions caused by the interaction of reflected and incoming waves. Cusp formations on surf beaches— such as these at Pearl Beach on the New South Wales central coast—are also often associated with the presence of rip currents. The effect is a scalloped waterline, with a series of crescent-shaped depressions regularly spaced along the beach face. The scooped-out areas may be only a few metres wide; or could reach for hundreds of metres.

Shock waves that cross the ocean

VIOLENT disturbances of ocean water occur with earthquakes and volcanic eruptions in or around an ocean basin. After such an event, waves hundreds of kilometres long and up to half an hour apart race from the shock zone at speeds approaching 800 km/h. Quite commonly but, in fact, wrongly called 'tidal waves', they are known to scientists as tsunami. The name comes from the Japanese words *tsu*, meaning port, and *nami*, meaning waves.

In mid-ocean, tsunami may be only a few centimetres high, and they are often so low away from the coast that their passing may not be noticed. But even over the deepest ocean they still slow and steepen—like all waves in shallowing water. They have time to build to terrifying heights—sometimes more than 30 metres—before running ashore for minutes on end with catastrophic effects. The highest recorded tsunami, which occurred off Alaska in 1964, measured 67 metres.

The coasts most menaced by tsunami are those facing and lying parallel to an earthquake fault line. The only area of Australia threatened this way is the east coast, which is aligned with major faults under the central South Pacific and on its eastern rim. But tsunami effects are largely buffered by the land mass of New Zealand and by the Great Barrier Reef.

Nearshore currents Powerful local water movements

No two parts of the coast are exactly the same. In places that look alike at first glance, shoreline features differ subtly—and swimming or boating conditions can vary drastically. In the interplay of waves and tides with the land and the sea bottom, each area has its own complex patterns.

The simplest local movement of water—and the one that most frequently surprises inexperienced swimmers—is the longshore current. This is the force that makes it difficult for a surf bather to stay between safety flags. It runs along any shore where waves break at an angle—and waves rarely come in exactly parallel to the beach.

When angled waves break they thrust water not only in a swash up the beach, but also in a persistent flow parallel to the shore. The current is spread right across the surf zone, but it is strongest about halfway between the breaker line and the beach. Its speed, which is related to the height and steepness of waves, may be as much as 1 metre a second. Longshore currents are not hazardous, however, unless they carry a swimmer into a deep channel or a rip.

Variations in the slope of the sea bed or the shape of a shore may cause unevenness in the height of a line of waves along a beach. When they break, the water level inside the surf zone is also uneven. That results in longshore currents of a different type: they run from high levels to low, and then they turn seawards to become feeders for rip currents.

Rips are strong, narrow currents running out through the surf zone to beyond the breakers. They flow at speeds up to 4 metres a second—a boon to board surfers seeking a free ride out, but a hazard for swimmers. People caught in rips exhaust themselves if they try to swim back to the shore against such a current. Confident swimmers are better off striking out sideways: rips are seldom more than 15 metres wide.

Weaker swimmers should conserve their energy and let a rip carry them out past the breakers. There, when the current slackens, it is easy to move to one side and make for a different point on the beach. Never rest for long on a sand bar—if the wave pattern changes even slightly the bar can collapse, with disastrous results.

Rip locations are not constant, however. They may come and go, or shift position, with changes in the direction of wave approach. And they do not always run straight out to sea: if the waves break at a considerable angle to the beach, rips are angled away in the opposite direction.

Tide movements are seldom of much significance in comparison with wave-induced currents near a mainland shore. In shallow estuaries and around islands and headlands, however, the effects of tidal currents are more pronounced, and sometimes startling.

Speeds of tidal currents fluctuate with the rise and fall of the tide, and there are usually two

Rips are formed as the mass of water pushed up to a beach by breaking waves finds its path back to the sea in narrow, fast-flowing currents. Water runs down the beach, and sideways along the beach face, creating longshore currents which feed rips as they travel seaward through the surf zone, and between channels in any sand bars. The current dissipates beyond the breakers at the rip head

Twin, parallel rips push water seaward from Dee Why beach, north of Sydney. The two channels of deep, fast-moving water interrupt the lines of incoming waves. Plumes of sand, carried from the beach by the currents, spread out into the calm water beyond the breaker zone. Rips like these are usually less than 15 metres wide, and may be moving as fast as 4 metres per second

Channelled tidal races, such as this one at Walcott Inlet in the Kimberleys, WA, can reach 28 km/h

The empty threat of 'undertow'

STANDING in the shallows, you feel the seaward backwash of broken waves tugging at your feet. Just ahead of a sharply steepening wave, you may feel water being drawn backwards into it. And if a breaker dumps you, its churning motion pulls you down and away from the shore for a moment. But it is not undertow. No subsurface motion exists that can take people out to sea against the advance of waves on a beach. If the word undertow is used to describe a real danger, it is usually a mistaken reference to a localised rip, or to the existence of a channel with a strong ebb-tide current.

maximum and two minimum rates during each cycle. The currents reverse themselves so quickly that there is scarcely a moment when they are not running. In deep water their top speed is seldom more than about 1 km/h. Even in shallow water, as long as it is not confined, a tidal current rarely exceeds 7 km/h. But where tides are channelled, the currents can easily achieve twice that speed.

In areas of extreme tide range, such as north-western Australia, a channelled tidal race may reach 28 km/h. In the rocky estuaries of the Kimberleys district of Western Australia, water velocities on that scale produce tidal bores —steep-fronted, breaking waves that run far upriver. Dangerous bores, to be avoided by small boats, are usually noted in the official sailing directions for more frequented areas.

Fast tidal races also produce dangerous eddies and whirlpools. Vigorous eddies are encountered in Cambridge Gulf, the approach to the port of Wyndham, WA. There the tidal current reaches 17 km/h. Even in areas where the tide range is much less—in Sydney Harbour, for example—eddies frequently make boating tricky.

One area where tidal currents can be particularly surprising is around islands ringed by barrier reefs. However slowly the currents move in deep water at the edge of a reef, they may run over its shallow coral terraces at speeds as high as 7 km/h. When they are at their maximum speed, alternating eddies form and break away at the downstream margin of the reef.

Barrier reefs normally lie near mean sea level—the mid-tide height—and are uncovered at low tide. Often during high tide they are covered by less than 1 metre of water. For a major part of the tidal cycle, breakers carry water across the reef and keep the lagoon level above the sea level outside. So there may be a continuous flow of water out through channels in the reef, even when the tide is coming in.

Where a coral barrier is always above the water level, forming an atoll, there is no water inflow from breakers. Then the lagoon behaves like any bay with a restricted entrance: if the passage of a large lagoon is narrow, powerful tidal currents will flow through it.

Bars rebuild a beach

AFTER storm waves have left a beach, nearshore water circulation starts returning lost sand. Complex oscillations formed by rip currents and surface currents caused directly by winds blowing over the water, deposit sand in a series of half-loops, called crescentic bars, which are fully formed in about two days. They may remain static for weeks, but gradually they link up with beach cusps and the troughs between fill with sand. Eventually the bars are cut by channels. They decay, and all the sand is pushed on to the beach.

Crescentic bars about to decay and deposit their sand on to the beach at Redhead, near Newcastle, NSW

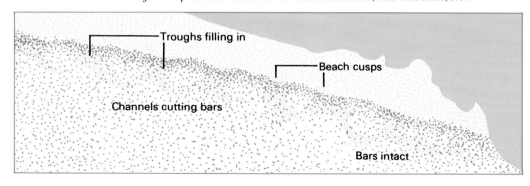

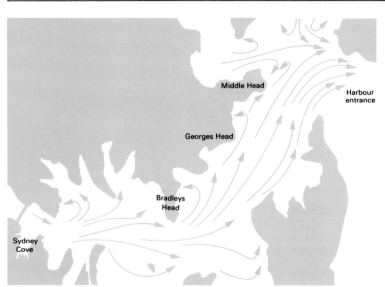

Wherever an estuary, bay or lagoon has its access to the open sea restricted by a narrow entrance channel, strong tidal currents can occur as the level within attempts to adjust to the level outside. This is most noticeable in the rocky estuaries of north-western Australia under extreme tidal ranges. But even in areas such as Sydney Harbour, where the tide range is much less, strong eddies can form, although they are much less dangerous. In this chart of the tidal pattern in Sydney Harbour at maximum ebb tide, eddies can be seen forming around Bradleys Head and Georges Head

Wind and weather patterns

The interaction of ocean and atmosphere

All weather stems from differences in air temperature and pressure. The earth's surface forms the bottom of an ocean of air, extending about 160 km above it. Although the gas molecules of the atmosphere are light, collectively they exert enormous pressure on the earth—about 10 tonnes per square metre at sea level. People are unaware of it because the pressure is not merely downwards: it is equal in all directions.

Air heated from the sun's radiation on the earth's surface expands and rises, carrying evaporated moisture if it is over an ocean. Expansion reduces its pressure, and this loss of pressure—not the height to which the air rises—causes it to cool and contract. Moisture condenses in clouds of water droplets. As contraction goes on the air sinks, and its increasing pressure raises its temperature again.

The sun's radiation promotes permanent convection systems which carry air from equatorial to subtropical regions at high level, and back to the equator at low level. This creates belts of sinking, high pressure air in both hemispheres, centred about latitude 30° but shifting with the seasonal track of the sun, and constant north-east or south-east 'trade' winds. There are further convection systems between the subtropical belt and the polar regions, causing strong airstreams from the west above latitude 40°.

Locally, however, the sun's effect is intermittent, especially over land. So the result is patchy: neighbouring bodies of air behave in contrasting ways. Sinking air creating a warm, calm, pressurised 'high' may be followed in a day or two by a cold, stormy, depressed 'low' of rising air. Moving pressure systems maintain their contrasts for days because of the time air takes to rise—to 15 000 metres above sea level—and sink again.

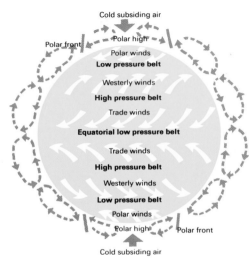

Surface winds and vertical convection systems create the basic pattern of global air movements

Prevailing winds are evidence of the movement of air of different origin, temperature and moisture in vast, consistent patterns. They play a big part in determining the basic climate of a coast. But its day-to-day weather is more noticeably affected by incidental, ever-changing winds created by a local unevenness of air pressure.

The air seeks to equalise pressure by flowing from a high to a low, but it cannot do so directly. The earth's rotation bends the airstream into an almost circular curve. Winds spiral gently out from a high until they are close to a low. Then they spiral in towards it much more rapidly.

At the same time, both the high and the low are moving. The distance between them may be changing, and each of them may also be changing in shape and intensity. So the direction and force of the winds they produce are highly variable in any one place. They can be forecast only by trying to predict exactly where the pressure systems will go and how they may by modified.

Winds around highs and lows spiral in opposite directions. In the Southern Hemisphere their motions are counter-clockwise around a high and clockwise around a low. High-pressure wind circulations are called anticyclones, and all low-pressure systems are technically cyclones. But those originating outside the tropics are normally termed depressions.

Subtropical anticyclones, separated by troughs of low pressure, move fairly regularly across Australia in a generally eastward direction. They are particularly well defined because they have formed from air sinking on to the flat surface of the Indian Ocean, and few mountains disturb them as they pass over the continent.

The anticyclone belt, shifting seasonally, is centred in late winter from around Geraldton, WA, to Cape Byron, NSW, and in late summer across northern Tasmania. On average, five individual highs occur every month, and each takes about five days to cross the continent. But at any particular time, a high may be almost stationary, or it may be travelling at more than 2000 km a day. The movement of one body of air is largely governed by the position of others.

Between highs and troughs there are frequently sharply defined boundaries—'cold

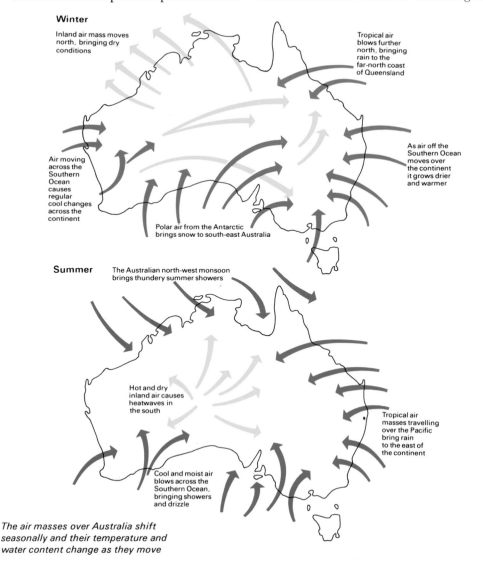

Winter

Inland air mass moves north, bringing dry conditions

Tropical air blows further north, bringing rain to the far-north coast of Queensland

Air moving across the Southern Ocean causes regular cool changes across the continent

As air off the Southern Ocean moves over the continent it grows drier and warmer

Polar air from the Antarctic brings snow to south-east Australia

Summer

The Australian north-west monsoon brings thundery summer showers

Hot and dry inland air causes heatwaves in the south

Tropical air masses travelling over the Pacific bring rain to the east of the continent

Cool and moist air blows across the Southern Ocean, bringing showers and drizzle

The air masses over Australia shift seasonally and their temperature and water content change as they move

fronts' marked in coastal regions by towering clouds, squalls, heavy rain and sometimes thunderstorms. Otherwise the weather in the anticyclone belt is dry and clear. Winds are light, and variable in direction.

South of the subtropical highs, and shifting seasonally in the same way, is an east-moving low-pressure system. Its major depressions are centred well towards Antarctica, but secondary lows and troughs bring disturbed winter weather to the south-western corner of Western Australia, to Victoria and Tasmania, and to New South Wales as far as its mid-north coast. Winter winds in these regions are mainly from the west, varying day by day from breezes to gales, and swinging from mild, drizzling north-westerlies to cold, showery south-westerlies.

North of the anticyclone belt, coastal regions are dominated except in summer by the strong, persistent flow of south-east 'trade' winds from the Pacific. Warm and moist when they cross the east coast, they are hot and parched by the time they reach the north-west. In Darwin they may blow at 50 km/h, and the accompanying dust haze may cut visibility to less than 2.5 km.

A third pressure belt rules summer conditions in northern Australia. The intertropical front—a 'weather equator' of rising air where the wind systems of the two hemispheres converge—starts to move south in October, carrying with it a string of highly unstable lows. The Asian northeast monsoon becomes the Australian northwest monsoon. From November to April, thundery showers saturate the far north. Winds are squally but light, except for stiff afternoon sea breezes—or unless a tropical cyclone develops.

Victoria and New South Wales, south of Port Macquarie, have Australia's most frequently changing coastal weather. Except in summer they lie just in the zone of disturbed westerlies, cold anticyclones and southern depressions. In summer a similar changeability comes from the troughs which separate warm anticyclones. Summer patterns may also be varied by the distant effects of tropical cyclones, bringing heavy rain and high seas.

Of all the coastal cities, Sydney is the most prone to sudden bouts of bad weather in summer. These spells come most commonly with south-easterlies after a cold front. Within about three hours, broken low cloud scuds in to the coast and showery squalls follow. Less commonly, a 'black nor-easter' with similar low cloud pattern may develop ahead of a trough.

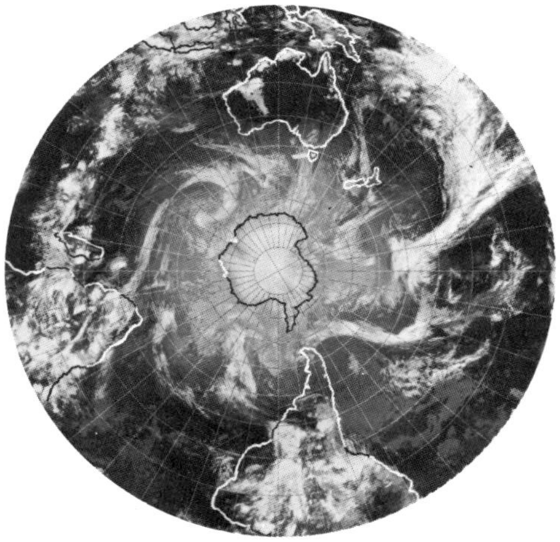

A view from 1450 km above the South Pole shows the summer cloud patterns

Simple ways to measure the wind

SAILING ship crews judged surface wind force from the sea's appearance. In the Royal Navy, various observations were graded on the Beaufort scale—named after an admiral—as a quick indicator of how much sail a man-o'-war could safely carry. Early aviators revised and extended the scale to include land-based observations.

Signs at sea	Signs on land	Description	Beaufort number	Speed (km/h)
Surface like a mirror	Smoke rises vertically	Calm	0	0-1
Ripples look like scales	Smoke drifts	Light air	1	1-5
Wavelet crests look glassy and do not break	Leaves rustle, wind vanes move	Light breeze	2	6-10
Large but short wavelets; crests starting to break	Leaves and twigs move constantly, flags stand out	Gentle breeze	3	11-20
Small waves lengthening; some foam crests	Dust and loose paper are raised	Moderate breeze	4	21-30
Moderate waves obviously longer; many foam crests	Small trees sway	Fresh breeze	5	31-40
Large waves start to form; perhaps some spray	Power lines whistle	Strong breeze	6	41-50
Sea heaps up; foam starts to blow	Big trees sway	Moderate gale	7	51-60
Spindrift foam blown in well-defined streaks	Twigs break off; walking impeded	Fresh gale	8	61-75
Dense streaks of foam; sea starts to roll	Slight structural damage—roof tiles, etc.	Strong gale	9	76-87
Waves with long, overhanging crests; foam in sheets; heavy rolling	Trees uprooted	Whole gale	10	88-100
Waves high enough to hide medium-sized ships; all crests blown into froth; sea covered with foam patches	Widespread damage	Storm	11	101-120
Air filled with foam and spray, seriously impairing visibility; sea completely white	Severe damage—weaker structures demolished	Hurricane	12	over 120

Old sayings that foretell bad weather

BEFORE weather watchers could exchange information quickly and meteorology was developed as a science, farmers and fishing folk passed weather lore to new generations in little rhymes or sayings. Many have a scientific basis and apply in southern Australia—especially those which indicate rain:

'A red sun has water in his eye'
The probable cause of redness, apart from bushfire smoke, is water droplets screening out other light waves. Moist air is condensing, clouds will form and rain may follow.

'Red sky at night, Sailor's delight; Red sky in the morning, Sailor's warning'
At sunset, light reflecting from high clouds indicates that the western horizon—over which most weather approaches—is clear. The same occurrence at sunrise means the eastern horizon is clear but clouds are building up on the weather side.

'Take shelter when the sun (or moon) is in his (her) house'
The 'house' is the halo sometimes seen around the sun or moon. Invisible, high-altitude cirrostratus cloud is forming. Heavier cloud will build downwards and rain may follow.

'When the stars begin to huddle, The earth will soon become a puddle'
If cirrostratus cloud starts to form at night, it may blot out stars of lesser magnitude and blur the light from major ones. So familiar groups seem to move into clusters.

'Rainbow at morning, Shepherd's warning; Rainbow at night, Shepherd's delight'
Rainbows, the result of sunlight striking water droplets, are visible to people with the sun at their backs. So a rainbow in the morning means moisture in the west—the usual weather quarter. An evening rainbow is in the eastern sky and probably means the rain is going away.

'Sunshine and showers, Rain again tomorrow'
When rain is interspersed with sunny periods, especially near the coast, the moist airstream is unstable and cumulus clouds are being built up by surface heating. Such conditions often last for more than a day.

Thunderstorms, with high-piling cumulonimbus clouds, are the most common—and most consistently damaging—weather system over the Australian coastline

Storms and cyclones Threats to life, property and beaches

Coastal regions of Australia, so often the meeting ground of air masses of different moisture and temperature, are prone to some of the world's most violent weather. It can produce winds to rip apart houses, bolts of lightning that spark raging bushfires, hail to devastate crops, and rain torrents and floods that wash away buildings, livestock and roads. And it whips the ocean into storm surges and waves of enormous force, hastening the erosion of coasts and sometimes destroying beaches completely (*see* Beach Erosion, overleaf).

In terms of loss of life and property damage, the tropical cyclone is the most dangerous weather system on earth. But on average only five or six each summer have any marked effect on the Australian coast. Tornadoes rarely strike populated regions, and never attain the wind speeds that make them so terrifying in the United States. Gales and flooding from intense southern depressions affect only a limited area. In total

impact—high frequency, wide occurrence and damaging effect—Australia's worst weather system is the thunderstorm.

Thunderstorms begin as small clumps of fleecy cumulus cloud. Cumulus normally blows away or evaporates readily, but if there is a tall mass of unstable cold air above the warm, moist air that is forming the cumulus, and if something pushes from below—a mountain slope acting as a wedge, or a dense cold front moving in—a vigorous updraught starts. Cumulonimbus clouds pile higher, their moisture cooling and condensing beyond the point at which rain would normally be produced. Ice crystals form instead.

At the storm's mature stage, so much ice and water collect that the updraught can no longer support their weight. They sink, and forceful downdraughts start. These can produce surface winds of 110 km/h and more, with phenomenal rain and sometimes hail. Cold low-level air spreads for kilometres ahead of the storm.

Air turbulence and the freezing process break up water particles and regroup them so that some parts of the cloud system have a positive electrical charge and some are negative. Early in the storm's life, huge sparks flash from positive to negative zones. Their reflections are seen as 'sheet' lightning. When the storm is mature, directly visible 'fork' lightning flashes between the cloud and the gound. The electrical charge may be as much as 30 million volts. It heats the air along its path to about 10 000°C, causing instant expansion and pressure waves that are heard as thunder. The sound travels at about 0.3 km a second, and can sometimes be heard more than 40 km away.

In the storm's dying stages, rain gradually eases and the remaining ice crystals are blown out by high-level winds into a cloud of flat-topped, anvil shape. The usual duration of one system is about half an hour, but it may start a chain of storms lasting for hours.

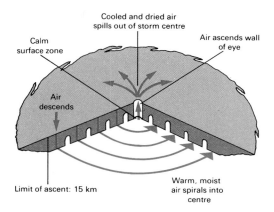

Starting over warm water, the great majority of cyclones stay at sea until they weaken over cold water. The 'eye' of a tropical cyclone is a column of rising air, surrounded by a fast-spinning wall of cloud and bands of other cloud spiralling towards it

Labels on diagram:
Cooled and dried air spills out of storm centre
Calm surface zone
Air ascends wall of eye
Air descends
Limit of ascent: 15 km
Warm, moist air spirals into centre

Warning signs of a tropical cyclone

UNEXPECTEDLY heavy swell in tropical waters may be the first visible sign of a distant cyclone. Any marked increase of wind should be taken as a reliable warning. The most dangerous winds—as well as the safe 'eye'—will be to the left of a person facing the wind. At close quarters, a cyclone system may be seen as bands of cloud arranged along the wind and spiralling in to a dark, unbroken mass. But the eye is seldom exactly in the middle, so barometric pressure readings are the surest indicators of an approaching or developing cyclone. It will cause an abrupt disturbance, followed by a general, continuing fall in pressure. Weather stations in Australia's north are constantly alert to the danger of cyclones during their summer season. Special radar allows the paths of approaching storms to be tracked, so that warnings can be broadcast well before the vicious winds strike.

As each new cyclone menace is reported, meteorologists allot it a name from the year's agreed alphabetical list. The practice of giving cyclones names began in Queensland in the 1890s and was followed by the Americans in World War II. In 1975 officials decided to alternate male and female names.

Tropical cyclone tracks, July 1979 to June 1980

Destructive tropical cyclones—also called hurricanes or typhoons in some parts of the world—start when existing depressions move over unusually warm patches of water. The normal process of rising air and falling pressure is intensified, and the heat of evaporated moisture is converted into wind energy that pulls the surrounding air into a tight, fast spiral.

A tropical cyclone's violence comes not from freakishly low pressure—some ordinary depressions are just as low—but from its compactness. Variation from highest to lowest pressure may be crammed into a diameter of less than 150 km in the early stages, resulting in winds so strong that they smash measuring instruments: their speed must be assumed from the impact of flying debris. Cyclone Althea recorded gusts of 194 km/h at Townsville in 1971.

Dangerous cyclone development requires open sea with a surface temperature of at least 27°C, high humidity, unstable air, and rotational wind deflection caused by the earth's movement. Only in two belts, between about 5° and 20° each side of the equator, do all those conditions coincide. Near Australia, the likeliest areas are to the north-east and north-west. Some cyclones originate to the north, in the Timor and Arafura Seas, and a few in the Gulf of Carpentaria, but they rarely occur before December or after March in any of these areas, and the great majority remain at sea until their force weakens over bodies of cold water.

Tropical cyclones never form over land even when conditions are very unstable. Surface friction slows the very low level air flows and too little water vapour is available to create a sufficiently high humidity. Water vapour is essential because cyclones derive much of their energy from the heat given off as the vapour condenses.

As a tropical cyclone develops, a spiralling mass of dense cloud forms, reaching from about 300 metres above sea level to 15 000 metres. The cloud base may descend to the sea with the rain torrent that soon sheets down, driven by violent winds. Lightning is frequent at first.

In a fully developed system there is an 'eye' of light winds or complete calm, more or less in the middle. It is a rainless area of fairly clear skies, averaging about 35 km in diameter in Australian waters, caused by condensed air sinking from the top of the cloud column. By this time the whole system is moving across the ocean, usually at less than 30 km/h.

The changing courses of tropical cyclones are determined by the locations of other pressure systems, which are themselves moving. A cyclone travels towards its side of steepest pressure gradient—where the rise to normal pressure occurs in the shortest distance. The general direction is easily seen on a weather map from the crowding of isobars, or lines of pressure.

When a cyclone moves outside the warm waters of the tropics, its width increases and its winds slacken. If it moves over land—even if still in the tropics—it is also quickly stretched and weakened. Its force is usually spent on the coastal region. There the destruction may be massive—because of the effect on the sea.

Storm surges of 5 metres above normal tide level, topped by waves 7 metres tall, are commonly reported. How disastrous such a surge may be depends on whether it coincides with high tide. The biggest surge reported in Australia, at Barrow Point, N. Qld, in 1899, was said to have swamped a policeman on a ridge more than 13 metres above normal sea level.

A tornado is most likely to form at the base of a high cumulonimbus thunderstorm system. Its fierce rotation results from a twisting of the updraught that feeds such a storm. A narrow funnel, widening towards the cloud, creates a small zone of such low pressure that movable objects —including people—can be sucked up in the spiralling column of air.

Tornadoes are so localised and destructive that central pressures and wind speeds cannot be measured. Pressure may fall below 800 millibars—compared with an average of 980 in tropical cyclones and 1013 in normal air. Their track of destruction may be only a few metres wide, and they usually occur in sparsely populated inland areas. Seen out to sea, they are often called waterspouts.

Willy-willies are small, short-lived eddies that can spin sand, dust and light debris up to about 2 metres from the ground. They are minicyclones created when air already of low pressure passes over a particularly hot patch of ground. Some people call them 'dust devils'.

Tornadoes can occur on coasts and inland

Beach erosion

When shifting sands are not replaced

Sand movement is as natural as the weather. Beaches are fluid zones that respond to wave and wind action, sometimes losing material and sometimes gaining it. Sediments added during calm weather are taken offshore in storms, to be replaced during the next quiet spell. In Australia this normal cycle of cut-and-fill is accompanied on the east and west coasts by an overall northward transport of sand. The majority of strong waves strike those coasts at a more or less southerly angle. Sand pulled from a beach is carried by longshore currents and most often returned to the shore at a point farther north. The loss is made good by other sand from the south—as long as the supply is adequate. If it is not, long-term erosion sets in and the shoreline recedes.

The past century has been a period of widespread erosion and coastal recession. Reports have come from areas representing virtually all the eastern coast south of the Great Barrier Reef, and from much of the west coast. Erosion arouses the greatest public concern in settled districts, when properties or holiday amenities are menaced. Aggravated storm damage and slower recovery are noted where human works and behaviour interfere with beach structure and vegetation. But shoreline recession is occurring widely in remote areas and in protected coastal reserves and national parks. Clearly, the supply of replacement beach materials from the south is not sufficient at present to compensate for the

A satellite view of the New South Wales central coast taken from a height of 920 km above the Earth. The photograph stretches from Newcastle Bight and Port Stephens in the south to Port Macquarie and the Hastings River in the north. The hook-shaped beaches, narrow at the southern end and broad at the north, are formed by waves that arrive consistently from the south

heavy and continuing northward loss of sand.

Urgent problems created by erosion are problems only because people, in committing capital resources to the seashore, have misunderstood the nature of beaches. They may recede—or advance—for centuries. The wave movements to which they respond are themselves subject to variations in world climate patterns. Predominant wave directions can change. So can the sea level, depending on how much water is held in glaciers and polar icecaps. The position and extent of a beach signify only the net effect of physical forces at one particular time—not something that people can indicate on a map or a property title and expect to stay put forever. The human sense of equilibrium may be static, but nature's is dynamic.

The sea off eastern Australia has been near its present level for only about 6000 years. During the most intensive phase of the last ice age, about 20 000 years ago, it was more than 100 metres lower. Rivers carved valleys across the land that was exposed. The return of the sea 'drowned' those extended river systems and made deep inlets where there had been shallow estuaries. For that reason, many rivers no longer carry material eroded from inland rock—a major contributor to beach supply—all the way to the coast. Instead they deposit rock debris and sediments in the upper parts of estuaries, where the water first deepens.

On many parts of the coast, from Gippsland in eastern Victoria to southern Queensland, there are dual barrier-beach formations. They consist of sand mostly of marine origin, including a sub-

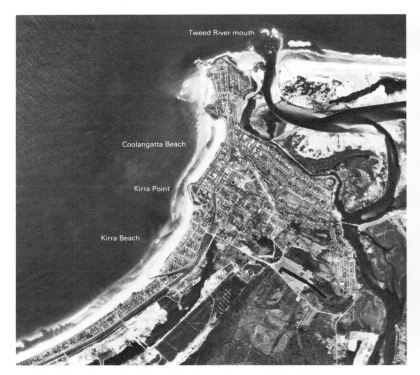

Sandy beaches around Tweed Heads and Coolangatta in 1962

Training walls impeding sand drift led to severe beach erosion by 1971

stantial input of material derived from the shells or skeletons of marine animals. Inner barriers were deposited about 125 000 years ago, when the sea was last near its present level. Modern barriers, established a little more than 6000 years ago, formed seaward of the ancient ones. Troughs of low-lying land were left in between. They became swamps and lagoons, typified by the Gippsland Lakes and the chains of waterways and wetlands on the NSW central coast. Such troughs act as traps for river-borne sediments that would otherwise have reached the coast. They also absorb wind-blown beach sand.

When the sea level was slightly lower than at present, Australia's eastern shores were probably one long barrier beach coast, with dunes stretching along the base of what are now the familiar cliff faces of central and southern New South Wales. As the sea level rose massive amounts of sand were lost when waves and tidal forces began to push barrier material into the deep inlets of newly drowned estuaries. The barrier system, with its easy northward flow of material, was broken at every such estuary—at Sydney's big sea inlets, for example. At the same time, rocky headlands began to interrupt the longshore drift pattern. More barrier material was pushed inshore between promontories, forming mainland beaches. Isolated longshore currents redistributed the material, scouring the southern ends of beaches and heaping sand to the north. Dunes and ramps of sand climbed cliff faces, spread over hilltops and spilled down the inland side. Sydney's eastern suburbs are founded on marine sand pushed up ramps that have long been stripped away.

Most of the conditions for large-scale beach depletion and shoreline recession are set by nature. There is nothing people can do about them. But the most active cause of further sand loss, contributed to by human activities, is the movement of destabilised dunes. Phases of dune migration seem to have been interspersed by periods of coastal stability for the past 4000 years. The changes were probably related to variations in the frequency of storms. If the cycle of storm-calm-storm cutting and filling is repeated too rapidly, plants may not have time to colonise regained sand and trap wind-blown sand at the back of the beach to rebuild foredunes. Without plant cover and foredune shelter, the inner dunes are mobile. Strong winds can drive them inland to swamp and kill any vegetation in their path. In that way formerly stable surfaces are also mobilised, and even more sand migrates. People destroying dune vegetation run the risk of triggering massive sand movements.

Man-made obstructions to normal longshore drift can cause dramatically sudden local erosion. A groyne built out from a beach, for example, traps sand on one side. But sand moving away from the other side cannot be replaced. The updrift beach, starved of materials, is progressively scoured by strong wave action. Such a situation has caused alarm on Queensland's lower Gold Coast since the 1960s. The region should not have much of a problem with erosion: its rivers supply plenty of sediments to the coast, and losses of sand into estuaries and inland-moving dunes are minor. But in 1964, to stabilise the Tweed River entrance for navigation, projecting training walls were built. The net quantity of sand supplied to beaches at Coolangatta and beyond decreased immediately. By 1967 they were unable to recover fully from storm effects. And the remedy, applied after severe storm damage in 1972, was worse than the ailment. A groyne built out to sea at Kirra Point trapped 300 000 cubic metres of sand on Coolangatta Beach within two years. But 500 000 cubic metres were lost from Kirra Beach, updrift of the groyne. The region's beaches, crucial to its tourist industry, are now maintained in their pre-1960s state by pumping enormous volumes of sand through a pipeline from the Tweed estuary, at heavy expense.

Dramatic changes to ocean beaches beside the mouth of the Tweed River, on the border between New South Wales and Queensland, demonstrate some of the problems caused by man-made alterations to the coast. In 1962 (far left) beaches to the north of the Tweed estuary had broad stretches of sand. In 1964 training walls were built at the mouth of the river to stabilise it for navigation. By 1971 (centre left) much of the sand had left Coolangatta Beach. A groyne built at Kirra Point in 1972, and another beside it (above), have solved Coolangatta's problem, but now the south end of Kirra Beach has all but disappeared

What can be done to save beaches

ANY approach to erosion that views the coastline as a fixed boundary is doomed to failure, or at best to be a never-ending drain on funds. But some steps can be taken to aid natural restoration fairly cheaply, and to reduce harmful human impact:

- Legal protection of foredune vegetation and the active encouragement of suitable plants on the upper parts of beaches, to reduce wind-blown sand losses.
- Measurement of a beach's sediment 'budget'—its income and outgoings of material —before positioning engineering works such as breakwaters and groynes.
- Zoning aganst future building in erosion-prone areas, to forestall community demands for costly and often fruitless protection measures.
- Educational emphasis on the dynamic nature of the shoreline, so that its changeability is respected and normal processes need no longer be regarded as disasters.

PART 3

Advice for holidaymakers

Seaside recreation is easy for most Australians. Ample beaches, coastal parks and inshore waters are seen not merely as holiday playgrounds but as enhancements of daily life. It is doubtful, however, whether many people take advantage of all their opportunities.

Leaving aside the limitations of expense and physical disability, there are benefits in exploring the fullest range of leisure activities. But the sea is an alien medium: it can be hostile, and so can its shores.

The drawbacks and dangers of inexperience cannot be lightly dismissed.

Information in the following pages is aimed at helping readers make more of the coast, without placing them in jeopardy.

It is presumed that they will also seek the best local advice before venturing into the unfamiliar.

They are urged to acquaint themselves fully with their rights of access and use, and to respect the rights of others.

And it is hoped that they will treat a fragile environment with all the care that a national treasure deserves.

Late afternoon sunlight turns the sea to the colour of liquid gold

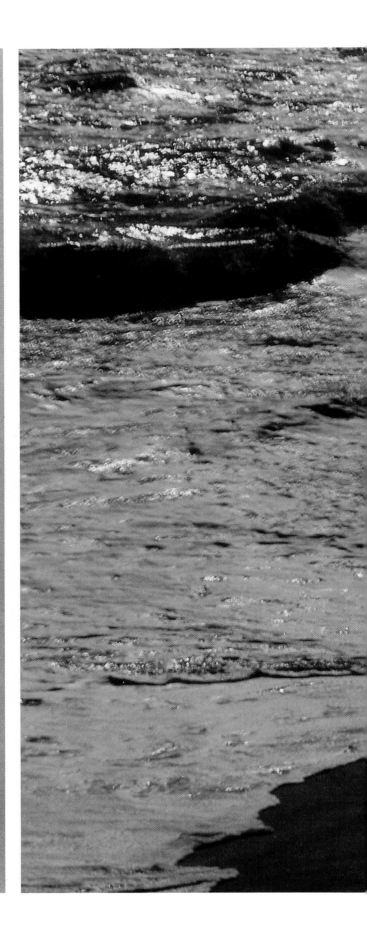

Who owns the coast? Answers to a complex question

The expanses of land around the Australian coast which have avoided the auctioneer's hammer and the developer's bulldozer remain unalienated public lands. They are necessary not only to preserve indigenous plants and animals, but also to provide valuable recreation space for an expanding human· population. Before governments were concerned with preserving the community's right of access to river banks, bay shores and ocean coasts, private ownership of waterfront property was not discouraged, and quite often only the narrow strip between low and high water marks remains public. Today, some coasts are not easily accessible because pasture lands back on to beachfronts, fences create barriers to public waterways, and industrial estates and port facilities create daunting obstructions.

Even the regulations governing public land form barriers of their own, with a maze of restrictions covering access, camping and caravanning, fire-lighting, vehicle entry and fishing. Consistent regulations face travellers all around the coast, but exceptions to the rule and temporary restrictions are frequent. When in doubt, always apply for information to regulating authorities, all of which have offices in the state capitals and branches in major towns. In some cases visitors may have to apply to a resident manager, ranger or forester for specific and seasonal restrictions.

Laws of trespass
It is generally not a crime simply to enter someone else's land whether it is privately owned or leased. The owner's only recourse is to sue for damages caused, though force in proportion to any danger or damage threatened may be used to eject a trespasser. Only if violence is threatened or appears to be threatened can injury to a trespasser be justified. Reasonable force may also be used to evict squatters, such as campers, who try to stay on a person's property without permission, and a caravan may be towed away if its owner refuses to leave. But no damage should be done to the trespasser's property. Laws relating to trespass on government installations such as port facilities, lighthouses, research stations and military reserves involve special offences and in some instances trespass on federal government property can incur a jail sentence of up to three months.

Crown land
Ocean beaches and the foreshores of tidal rivers and lakes are all part of Crown property. Like all unoccupied Crown land, they are generally accessible to the public, though entry may be restricted to paying users in places where commercial camping areas, boat ramps and other facilities have been established. Along popular city beaches, boating may be prohibited from nearshore waters during daylight hours to avoid danger to swimmers, but anglers are permitted inside the marker buoys after sunset. Beaching of boats is allowable in emergencies.

Where private property adjoins a tidal foreshore, public pedestrian access is preserved, although private ownership may extend to the high water mark. The point reached by water at a mean high tide can be accurately defined only by a surveyor, but can often be judged by the extent of land vegetation or marine growth on rocky foreshores.

Clubs or individuals may have permits or leases allowing jetties or club houses to be built over the foreshore for mooring and fishing. Permission to occupy this land must be obtained in the form of leases or licences which generally relate only to the structure itself. If public access to the foreshore is blocked, people have right of passage over the structure. In some regions, Port Phillip Bay for example, the public also has the right to embark and disembark from all private and public jetties. In many places there is a reserve 30 metres wide adjoining the mean high water mark. This may extend up to 150 metres or more inland and may be difficult to distinguish from the adjacent privately owned land. Where there is doubt about the status of foreshore land and the structures on it, a local government authority or lands department should be consulted.

Aboriginal lands
Most of the big sections of coast reserved for Aboriginal communities, or held freehold by them, are well out of populated areas. Some are only accessible by sea or air and there is little conflict with the routes taken by all but the best equipped and most adventurous travellers. Where the reserve lands are easy to get to, in areas of coastline attractive to tourists, they must be treated at all times as the property of their residents. The state offices of the Department of Aboriginal Affairs will direct people to the appropriate authority for the granting of entry permits, though few are issued for recreational purposes and the Aboriginal communities themselves review all applications. Transit permits are normally freely available and expeditions by scientific groups and wildlife clubs are given special consideration. Travellers to Cape York are provided with a camping ground within the Aboriginal township of Bamaga, but it is advisable to apply in writing to the community's council chairman giving comprehensive details of your proposed trips. On Bathurst Island the Tiwi people's community actively encourages visitors on scheduled air tours from Darwin and permission for entry is automatically included with tour bookings

---

Mining the rich 'black sands'

SAND mining leases are granted under the authority of state government mines departments, like any other mining right. Leases are held on extensive tracts of coastal Crown land, including some in national parks. Modern leases require mining companies to restore worked-over dunes as nearly as possible to their natural state. Since ecological objections aroused public protest in the 1970s, some leases have been terminated by agreement. In the case of Fraser Island (see page 331) the Federal Government halted mining by using its power to control exports. The unworked leases are still held, however. If profitable local markets could be found, a resumption of mining could be proposed and environmental arguments would start all over again.

Beach mining began in 1870, when gold was found in deposits of dark, heavy minerals at Ballina, NSW. 'Black sands' occurred then in surface outcrops called sniggers. Such easily found deposits were cleaned out by miners who extracted gold, tin and platinum. They dumped the major components—rutile (titanium dioxide), ilmenite (titanium iron oxide) and zircon (zirconium silicate). In roughly equal proportions, those three compounds comprise about 97 per cent of the heavy minerals that work their way to the bottom of Australian quartz sands. Their density is about twice that of quartz, and their grain size about half.

Soon after the turn of the century, titanium began to be sought after as the basis of white paint. Rutile and ilmenite were wanted as furnace linings, or as welding fluxes. Zircon became valuable as a lining material or a ceramics glaze. Rutile fetched high prices in the 1950s, with the use of titanium in jet engines.

Mining at Myall Lakes involved one of the largest dune systems in the Southern Hemisphere. The 110-metre high dunes were blown there only about 2000 years ago. It is hoped that replanted areas (right)—seen here after five years—will eventually return to their original condition (crest of dune, left)

Parks and reserves

Australia's first national park, Royal National Park near Sydney, was declared in 1879 with a Crown grant to the park's trustees exhorting them to use the land for the recreation of the inhabitants of the colony. Authority was given to establish lawns, ornamental gardens, a zoo, cricket pitch, racecourse and rifle range—which created a large bushland amusement park. The management of national parks has changed greatly over the past 100 years; interference with the natural environment to provide facilities for the community has been tempered by a greater appreciation of conservation requirements. Park administrations are now keenly aware that they hold the key to the survival of rare and vanishing wildlife species and the preservation of representative samples of all major habitats, as well as areas of geological and historic significance.

Many coastal reserves still principally aim to fulfil the recreational needs of the public—Victoria's Coastal Parks, Tasmania's State Recreation Areas and Coastal Reserves, State Recreation Areas in New South Wales and some of the Environmental Parks in Queensland. Such areas are normally narrow coastal strips with some land left in its natural state, but with picnic areas, walking tracks and camping grounds provided, and waterways where motorboating may be allowed. Some of the older national parks, such as the Royal in New South Wales, Victoria's Wilson's Promontory National Park, and Yanchep National Park in Western Australia, retain a legacy of facilities from days when their role was largely to cater for family holidays and recreational sportsmen. Newer national parks, with extensive areas of forest and heathland, are more firmly dedicated to the preservation of the natural environment—an important goal in Australia, where plants and animals are rapidly disappearing even in areas of little or no settlement.

Such conservation areas must be large enough to ensure that the environment is undisturbed by man's activities and that the ecological balance of plant and animal communities is maintained. Research has suggested that only areas of 20 250 hectares or more are likely to support the range of plants and animals that are representative of a particular Australian habitat. The largest proportion of all national park area is consequently left in its natural state. Vehicles are allowed only on existing tracks and roads provided for access to camp sites, picnic grounds and along scenic drives. Use of off-road vehicles, such as trail bikes, dune buggies and four-wheel drives, away from existing tracks, is expressly forbidden because of the threat to soil and vegetation.

Occasionally conservation requirements may lead to the closure of parts of a park. Overuse and damage by fire require long periods free of disturbance for plant regrowth and animal recolonisation. Areas of special conservation significance—the breeding site of a rare bird or the habitat of an endangered plant—may be permanently closed. Such areas include the wetlands of coastal lagoons and estuaries, which are a sanctuary for waterfowl during the interior's

A female noisy scrub bird and nest

Preserving endangered wildlife

As MORE and more of Australia's coastal fringe is developed for housing or industry, it becomes increasingly important that some areas of natural landscape are set aside to conserve the plants and animals that live there. Occasionally the demands of conservation may conflict with the wishes of holidaymakers. Access may have to be forbidden or restricted in areas where a delicate natural habitat may be destroyed or rare animals frightened away by the presence of people. In some cases, such as that of the noisy scrub bird in Western Australia, such action may be necessary to save a species from extinction.

In 1961 plans for a new township to be called Casuarina at Two Peoples Bay, just east of Albany, were abandoned after new sightings of a bird thought to be extinct since 1889. The 4639 hectares around the bay still carry the only known population of noisy scrub birds, *Atrichornis clamosus*, and were declared a nature reserve in 1966 to protect the species. Most of the population of about 72 breeding pairs and 20 non-breeding males lives in densely vegetated gullies in the Mount Gardner Peninsula, part of which has been declared a prohibited area to prevent interference with research programmes. No public entry is permitted into this part of the reserve and there are clearly marked signs on the access tracks. But about half the peninsula is a limited access area, and may be entered on foot by birdwatchers wishing to catch a glimpse of the shy and secretive bird. Its brown colouring and dark cross bars blend in with the vegetation and make it extremely difficult to see; it rarely flies, moving mainly in the thick, low scrub. But the loud song of the male bird is a strong and persistent reminder of its presence, and can be heard over a distance of nearly 1.5 km on calm days.

dry months, and many rugged and mostly inaccessible offshore islands where migratory birds and seal colonies breed for short seasons. Only people with genuine scientific interests are issued permits to enter these areas. Parks known as fauna sanctuaries, nature reserves, or conservation parks, unlike national parks, allow only limited public access, and camping is often prohibited or restricted to small areas and for short periods such as school holidays, when special consideration for camping permits is given to groups involved in educational wildlife projects.

Marine parks control activities below the waterline and aim to restrict spearfishing, specimen collecting and some surface fishing in favour of pastimes such as snorkelling and scuba diving. Australia's largest marine park, The Great Barrier Reef Marine Park, was empowered in 1976 to provide protection for the delicate coral formations by controlling tourist operations; some vulnerable areas have been made off-limits for boating and fishing.

Permits must generally be obtained for camping at organised camp sites in national parks and it may be necessary to make bookings well ahead, especially for holiday periods. For Wilson's Promontory National Park bookings for the busy Christmas season are open only during July, after which a ballot is held to allocate the camping and caravan sites. Even the traffic on walking trails in heavily used parks is strictly controlled.

State forests

In State Forests, multiple-use management ensures the country's timber industry a continuity of supply, while providing for recreation and education as well as the protection of wildlife habitats. The forests are most widespread in humid coastal regions; many adjoin national parks, where they act as conservation buffer zones. State Forests are normally open to the public and, with fire trails and former logger routes, are well served by tracks for vehicles. Many have recommended scenic drives, and developed areas for camping. Others permit hiking trips into remote regions where there are no facilities. Check with the local forestry office, where maps and information on the best routes to take, spots to see and locations of picnic grounds, as well as advice on logging and fire restrictions, may be readily obtained. Particular care in State Forests is recommended for drivers unused to rural roads which are often narrow and winding, offer poor visibility and are used by heavy trucks. Only firm gravel roads should be used during wet weather as many forest roads become slippery after even light rain.

Lighting campfires

Campfires are allowed in national parks, state forests and on Crown land for cooking and warmth, but should be kept small to conserve wood and, wherever possible, portable stoves should be used. Great care and attention should be given to the siting and extinguishing of fires and to the exact legal requirements in each state.

On days of total fire ban no fires are permitted in parks and forests. In campgrounds and picnic areas fires may be lit only in the fireplaces provided, or as directed by signs. Where there are no properly constructed fireplaces, fires should be contained in a trench at least 500 mm deep. All flammable material on the ground or overhanging the fire within a distance of 3 metres must be removed before the fire is lit. The fire must not be left unattended and must be completely extinguished, preferably with water, before leaving. Trenches must be filled in.

Water safety Surviving in the surf and still water

It is safer to swim at a beach patrolled by members of the surf lifesaving association or professional lifeguards than it is to take a bath, according to statistics published on accidental drownings in Australia. More and more people, however, are venturing to unpatrolled and remote areas, where the surf may be better but the statistics are worse. In the decade of the 1970s there were no drownings on patrolled beaches, while an average of eight a year occurred at unsupervised surfing spots.

Groups who venture to isolated beaches must remember that they have the responsibility for their own safety. It is important to understand the sea, the surf and the formation of beaches, and to be able to recognize any danger signs that may be present. Anyone using the sea must also know their own swimming ability and level of fitness. Reasonable pool-swimmers may perform poorly in the surf, where there are no edges, the bottom is irregular, the water continually moving and the depth forever changing.

Swells erode the sandy face of a beach and carry a great deal of it seawards to deposit it as offshore bars or sandbanks. A sandbank absorbs the force of incoming waves so that the eroding action of storms is lessened. But even when a sandbank is present, turbulent waves are constantly moving masses of water towards the shore, all of which must return seawards. Much returns in the rip currents which form channels through the sandbanks. Where curved beaches end at rocky outcrops—either natural or man-made—corner rips sweep the water along its face. Most people have heard of rips, but will be unable to avoid their dangers unless they can recognise them.

Before entering the water always spend some time watching a beach and its near-shore waters to try and spot any rips. If you plan to surf at an unpatrolled spot, find an elevated place at the back of the beach, or on a headland, and study the water until the pattern of banks and rips becomes clear. Rips can usually be seen from the beach, but they may be obscured by heavy seas, onshore winds and high tide. At such times you cannot be confident of your safety in the water.

The waves and water over a rip are obviously different from those over adjoining sand banks. A headland view of a rip at the centre of Maroubra Beach, NSW (top) clearly shows a band of foam and churned-up sand moving seawards in the current. Foam towards the furthest line of breakers indicates the point at which the rip has reached its head and begun to dissipate after passing through a channel in the sand bank. Choppy water interrupts the pattern of the surf over the same rip seen from the beach (centre). Waves break irregularly over the channel, do not roll and are often out of line with those in surrounding water. On other beaches the colours of rips may be darker because the water is deeper. At times they may look clear and undisturbed, and thus attractive to swimmers. Do not fight against a rip, but allow it to carry you out until it weakens. Strong swimmers can move diagonally out of a rip, but weaker swimmers should swim parallel to the beach and then back to shore. Children must not leave their surfboards if carried out on a rip, but stay with them till help arrives as their support may be vital

A corner rip at Avoca Beach, NSW, sweeps a deep channel of darker water along the face of a man-made rock pool. Large waves break regularly to the left of the rip which appears deceptively calm

What happened on Black Sunday

STABILITY of an offshore sandbar cannot be taken for granted, even in the best of weather. A bar modifies the interaction of incoming and reflected waves, but only up to a point that they can tolerate. If it is interfering too much with their movements, they may change their patterns and suddenly destroy it.

At Sydney's Bondi Beach on 'Black Sunday'—6 Feb 1938—about 300 novice surfers using a bar had it dissolve beneath their feet after a spontaneous change of wave movement. They were left well out of their depth, and most were panic stricken. Surf club members, on the beach preparing for a race, went quickly to the rescue but five people drowned.

In a medium to heavy surf, rips can alter rapidly, creating very hazardous conditions. In a small surf, rips are fairly stable and predictable, but even so they should not be trusted.

If you are caught in a rip, calmly swim or scull sideways towards a sandbank. If possible, signal for help by raising one arm. There is little point in shouting for help because it causes fatigue and cannot be heard above the noise of waves. While waiting for help, lie face up in the water and float with your head partly submerged. A relaxed horizontal position aids flotation and the body's natural buoyancy will keep your face above water with a minimum of effort. Treading water—moving the legs as if walking upstairs and pressing outwards and down with the arms—gives a better view, but it is tiring.

On unpatrolled or deserted beaches, where there is no help available, you must be able to swim out of rips by yourself. Conserve strength as much as possible and do not fight against the current. As the rip reaches its head, on the seaward side of its path through the sandbar, the current will dissipate. Swim parallel to the shore for about 30 metres before turning back towards the beach. At low tide sandbars close to the edge of a rip may only be covered by shallow water and if you are in difficulty you can use them to rest on while making your way back to the beach.

The breast stroke is less fatiguing for the return swim than the crawl, and it will still enable you to maintain a reasonable speed. Use side stroke and back stroke for relief. Turn your head away from the wind and breathe in a regular rhythm. If possible swim out of a rip in the same direction as the longshore current is flowing. This is the current which is commonly noticed moving along a beach. It carries swimmers away from their point of entry and may sweep them into a rip or deep channel. When returning to the beach be careful not to swim back into a rip. Not all rips run at right angles to land. If waves strike the shorelines at an angle, the rip, too, will be angled away from the beach.

Children who are carried out of their depth by rips often jump off their surf craft and try to swim against the current. This is exactly the opposite to what should be done. Instead they should stay with their craft, paddle to calm water—even if it is beyond the breakers—raise an arm and wait for help. In such circumstances a surf mat is as important as a life jacket. A flexible strap attaching a surf craft to an ankle or wrist is a valuable additional safety device.

While the hazards of ocean swimming are usually obvious, rivers, bays and lagoons conceal their dangers beneath still waters. Most fatal drowning accidents occur in sheltered waterways—often in peaceful conditions. The misuse of power boats in swimming areas and the consumption of alcohol before swimming, particularly from houseboats, are major causes of accidents. The currents of fast-flowing rivers discourage most swimmers simply because they look dangerous. But slower streams and enclosed waters are often just as hazardous. The main problem is usually visibility. You risk severe spinal injuries if you dive into cloudy water without first checking its depth.

The beds of lagoons and rivers are often soft and weed-covered—oozing mud and tangled weeds can trap swimmers just as securely as heavy branches. Panic and quick, jerky movements may only tighten the grip of weeds. If trapped, gently unravel the weed with as little agitation of the water as possible.

Muscle cramp can disable a swimmer in deep water or rough surf and can cause drowning.

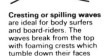

Cresting or spilling waves are ideal for body surfers and board-riders. The waves break from the top with foaming crests which tumble down their faces

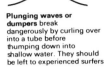

Plunging waves or dumpers break dangerously by curling over into a tube before thumping down into shallow water. They should be left to experienced surfers

Surging waves often run ashore without breaking, and they can suddenly swamp children playing around rocks, or break on them near the water's edge unexpectedly

Three types of waves—spilling, plunging and surging—are commonly seen on ocean shores. Never underestimate the power of waves which can often appear small when seen from the shore. Dive under waves when surfing—trying to keep your head above water wastes energy

These painful spasms usually occur in the legs, and are more likely to happen to people in cold water and after strenuous exercise. Eating always impairs physical performance because greater quantities of blood are diverted to the digestive system, leaving less for other muscles that need it during physical exertion. Light refreshments or snacks, rather than a full picnic meal, are better for a day at the beach. If attacked by cramp either float on your back or scull gently with your hands in a breast stroke motion and signal for help. Relieve the pain of cramp in the thigh by straightening your knee and raising your leg to stretch the muscle. For cramp in the lower leg, straighten your knee and draw you toes upwards towards your shin. Apply a cold-compress or ice-pack wherever possible, and in hot conditions drink a tumbler of water containing half a teaspoon of salt to aid recovery.

Water safety signs
A new set of standard symbols is being introduced on Australian beaches to replace the multitude of different symbols and word signs used by local authorities. When the symbol is shown in blue it indicates that the nominated sport or activity is permitted and that the area is considered safe. When the symbol is shown in a red circle with a diagonal line through it, the sport is prohibited because conditions are unsafe or there may be danger to other people. On patrolled beaches swimmers must remain in the supervised area which is marked by red and yellow flags. Leave the water when the shark flag is shown or its accompanying siren is heard

Swimming

Fishing

Water skiing

Surf craft riding

Scuba diving

Shark alarm flag

Patrolled swimming area

Fishing for leisure/1 Where and when to find the fish

Fishing is by far the most popular water sport in Australia. An estimated 30 per cent of Australians are recreational anglers. A survey held in NSW in 1977 revealed that 26 per cent of the population had fished in the sea at least once within the year. Sixty per cent of New South Wales boys between the ages of 13 and 17 fished for leisure, and altogether New South Wales fishermen spent 20 million days a year fishing for fun. Wherever there is reasonable access to the bays, beaches and rock platforms around the Australian coast, someone can usually be found waiting optimistically for a bite. However, two basic problems confront the amateur angler—where to find the fish, and what tackle to use.

The most popular recreational fishing areas are the thousands of estuaries and bays around the coast, where lines are cast from the shore, jetties, wharves, rock retaining walls and boats. From boats the best fishing is in the main channels of rivers, streams and inlets. Spots near weeds, rocks and mangroves attract fish, as they are major feeding areas. Around wharves and jetties the supporting piles may be heavily encrusted with mussels, sea squirts, weeds and the other marine life that fish feed on. The species commonly caught within these partly enclosed waters are flathead, bream, tailor, mulloway, whiting, luderick, garfish, leatherjacket, and flounder, all of which make excellent eating.

Surf fishermen will catch most of the species above, but success among the waves requires an ability to recognise the water conditions each fish is likely to favour. Patches of dark water usually indicate the deep channels, where tailor and Australian salmon search for food along the edges. Mulloway travel the rips and gutters of a beach where they can feed on unwary tailor and whiting, and they may also move along the water's edge seeking out one of their favourite foods—beach worms. Flathead and whiting partly bury themselves in the sandy bottom of shallower zones, covered by the froth and foam of breaking waves, and often within a few metres of the shore. Bream spend most of their time foraging for crustacea, molluscs and worms dislodged by pounding waves, particularly among submerged rocks at the corners of beaches.

Rock fishermen can hope to catch snapper, rock cod and bream, while the more experienced and adventurous will attempt to catch tuna, kingfish, mulloway, and even marlin. Rock fishing can be hazardous, and great care should be taken to make sure the area is safe before stepping on to an exposed rock platform or ledge. Spend some time watching the sea's behaviour to see if the platform is a safe one. Even an apparently placid sea can produce freak waves which will submerge areas that were previously merely splashed by spray. Boots fitted with spiked metal strips give a better foothold on slippery rocks than rubber-soled shoes. Wet granite is extremely dangerous, no matter what footwear is worn. If a wave sweeps across the rocks, stand on one leg to present less surface area to the water, and so reduce the chance of being knocked over. If washed into the sea, do not remove shoes or boots as they will be needed to get a purchase on the rocks when clambering ashore. In smooth waters it may be safe to allow a rising swell to wash you back on to the rocks. But in rough seas swim away from shore to avoid being pushed under the waves, or dashed against the rocks.

Most fishermen choose a rod and reel rather than the simple handline wound on to a cork or bottle. Whether a rod or handline is used, choose tackle that suits the kind of fishing being carried out. No outfit is suitable for all conditions.

Surf and rock fishermen usually use hollow glass-fibre rods, 3.4 to 3.8 metres long. Any of the three basic reel types—threadline, overhead revolving spool, and sidecast—can be used, provided that the spool has a minimum line capacity of at least 250 metres of nylon line with a breaking strength of 10 kg. The position of the reel on the rod should suit the reel type—low for the sidecast, medium for the threadline, and high for the overhead. Estuary fishermen find shorter rods ranging from 2 to 3 metres best. Reel size, too, can be smaller—use any of the basic types with a spool capacity of 250 metres of 5 to 7 kg nylon. The most popular reel is the threadline because it is easy to use.

There are few poisonous fish in Australian waters. Nevertheless, if you cannot identify a fish, or find advice on its edibility, it is safer to throw it back. In tropical areas a type of poisoning known as ciguatera can kill people who eat the flesh of some reef species (see page 67). In southern waters the spiky toad fish, also known as the puffer, should never be eaten as its flesh is highly toxic and can cause a rapid death.

Some fish have venomous spines which can cause violent pain if they penetrate the skin. Catfish, bullrouts, fortescues and stonefish are common species that may be encountered. Do not even handle these fish. Release them by cutting the line just above the hook, which will event-

Choosing the best rig

IT IS important to find the best rig—a combination of hooks, swivels, sinkers and traces—to attract, play and land each species of fish. Fish behave differently as conditions change, so one rig will always be better than others in any set of circumstances. All the rigs shown have been successful, but they should only be used as a starting point for more experiments.

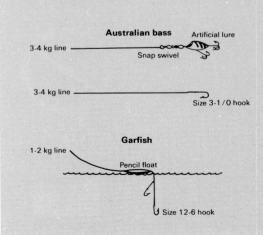

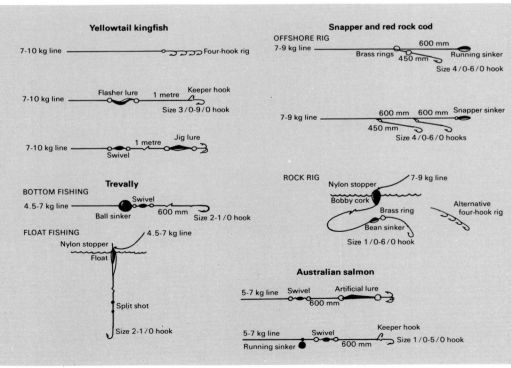

ually rust and drop out without harming the fish.

The 22 fish species most commonly caught in Australian coastal waters must each be fished for differently. Behaviour patterns differ widely, so a knowledge of where and when fish are likely to be feeding, and what the most tempting bait is will all increase the chances of success. The best arrangement of tackle may differ with location, so experiments are recommended. The size and placement of swivel, rings, hooks and other tackle shown in the illustrations below have all proved successful.

Dusky flathead Mud flathead, Estuary flathead, River flathead, Black flathead *Platycephalus fuscus*
Sandy bottoms, sparsely patched with weed beds, are the favourite haunt of flathead. These fish move slowly across the bottom searching for food, or lie partly buried waiting for small food fish to swim by. Boat owners can drift with the current and allow the bait to drag along the bottom. Flathead frequently lie on the edges of sandbars waiting for fish that retreat to deeper water as the tide recedes. Small, live poddy mullet and yellow-tail, yabbies and prawns are excellent baits, as are fillets of fresh mullet, and whole garfish or blue pilchards. Any artificial lure that resembles a small baitfish, either in shape or action, will attract flathead. Their large mouths will easily accept big hooks, sizes 5/0 to 7/0 are popular. Do not use a wire trace, and the breaking strength of the line need be no higher than 7 kg.

Silver bream Yellowfin bream, Sea bream, Black bream, Surf bream *Acanthopagrus australis*
The delicate flavour of its flesh makes the bream a keenly sought species. They are very timid fish, and are more active after dark, when they should be fished for on a rising tide. Bream roam the shoreline, especially where there are oyster and mussel covered rocks, and they are often taken alongside bridge and wharf pylons. The edges of sandbars and weed beds are other worthwhile hunting grounds. Baits are many, but the best are blood worms, live saltwater yabbies and prawns, fresh mullet or garfish fillets, mullet gut and dough. Small hooks are best—sizes 2, 1, 1/0 or 3/0—and the breaking strength of the line should not exceed 7 kg.

Tailor Skipjack, Tailer, Chopper, Bluefish *Pomatomus saltatrix*
Recognised as one of the most voracious fish in the sea, tailor roam constantly at all depths in search of food. They have no specific habitats, but their presence is often betrayed by gulls and terns as they fight over scraps of torn fish, chopped to pieces by a passing school. Tailor will readily take pilchards and sea gar-fish, and are easy to catch with silver spoon or minnow-type lures. They invariably attack the tail of the bait, intending to disable their prey and make it easier to de-vour in a subsequent attack. The sharp, constantly chopping teeth can easily sever a nylon line, and a wire-trace between the main line and the hook is essential when single hooks are used, but not necessary when using a lure or ganged hook. Tow a lure, or bait, 10 to 12 metres behind a slow-moving boat. If fishing from a stationary platform, keep the bait moving by slowly winding it back in. Hook size depends upon the bait. With blue pilchards or garfish baits, gang three or more size 3/0 to 5/0 hooks by passing the point of one through the eye of another. A 5/0 hook is not too big for fillet baits. Use a 7 kg breaking strength line.

Mulloway Jewfish, Silver jew, Soapie (when small), School jew, Kingfish (Vic.), Butterfish (SA), River king-fish (WA) *Argyrosomus hololepidotus*
A prize mulloway can weigh over 50 kg. In estuaries these fish can travel beyond tidal influence, and many are captured several kilometres from the sea. They favour the deeper water of holes and the stream centre, feeding on small luderick, whiting, squid, mullet, tailor, octopus, prawns, and yabbies. Blue pilchards, garfish, and fillets of fresh fish can also be used as bait. One of the best times to fish is at night when the tide is rising or slack. Large hooks, up to size 9/0, and lines of 15 kg breaking strength are necessary for big mulloway.

Sand whiting Bluenose whiting, Summer whiting, Silver whiting *Sillago ciliata*
Small in size but tough fighters, whiting are much sought after. Their habitats are similar to those of flat-head, but they are often found in much shallower water. Whiting will seldom take a fish bait, preferring worms, yabbies, or cockles. Light lines of up to 3 kg breaking strength and small hooks, sizes 6 to 1, are best. Keep the bait moving by winding the line in, casting out again, and repeating the process. Morning and evening are good fishing times. A tide rising over sandflats will flush out worms and small crustacea which attract these fish.

Luderick Blackfish, Nigger, Darkie, Black bream, Sweep *Girella tricuspidata*
Luderick will test any angler's skill. They feed mainly on green weed, sea lettuce and the minute marine organisms that cling to them, but they also occasionally take live yabbies and worms. Luderick are found close to shore near weed beds, reefs, rock retaining walls, and wharf or bridge pylons. The fish have very small mouths and dainty feeding habits so a size 8 or 12 hook must be used. Plait the hook with wisps of green weed and suspend it beneath a slim boat at a depth determined by trial and error. Fish on a rising to full tide. When a fish has been caught, cut its throat immediately to bleed it, or the flesh will deteriorate.

River garfish *Hyporhamphus regularis*
Eastern sea garfish Beakie *Hyporhamphus australis*
The flesh of these small fish is good to eat and well worth the trouble of removing tiny bones. They are usually found over weed beds or around jetties and wharves, and take small pieces of fish, worms, prawns, squid, bread crust or dough. Use a small hook, around size 12, and suspend it about 300 mm under a slim, lightweight float. Flashing silver or gold tinsel attract the fish to small artificial flies. To remove the bones prior to cooking, lay the cleaned fish gut down on a board and roll a milk bottle along the backbone. Turn the fish over and gently work the backbone and attached bones free of the flesh. Sea garfish make excellent bait for tailor.

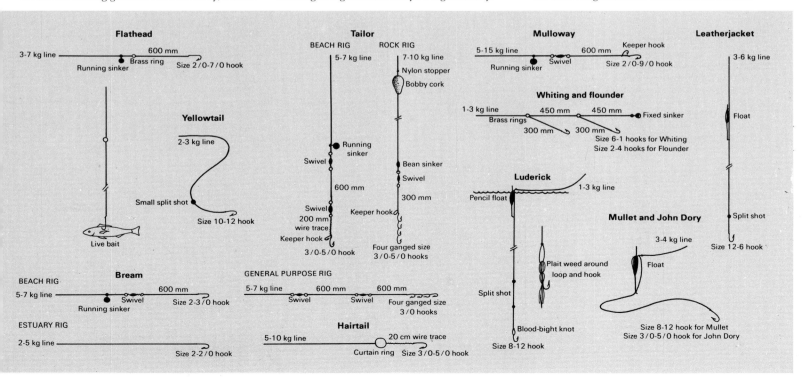

Fishing for leisure/2 Practical advice on bait and tackle

Chinaman leatherjack Yellow leatherjacket *Nelusetta ayraudi*

Scribbled leatherjacket Fantail leatherjacket, Fan-bellied leatherjacket *Alutera scripta*

Well-known scavengers, leatherjacket are found near jetties and wharves, around boat moorings, and in large weed beds. They will respond to any flesh bait, as well as to bread and cheese. They have a small mouth and incisor-like teeth so use a small hook with a long shank to prevent the fish from biting through the line. Float fishing is the most efficient method—suspend a baited hook, size 12-6, just above the sea floor. The flesh of a leatherjacket is tender and delicious. It makes an ideal food for invalids and children because the large bones are easy to see and remove.

Large-toothed flounder *Pseudorhombus arsius*

Considered a delicacy wherever it is served, flounder is principally a bottom dweller which feeds on worms, small crustacea and shellfish. Best baits are live yabbies and prawns used on size 2 to 4 hooks. The fish are poor fighters, and are often found to be hooked only when the line is reeled in to check the bait.

McCulloch's yellowtail Yellowtail, Yakka, Scad *Trachurus mccullochi*

Small yellowtail are abundant in most estuaries around the Australian coast and they are a popular bait fish.

They can be found around wharves and jetties, among moored boats, in weed beds, and close to underwater reefs in sheltered waters. The fish rarely exceed 200 mm in length, and they have a small mouth so a size 10 or 12 hook is adequate. Handlines are recommended. Best baits are small pieces of squid—which are tough and stay on the hook longer—peeled prawns, and worms. Yellowtail also respond well to small white lures hung in clusters from short leaders attached to the main line. As many as five or six fish can be caught at the one time by jigging the lures up and down. Mashed potato used as a berley will attract and hold yellowtail in the immediate fishing area, but it should be used sparingly—a teaspoon every 10 to 15 minutes—or they may stop biting. The fish may be kept alive in a tank, provided the water is changed regularly and adequate aeration is provided. Small battery-operated aerators can be used, but a constant flow of fresh seawater through the holding tank is more successful. Parents should not be concerned if their children, having caught a number of small yellowtail, want to cook and eat them. The flesh is delicious, although the bones must be removed carefully under adult supervision.

Silver trevally White trevally *Pseudocaranx dentex Pseudocaranx wrighti Caranx nobilis Usacaranx nobilis*

Silver trevally are a popular sporting fish because they are tough, determined opponents that never give in. They are caught in estuaries, off beaches and rocks, and

from the open sea near wrecks and reefs. Trevally are good table fish, but they must be bled immediately upon capture. To do this, simply cut the fish's throat. When fishing from a boat use a short 2 to 2.5 metre rod, and a reel holding about 200 metres of 4.5 kg breaking strain line. Fish weighing up to 2 kg can be caught with this equipment, but stronger line must be used for bigger fish. Rock fishermen should use long, light rods with reels carrying 6 to 7 kg breaking strain line. Good baits are fresh prawns, live saltwater yabbies, worms, and fillets of mullet, pilchard and garfish. Saltwater flies, metal spinners, or small lead-head jigs with a hair body are successful lures. Use a hook between sizes 2 and 1/0. Trevally have soft mouths and should be played gently to prevent the hook pulling out. Do not overcook the fish or the flesh will be dry.

Australian snapper Schnapper, Cockney bream-Red bream-Squire, as size increases *Chrysophrys auratus*

Young snapper are called cockney bream until they reach a weight of about 750 g. Adult snapper, with a fully developed snout bulge and bump on top of the head, can weigh up to 20 kg. Most large snapper are caught around coastal rocks and near offshore reefs, although the occasional stray can be caught from an ocean beach. Rock fishermen should use a medium to fast taper rod up to 4 metres long, a reel holding 7 to 9 kg breaking strain nylon line and hooks of sizes 4/0 to 6/0. Good baits for snapper are skinned octopus leg,

Gathering and preparing fresh bait

WHERE IT is difficult to buy bait, or to store it for long periods, anglers can successfully make their own or gather it around the shoreline. This not only saves money, but also provides the freshest bait possible. Stale bait is only useful as an ingredient in a berley—a mixture of various foods thrown on to the water to attract fish and hold them in the immediate fishing area. Mixtures of minced fish-flesh, bran, soaked wheat, minced prawns, stale bread, crushed shellfish, and a small quantity of tuna oil will produce a good, general-purpose berley.

Dough is one of the most popular baits for bream. Prepare it from flour and water and add a dash of tuna oil and a little cotton wool. The oil gives the dough a putty-like consistency, helps to keep it moist, and attracts fish, while cotton-wool keeps the dough on the hook. Use only sufficient to fill the bend of the hook.

Green weed and sea lettuce attract fish that live on marine algae. Sea lettuce grows abundantly on ocean rocks constantly washed by waves and can also be gathered in estuaries from submerged wharf pylons and rocks. It is normally plaited around the hook shank leaving a short piece hanging below the bend.

Pinkish-white saltwater yabbies are found in estuaries, where they live in burrows beneath sand and mud flats. They are caught with a specially made cylindrical pump. Place the mouth of the pump over a finger-sized yabby hole

and push it into the sand with one hand, while pulling the plunger with the other. This sucks sand, water, and yabby into the pump body. The contents are then ejected into a floating sieve, or on to the sand surface if the tide is out, from where the yabby can be collected.

Cunjevoi, or sea squirts as they are commonly known, are marine animals which grow on ocean rocks in the intertidal zone (see page 17). The animal's rough, leathery covering conceals a soft red flesh that is highly prized as bait. To reach the flesh, cut the cunjevoi from the rock with a knife and pull out the tough muscular tissue inside. The softer parts are difficult to keep on the hook, but can be toughened and preserved by salting down.

Beach worms grow to over 2 metres long and live in the sands of ocean beaches (see page 11). An hour either side of low tide is the best time to search for them. Wave a piece of fish flesh, attached to a cord, or in a stocking, in the water as a wave recedes. The worm's head will emerge from the sand as it searches for the bait, and it can be lured further from the sand using a smaller piece of bait held near its head. Quickly grip the worm behind the head with your thumb and forefinger and pull it firmly and steadily from the sand. Practice is needed to perfect the technique, as the worms are very quick at retreating.

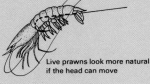

Live prawns look more natural if the head can move

Secure the head and tail of dead prawns or yabbies

Allow the ends of worm sections to move on the hook

Allow the fronds of baited sea lettuce to move freely

Arrange a strip of fish flesh on the hook so that the end is left free

Feed a small crab on to the hook to give it a natural position in the water

Break large crabs into small pieces so they can be used as bait

Bait live fish through the mouth, or in fleshy parts, to avoid damage to the spine

Make sure enough of the hook on ganged-rigs is left to penetrate the catch

squid, pilchard, garfish and slimy mackerel, live yellowtail, fresh prawns, crabs, and fillets of fresh mullet, bonito and striped tuna. Wherever possible do not use a sinker. A floating bait such as a blue pilchard on a series of ganged hooks, slowly reeled in, is most likely to attract snapper. If possible use a berley of chopped fish-flesh, crabs, prawns and squid mixed with stale bread and a dash of tuna oil. When rock fishing use a long-handled gaff to land the fish and reduce the risk of being washed into the water.

Red rock cod Cardinal scorpionfish, Red scorpion cod, Fire cod, Prickly heat *Scorpaena cardinalis*
Mottled reds, browns, and yellows decorate the red rock cod and camouflage it for life among rocks and seaweed. These fish are poor fighters but they can offer considerable resistance by opening their large mouths, expanding their pectoral and ventral fins and curling their tails to one side. The pressure of water against the fish's body has been known to snap light lines. The rock fishing rig for snapper will attract and hold the cod, but they will take almost any flesh-baited rig with hooks ranging from size 1/0 up to size 6/0, and even larger. The cod's mouth is so big that it has earned the nicknames swallow-all and mouth almighty. Venomous spines on the cod's fins can inflict a painful wound, so it should be handled with care, even when dead. The flesh is delicious, especially if lightly cooked and eaten cold.

Australian salmon Salmon trout *Arripis trutta*
These powerful fish grow to about 8 kg, but they are not a popular food fish because the flesh has a strong flavour. Juveniles are often caught in estuaries and bays and are called, colloquially, salmon trout or bay trout. Adults live in the open ocean and are popular sportfish with surf fishermen who find them one of the toughest adversaries. Use a 3 to 4 metre surf rod, a reel carrying at least 200 metres of 5 to 7 kg breaking strain nylon line and hooks of size 1/0 to 5/0. A sinker weighing 70 to 84 g will enable a long cast to be made. When fishing from a boat offshore use a 2.1 m rod and a line with a breaking strain of up to 6 kg. Best baits are sea garfish and blue pilchards, attached whole on ganged hooks, or small fillets used on single size 3/0 to 5/0 hooks. Chrome-plated hexagonal or round, sliced lures will also tempt Australian salmon. When fighting the fish it will be necessary to wind the line in quickly, so use a reel with a gear ratio around 6 to 1. Schools of migrating salmon encountered offshore will bite on a blue plastic squid lure, saltwater flies and feather jigs, cast from or towed behind a boat.

Sea mullet Bully mullet, Mangrove mullet, Hargut mullet, Poddy mullet, River mullet, Bullnose mullet *Mugil cephalus*
Mullet are one of the most common fish in the sea, but also one of the hardest to catch. They can be found in most estuaries and bays around Australia, and usually roam close to the shore or along the edges of sandbars where the juveniles, known as poddy mullet, fall prey to flathead, tailor, and mulloway. The gut of an adult mullet is a good bait for bream, and fillets of fresh sea mullet are a popular bait for most carnivorous fish. The mullet's basic diet is algae, but they can be caught using small pieces of prawn, fish flesh, and worms. Dough is an easy bait to prepare and is eagerly taken by mullet, especially if a berley of bread crumbs is used as well. Fly fishing, using small white or pink flies, is also successful. Use a size 8 to 12 hook suspended 200 to 300 mm below a float on a line of 3 to 4 kg breaking strength. A short spinning rod and reel are adequate. Mullet are determined fighters and skill is required to land them. The flesh has an excellent flavour, but when preparing it for the table make sure the black stomach lining is removed, because it can affect the taste.

Basic fishing knots

WELL-TIED knots distribute strain on a line through the knot, and avoid weak spots that might break under pressure. To obtain the utmost strength make sure the correct number of turns are completed, and that turns do not cross over one another, or slip out of place as the knot is being closed.

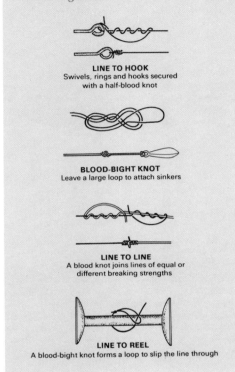

LINE TO HOOK
Swivels, rings and hooks secured with a half-blood knot

BLOOD-BIGHT KNOT
Leave a large loop to attach sinkers

LINE TO LINE
A blood knot joins lines of equal or different breaking strengths

LINE TO REEL
A blood-bight knot forms a loop to slip the line through

Yellowtail kingfish Kingfish, Kingie, Amberjack, Southern yellowtail *Seriola lalandi*
Strong, vigorous sporting fish, yellowtail kingfish can grow to 65 kg, but the average size encountered by most fishermen is about 5 kg. They can be caught with a fish bait, or with a lure towed behind a boat. Yellowtail are a good live bait, and small kingfish are sometimes used to catch the large record breakers. Strong size 5/0 to 9/0 hooks are needed to hold a large fish when live bait is used, and it pays to use a length of heavier line between the hook and main line when fishing over reefs. Kingfish have a habit of diving for the bottom where the line may be snagged and broken. Kingfish may also be caught with a jigged lure—a lure repeatedly dropped to the bottom and rapidly retrieved with a jerking pull. Metal jigs vary in weight and shape, but most are thin and long, with an average weight of 200 g. Colour does not seem to be important. Schools of kingfish roaming surface waters will readily attack red and white feather jigs or a pink plastic squid lure towed at speeds from 5 to 30 km/h. When one kingfish is hooked, the rest of the school generally follows and a large surface popper lure, cast to the surfacing school, should result in a strike. Kingfish can sometimes be caught with live bait cast into deep water from rocks along the ocean front.

Australian hairtail Ribbonfish *Trichiurus coxii*
Despite its forbidding appearance, hairtail is an excellent table fish which requires little preparation for cooking, as it has no scales. The undershot jaws of the fish's angular head are studded with razor sharp teeth and care must be taken to avoid a nasty cut. When a fish is landed, hold the line with a finger through the curtain ring near the end of the rig, grip the fish firmly behind the head and place it in a strong bag to prevent accidents. Hairtail are usually found in the deep water of bays and estuaries. When fishing from a boat use a stout handline of up to 10 kg breaking strength, and size 3/0 to 5/0 hooks. Rod and reel fishermen will find this an exciting fish to catch as it does not give in easily. Best baits are live yellowtail, prawns, gang-hooked garfish and blue pilchards. A steady supply of minced fish berley will attract and hold a school in the fishing area. The best depth for fishing can only be found by trial and error, but a good starting point is 6 to 7 metres. Hairtail take hold of a bait gently and move slowly away with it. If a fisherman strikes too early, the bait will be pulled from the fish's mouth. The best strategy is to let out a metre of line, and then strike. Use a wire trace as the hairtail's teeth will quickly sever even heavy nylon line.

Australian bass Australian perch, Estuary perch, Gippsland perch *Macquaria colonorum*
The sturdy fighting bass is found in coastal streams below tidal influence along the eastern seaboard from the Pumice Stone Channel in southern Queensland to the Gippsland lakes in Victoria. Above tidal influence, a similar fish—*Percalates novemaculatus*—can be caught using the same tackle and approach. Two good fishing outfits are a threadline reel spooled with nylon line of 3 to 4 kg breaking strength mounted on a light spinning rod, or a pistol-grip rod with a closed-face or baitcaster reel. The different kinds of bass lure are designed to move like food fish, frogs and insects, or small animals which have fallen into the water. Some lures are made to dive deep when they are reeled in, while others splash across the surface and are more popular for night fishing. Lines are best cast from a boat drifting close to the shore, slowly retrieved, then cast again until there is a strike. The lure should be dropped as close as possible to weed beds, overhanging trees, submerged logs and rocks where bass are likely to be waiting.

John Dory *Zeus faber*
John Dory consistently commands a high price at Australia's fish markets, and is always in demand for restaurants. This greenish brown fish is easily identified by the large dark grey spot on each side of its body just above and behind the small pectoral fins. They can grow to a weight of 4 kg, but most specimens are about 500 g. Their bodies are tall and thin and the head accounts for almost one third of the total length. The huge mouth is capable of wide and rapid extension. The best bait for John Dory is live yellowtail. Use a hook between sizes 3/0 and 5/0, and a light line with a breaking strength of 3 to 4 kg. Rod and reel fishing is usual, and it is worthwhile using a float to keep the live bait in midwater. John Dory are poor fighters. They are often taken around wharf and jetty piles, in weed beds and over reefs where they feed on small yellowtail, hardyheads, cockney bream, and other bait fish. The fish's skin is smooth and scaleless, so it is only necessary to remove the large head and intestines before cooking.

Prawn family *Penaeidae*, various species
Prawns mature in tidal estuaries and lakes in summer and are caught in shallow water at night as they move towards the sea. Carry a strong light so that prawns stationary on the bottom can be spotted easily, and use a triangular-framed net. Place the net behind the prawn and scoop it up quickly, or startle it with a movement of your foot so that it shoots backwards into the net. Drag longer nets against the current, with one prawner wading into waist-deep water.

Identifying your catch

Of the thousands of species of fish living in the waters around Australia's coast only a small percentage end up in an angler's creel. Many are considered unfit for eating and are simply thrown back into the sea when caught. On the Great Barrier Reef alone there are around 1400 species to be found. Most of these, however, are small fish, more suitable for an aquarium than for the dinner table. Some fish are toxic and if eaten can cause sickness and even death, so it is important to be able to identify your catch. The 22 fish illustrated below are the ones most commonly fished for and caught, either for sport or for eating. Many fish are known by a variety of common names, and these vary from place to place. Even scientific names can change when species are reclassified.

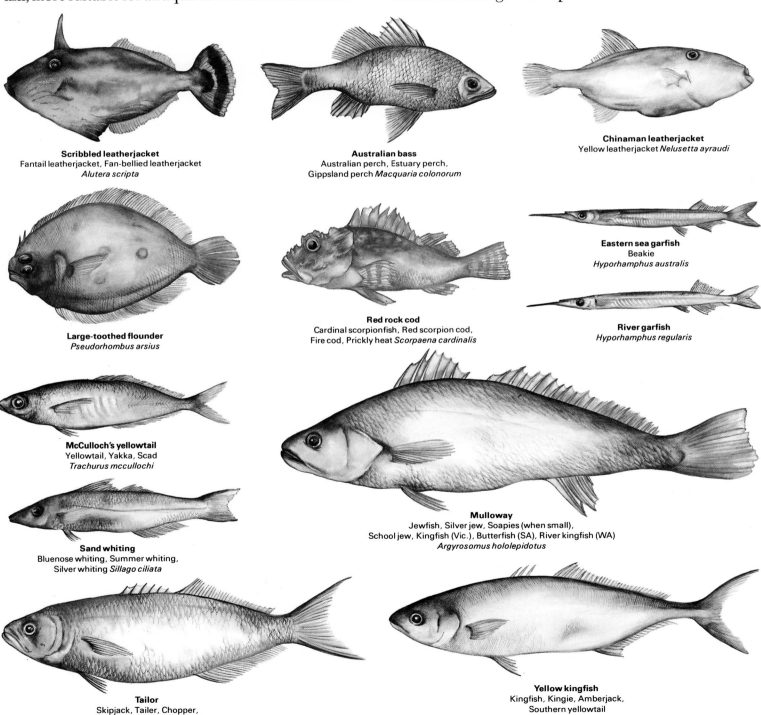

Scribbled leatherjacket
Fantail leatherjacket, Fan-bellied leatherjacket
Alutera scripta

Australian bass
Australian perch, Estuary perch,
Gippsland perch *Macquaria colonorum*

Chinaman leatherjacket
Yellow leatherjacket *Nelusetta ayraudi*

Large-toothed flounder
Pseudorhombus arsius

Red rock cod
Cardinal scorpionfish, Red scorpion cod,
Fire cod, Prickly heat *Scorpaena cardinalis*

Eastern sea garfish
Beakie
Hyporhamphus australis

River garfish
Hyporhamphus regularis

McCulloch's yellowtail
Yellowtail, Yakka, Scad
Trachurus mccullochi

Sand whiting
Bluenose whiting, Summer whiting,
Silver whiting *Sillago ciliata*

Mulloway
Jewfish, Silver jew, Soapies (when small),
School jew, Kingfish (Vic.), Butterfish (SA), River kingfish (WA)
Argyrosomus hololepidotus

Tailor
Skipjack, Tailer, Chopper,
Bluefish *Pomatomus saltatrix*

Yellow kingfish
Kingfish, Kingie, Amberjack,
Southern yellowtail
Seriola lalandi

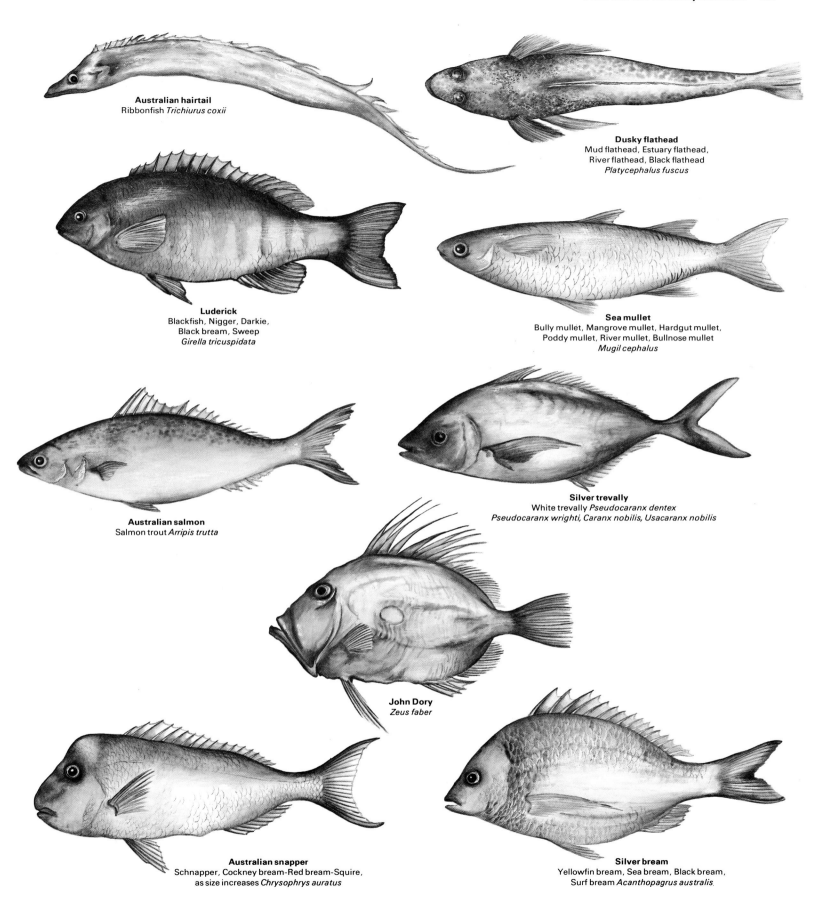

Australian hairtail
Ribbonfish *Trichiurus coxii*

Dusky flathead
Mud flathead, Estuary flathead,
River flathead, Black flathead
Platycephalus fuscus

Luderick
Blackfish, Nigger, Darkie,
Black bream, Sweep
Girella tricuspidata

Sea mullet
Bully mullet, Mangrove mullet, Hardgut mullet,
Poddy mullet, River mullet, Bullnose mullet
Mugil cephalus

Australian salmon
Salmon trout *Arripis trutta*

Silver trevally
White trevally *Pseudocaranx dentex*
Pseudocaranx wrighti, Caranx nobilis, Usacaranx nobilis

John Dory
Zeus faber

Australian snapper
Schnapper, Cockney bream-Red bream-Squire,
as size increases *Chrysophrys auratus*

Silver bream
Yellowfin bream, Sea bream, Black bream,
Surf bream *Acanthopagrus australis*

Inshore boating Vital preparations for a day on the water

Nearly 700,000 Australian families own a craft for sailing, paddling or power boating. Most are small and low-powered, used mainly for weekend recreation on bays and estuaries where boat owners are attracted by fine conditions and placid waters. But behind the apparent safety of sheltered waterways lie potential hazards which must not be disregarded. To prevent a holiday turning into a nightmare, every boat owner must be aware of the problems that can arise, and the steps that may be taken to avoid them.

The anchor, one of the principal pieces of equipment on the boat, is thought by many to be of use only for holding the boat in position while fishing over a favourite spot or picnicking on the shore. But the anchor is more than that—it is a vital safety aid. In the wide estuaries common to most of Australia's big rivers mechanical failure may result in a boat being caught in a strong outrunning tide and swept on to a dangerous bar at the entrance. Because most boats are too heavy or cumbersome to be rowed against such a tide, or against a strong wind, the only way to avoid disaster is to drop the anchor as quickly as possible. With the correct anchor and gear, a boat can be halted and held in position while repair work is carried out, or signals are sent for help.

Anchors of inappropriate design and weight, however, will not catch in the sea bed, and an anchor line which is too short will constantly pluck the anchor out before it can take a firm hold. While a sand-anchor may sometimes hold on a rocky bottom, a reef-anchor will not hold properly in sand or mud. A short anchor line which is quite adequate in a sheltered bay will be insufficient in deep water or against a strong current.

The best anchor lines are made of nylon or other synthetic materials and must be long enough to allow at least five or six times the water's depth to be paid out. The longer and heavier the anchor line, the greater the anchor's holding power. A length of chain about 3 metres long between the anchor and the line adds weight and prevents the line chafing on the sea bed, particularly over reefs. Any reputable dealer will advise on the correct type and weight of anchor for your particular craft.

A boat which is overloaded may appear stable in sheltered nearshore waters, but the wash of a passing vessel or a turbulent rip sweeping around

Long mooring lines must be used in areas where the tide range is large. Secure a boat at both bow and stern so that it can rise and fall with the water level

A long line, with a length of chain attached, helps the anchor to lie on the sea bed and dig in securely. The length of line hanging in the water forms a buffer against the tugging of the boat as it is buffeted by wind and waves—small shocks are absorbed by the line before they reach the anchor

a headland may push a wave aboard. When the boat's stability is upset it may be impossible to avoid further waves and the boat may soon be swamped. All boats should carry a notice indicating the maximum number of people to be carried, and this figure must be sensibly balanced with the amount of gear taken on board.

The effect of bad trimming is much the same as overloading. Move passengers or gear so that the boat is neither down at the bow nor at the stern—conditions which make any craft difficult to handle and impair its performance. A badly trimmed boat will use more fuel, strain the motor and provide an uncomfortable ride. In small boats correct trim is easily achieved by adjusting the positions of passengers or luggage, but larger craft need adjustable trim controls.

Naval charts and boating maps can help sailors avoid the hazards hidden in many deceptively safe waterways. If a boat is grounded on a mud-

bank it may result in little more than a scratched bottom, but to hit a reef, particularly at high speed, can cause serious damage to the craft and injury to the occupants. The reefs, sand banks, shoals and channels shown on maps allow sailors to plot a safe course, and prominent landmarks are shown to aid navigation.

For anglers, the location of wrecks and the contours and composition of the sea bed may give a good indication of the sorts of fish likely to be found in an area. Charts produced by the hydrographic office of the Navy are readily available for most major waterways, and boating maps produced by local authorities cover many popular rivers, lakes and estuaries.

In unfamiliar waters boat owners must seek local advice on sand bars and channels, as these may change considerably depending on the weather, the tide and the volume of water flowing into rivers and lakes.

Signalling for help

THERE are a number of internationally known distress signs that can be used in emergencies. These include raising and lowering outstretched arms, firing red flares or rockets and regularly repeated signals from a foghorn or gun. Flames and smoke from a container of burning tar or oil will attract attention by day or night. Distress sheets—bright orange rectangles marked with a black 'V', or a black square or circle—are valuable for attracting the attention of aircraft.

The gradient of any specially constructed launching ramp usually provides sufficient depth of water over a normal range of tides, so that a boat can be launched and retrieved without damage to its hull. Take care not to immerse the trailer's wheel hubs because bearings will rapidly corrode in the salt water, and this is potentially dangerous. Most ramps have areas nearby where preparation for launching can be carried out. Release tie-downs, check the motor, and load all equipment to prevent unnecessary delays on the ramp itself

Nothing has a greater effect on boating holidays than the weather. Apart from comfort, the weather can greatly affect the safety of any vessel. Check the forecast before setting out to avoid being caught in bad weather. This is particularly important for small boats in open waterways such as Melbourne's Port Phillip Bay and Brisbane's Moreton Bay, where choppy seas can quickly develop that will threaten all but the most seaworthy craft. However, local conditions can change rapidly and forecasts can be wrong, so it is wise to learn to recognise threatening weather patterns.

Most dangerous weather conditions give an indication of their approach with unmistakable sky signs. A cold front is usually accompanied by a build up of giant towering clouds. A line squall can appear as a fast-moving roll of cloud stretching across the sky. Local weather patterns may have their own peculiar signs which, if recognised early enough, give sailors time to make for port or for the shelter of a headland. Coast guards, members of yacht clubs and commercial fishermen are always willing to provide helpful information to visitors.

Many of the rules governing safe boating are covered by regulations and enforced by law. Speed limits apply in most popular waterways and around moorings, and boating may be prohibited altogether in swimming areas. One life jacket per passenger is obligatory on all craft, from the smallest dinghies to ocean-going yachts. An anchor, paddles and fire extinguisher may also be considered to be standard equipment in some areas. Alternative means of propulsion—a secondary outboard, sail, oars or paddles—are useful in case a motor fails or winds become too light to propel a yacht. A good sailing day with a brisk breeze can become a dead calm by the middle of the afternoon, and the shore may be a long way off. Carry a spare length of rope to repair rigging, or a shear pin in case the propeller hits an obstruction in the water. Such precautions can mean the difference between getting back to shore on time or spending hours waiting for a tow. Report trips into offshore waters to the water police or coastguard. Detailed plans of the route to be travelled and expected time of arrival are necessary, so that a search operation can be started if a boating party fails to confirm its safe arrival.

Four basic knots that boat owners must master

BOATS must be securely tied to anchors and mooring points for safety. The knots that are used must remain firm whether the rope is wet and taut, or dry and slack. Modern synthetic ropes have a slippery surface and this must also be taken into account. A good knot must release easily when the direction of pressure is reversed, so that a quick reaction to emergencies is possible. Each knot serves a different purpose—everything from mooring a boat to a jetty to joining two pieces of rope together—and all boat owners must be familiar with the four most common ones. These are the reef knot, the clove hitch, the bowline, the round-turn with two half-hitches. Practice tying the knots at home until the sequence of operations becomes second nature.

Reef knot
Joins two pieces of rope of similar size. Will not jam. Release by pushing strands of one rope into the knot

Round-turn and two half-hitches
Safe, efficient way to securely fasten a rope to small fixtures such as jetty rings and nails

Clove hitch
Simple knot used to attach a rope to a fixed object. Release knot by easing pressure on either end of the rope

Bowline
Mainly used at the end of a rope to make a non-slip loop for dropping over mooring posts on a wharf or jetty. Release by pushing rope into knot

Coastal hazards Dangers that can be avoided

Coasts are risky places—mainly because so many people using them are visiting unfamiliar territory and experiencing an unaccustomed climate. Often people are literally out of their element, venturing on and into water that holds its own menace, as well as concealing dangerous creatures. But nearly all trouble can be avoided with some knowledge of where hazards may be found, and the exercise of common sense and caution. The problems that most frequently lead to drowning are discussed earlier in this section, and resuscitation is dealt with overleaf, as are other first aid treatments, including those for many stings and bites. Two special menaces of tropical coasts are saltwater crocodiles, which can kill with a blow from their tails, and box jellyfish, whose stings require trained assistance.

Sun effects—sunburn, sunstroke and heat exhaustion—are characteristic of coasts only because most people wear less clothing and spend more time basking than usual. Screening creams provide the best protection against burning. If washed off by perspiration or bathing, they should be reapplied at once. Sunstroke is a breakdown of the body's heat-regulating system: victims do not sweat. Heat exhaustion is a failure of blood circulation to the extremities, caused by loss of body salt and fluid, and is more common among the chronically ill or elderly. People prone to either sunstroke or heat exhaustion should seek shade and cooler air, and perhaps limit their travelling to temperate regions.

Infections start easily from coral cuts in the tropics, from wounds inflicted by some of the relatively harmless marine stingers or spiked fish, and from insect bites. Shoes should be worn on reefs and in tropical waters. The use of insect repellents is advisable, even by people who are not irritated by itching bites. Mosquito-borne

Cone shells must be left alone—the poison injected by tropical species is usually fatal

diseases include dengue fever in the tropics and the related Ross River fever in subtropical Queensland. And in remote parts on the north coast, pockets of malaria may still be found.

Stinging jellyfish, other than the tropical box jellyfish, are unlikely to cause death. But heavy doses of their venom can cause severe and prolonged pain and may bring about collapse. Corneal scarring may result from a sting across an eye. Swimmers should note that the prevalence of most such jellyfish increases with the water temperature: risks are greatest in late summer. At least six Australian species of *Conus*, the **stinging shellfish,** are known to be dangerous. They shoot out hard, barbed spears that pump venom. The most lethal are found on tropical reefs, where they bury themselves in sand by day. All known species contain some venom and none should be handled before making certain that the living animal is not still inside.

Of dozens of species of venomous **stinging fish,** the deadliest are stonefish, *Synanceia*. Though big—up to 500 mm—and bulky, they are virtually impossible to see in their coral reef or mudflat habitats, because they are coated with slime and algae and sometimes partly buried in sand. They have 13 sharp spines along their backs, each

linked to two venom glands. Stonefish are distributed throughout the tropics and south to Brisbane, most stings occurring at Easter or during the August school holidays. Strong footwear is the best protection. Fishermen should learn to identify stonefish, and not grab too quickly at whatever they hook or net. Stinging fish common in cooler waters—catfish, bullrout, fortescue, cobbler, red rock cod, flathead, goblinfish, old wife and many more—do most harm to anglers and trawlermen handling them accidentally, especially at night. Their venom is much less dangerous than that of the stonefish and other tropical species, but it may cause a collapse leading to drowning. Stingrays, though venomous, do most of their damage by the wound they inflict. Feeding on the sea bed and often motionless, a stingray drives its long, spiny tail directly up at anyone treading on it. Some species are found all around the coast. They are unlikely to feed where many people are swimming, but a close watch should be kept in lonely waters. One species of shark, known as the Port Jackson but

Camouflage renders the stonefish almost invisible

The ocean's most feared menace

The possibility of shark attack probably worries Australian surf bathers more than any other seaside hazard. Yet the chances of being bitten are extremely remote. In the decade from 1970 there were only 20 attacks in Australian waters, of which five were fatal. Many city beaches have now been made even safer by meshing—with a net suspended in the water a few hundred metres from the beach for part of its length. The net is not intended to seal off the beach completely, but to provide a trap for any sharks in the area. Sharks must keep moving so that water can circulate through their gills; if they are caught in a net and immobilised they quickly drown. Nets are retrieved at regular intervals, dead sharks removed and damage repaired. Since meshing was introduced in Sydney in 1937 there has not been a fatal attack on any of Sydney's 60 km of ocean beaches. In recent years the number of sharks caught in nets has declined considerably, in Sydney from 224 in 1951 to 43 in 1969, and some experts think that the nets may discourage sharks from establishing territories. Attacks are very rare in waters where the surface temperature is below 21°C, so the seasonal patterns of water temperature variations are a good guide to the periods when bathing is most likely to be safe.

Shark attacks follow the seasonal warming of southern waters. Bathers should remember that shallow bays are often warmer than the surrounding ocean

▨ Temperature above 21°C   ▨ Temperature below 21°C   ● Shark attack sites

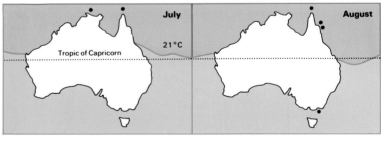

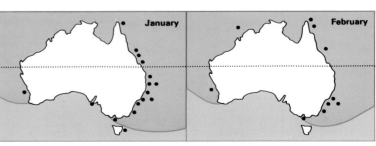

Vivid circles of colour make the blue-ringed octopus easy to identify. These creatures are very common

When a fish feast may be poisonous

CIGUATERA poisoning, much publicised since the late 1970s, has always been a risk on tropical coasts and islands. Toxins originating in coral reef algae and small marine animals are passed from fish to fish in the reef food chain. The bigger the fish, the greater the accumulation of poison. More than 300 species could have it, but the highest concentrations are believed to be in the liver and other internal organs of red bass, chinaman and paddletail—none of which are permitted to be sold commercially—along with barracouta and moray eel.

Symptoms of ciguatera poisoning usually include numb and tingling fingers, numbness around the mouth, burning or tingling of the skin in cold water, muscle and joint pain, vomiting, diarrhoea and headache. Death is unusual but a lengthy treatment in hospital may be necessary. The disease can have a debilitating effect for months. Fish eaters visiting the tropics should not eat large portions from the bigger reef fish, and they should never eat repeated meals from the same fish. Whatever the species, the internal organs of reef fish should never be eaten.

distributed throughout temperate waters, has a venomous spine in front of each of the two fins on its back. Its struggles when hooked or speared can drive a spine centimetres into a fisherman's flesh. Pain and muscle weakness from the poison may last only a few hours, but the ragged wound is easily infected. Both the tiny southern blue-ringed octopus and its bigger tropical relative have been known to kill humans with the venomous bites of their beaks. The deaths were entirely avoidable. This easily identified animal is harmless in the water—it bites humans only if it

is picked up, usually after having been stranded in a rock pool by low tide.

More than 30 species of **sea snake** are found in tropical Australian waters but only two are distributed as far south as Cape Leeuwin or Bass Strait. Their fangs deliver meagre amounts of venom but it can be extremely toxic, causing death by muscle destruction. No one inexperienced in handling snakes should pick one up, and prawning or fishing nets should be handled with care, especially at night.

Coastal **land snakes** in temperate regions

include the Western Australian dugite and the Sydney broad-headed snake, both of which are highly venomous though unlikely to cause death. The broad-head likes to hide in dry rock crevices or under boulders and slabs. The taipan—the longest venomous snake in Australia, and invariably lethal with its bite until an anti-venom was developed in the 1950s—inhabits north-eastern and northern coastal areas. Normally timid, it flees when approached, but is likely to strike if cornered, snapping three or four times with fangs up to 13 mm long.

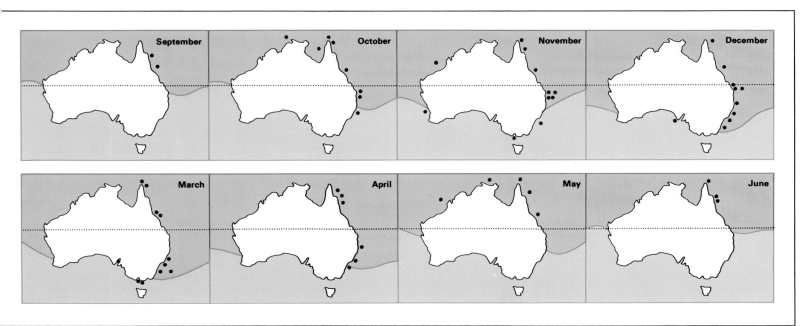

Emergency action Skills to save a life

A drowning person's breathing and heartbeat may stop, but they can still be revived. Resuscitation has to begin as soon as possible—in the water if necessary—to restore the supply of oxygen to the blood, restart the heart and keep the blood circulating around the body. Victims of suffocation, electric shock, heart attack and some poisons and venoms can also be kept alive.

Place the victim on their side on a firm, level surface and clear the throat to prevent any food, blood or mucus going down into the lungs. If the patient is unconscious, make sure the tongue does not fall backwards and block the throat. Use your fingers to scoop out any particles behind the tongue. Take out any false teeth. Tilt the head backwards while supporting the jaw with the other hand, keeping the face pointing slightly down so that any mucus or fluid can drain out of the mouth. Then put the person on their back. Kneel at the head and put the palm of one hand on the top of the victim's head while supporting the chin with the other, and tilt the head back so the tongue will keep out of the way and air will be able to enter freely.

Pinch the victim's nostrils closed with your thumb and forefinger, all the time keeping the head tilted back. Take a deep breath, open your mouth as wide as possible and put it over the victim's mouth, making an airtight seal. Blow into the mouth strongly.

Take your mouth away. If the victim's chest is not rising, check if the airway is clear. Then put your mouth back over the victim's and breathe into the victim five times, as fast as you can.

Check if there is any pulse beat by feeling for the carotid pulse in the neck (as shown). If there is a pulse beat, continue with mouth-to-mouth respiration at 12 breaths a minute. It may be necessary to continue for a long time. Check the carotid pulse every two minutes.

If there is no carotid pulse, mouth-to-mouth respiration should go on and heart massage should begin immediately. Kneel beside the victim. Find the lower half of the breastbone. Put the heel of your other hand over the first hand. With arms straight, lean forward and press down on the breastbone so it goes down about 50 mm. Keeping your hands in position, lean back and release the pressure. Continue the process rhythmically, pressing down *at least* once a second. The best

rate would be around 80 times a minute.

If you are alone with the victim, after 15 chest presses move to the head and use your mouth to inflate the lungs twice. Continue with 15 chest compressions then two lung inflations in turn.

If there are two people available they should kneel on opposite sides of the victim. One person does five chest presses, one every second—to get the timing right, count out loud 'one thousand, two thousand' and so on. The other person then makes one chest inflation using mouth-to-mouth.

If the victim is a child, only one hand should be used for chest compressions, and they should be given a little faster. The breastbone should be pressed down only 20 mm. Do not press a baby's breastbone down more than 10 mm.

If breathing begins, put the victim quickly into the recovery position (as shown). Vomiting will often occur now. Keep the throat clear. Watch the person continually to check if the breathing is satisfactory. If not, replace on the back and begin resuscitation again. Check the pulse every 2 to 3 minutes. To stop loss of body heat, cover the victim with a coat or blanket. Stay with the victim until qualified help comes.

How to give mouth-to-mouth resuscitation

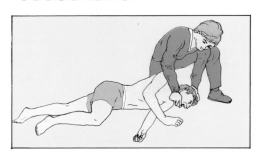

1 Resuscitation can begin in the water if necessary. Once out of the water, place the victim lying on their side on a firm, level surface. Keep the head tilted to help clear the airway

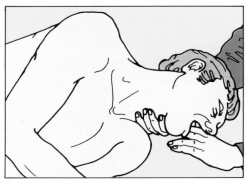

2 An unconscious person cannot prevent food or mucus passing down the throat into the lungs, so clear the mouth behind the tongue

3 Once the airway has been cleared, turn the patient on their back. Supporting the chin, tilt the head so that the tongue is clear and air can enter the lungs

4 While the head is still tilted back, pinch the patient's nostrils. Take a deep breath, hold it, then put your mouth firmly over the victim's and blow strongly

5 When you take your mouth away, check to see if the patient's chest is rising, and listen for any exhalation of air. Repeat resuscitation until breathing resumes

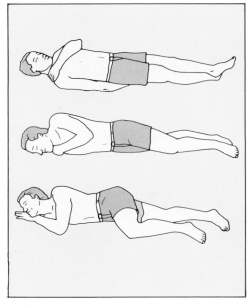

6 The recovery or coma position keeps the airway clear and stops vomit getting into the lungs. If you have given mouth-to-mouth resuscitation and heart massage and restored a victim's breathing and heart beat, they will be lying on their back.

To put the victim in the recovery position, kneel at the victim's side and pull their further leg over the one nearest to you. Then place the arm further from you across the chest to the shoulder area. Position the other arm down along the torso (with the palm upwards). Next pull the victim on to the side that is nearest to you. Pull the underneath arm down behind the back. Bend the top leg. Put the arm of the top hand under the chin, supporting the chin but with the hand clear of the mouth. Tilt the head slightly backwards to keep the airway clear

The technique of heart massage

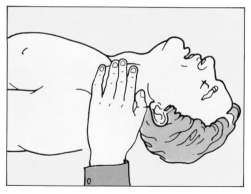

1 To check for heartbeat, place your hand palm downwards across the side of the victim's neck and feel for the carotid artery pulse between the Adam's apple and the neck muscles

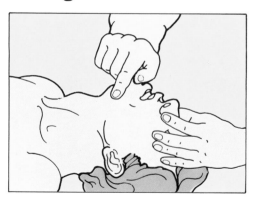

2 Before applying external cardiac compression, place the patient on their back on a flat, firm surface and remove any restricting clothing. Check that the airway is clear, then tilt head well back

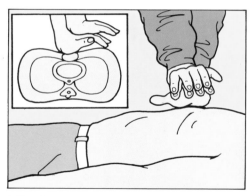

3 Kneeling to one side, place the heel of one hand on the middle half of the patient's breastbone. Keeping palm and fingers raised above the chest, place heel of other hand on top of first hand

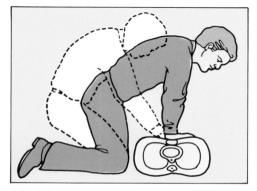

4 Straighten arms and push down on the breastbone, depressing it about 50 mm. Keeping your hands in position, lean back and release pressure on chest. Repeat at least once a second

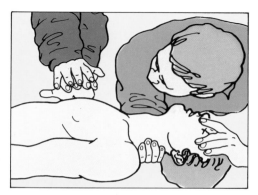

5 If two people are available, one should apply mouth-to-mouth resuscitation while the other continues heart massage, working together at the rate of 1 air inflation to 5 compressions

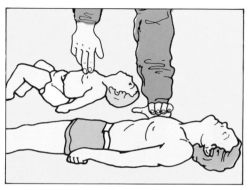

6 On a child, use only one hand and increase the adult rate of cardiac compressions, with less depression of the breastbone. Do not depress a baby's breastbone more than 10 mm

Aiding a shark attack victim

MOST shark attacks are survivable if help is at hand. Rescuers are hardly ever harmed. But people must condition themselves to the horrifying appearance of some wounds, to avoid panic.

Bleeding must be staunched quickly. If the victim cannot be brought ashore immediately, use your fingers to press hard into or just above any point where blood is spurting. Once ashore, do NOT try to get the victim to hospital. Move him only out of reach of waves and lay him on the sand with his head lowermost.

Apply a tourniquet above the wound, over a long bone—not a joint. You can use a belt or a strip of cloth or rubber, but nothing as narrow as string or shoe laces. If heavy bleeding continues, use pressure by hand or pack cloth of any kind over the wound. Do NOT remove blood-soaked dressings—press more cloths on top. Then call an ambulance.

While waiting, cover the victim lightly but give him nothing to eat or drink. If he is wearing a wetsuit, leave it on. Monitor the victim's breathing and be ready to give mouth-to-mouth resuscitation.

Venomous bites and stings

Snakebites and most serious marine stingings can be combated with good first aid. The aim is to slow the spread of venom and the onset of paralysis until qualified medical treatment can be given.

Never cut into a snakebite wound or cut away injured tissue. That does more harm than good. Do NOT try to remove clothing covering the wound—movement will spread the venom. Do NOT wash the wounded area. Surplus venom splashes on the skin cannot hurt the victim and it will help in quick identification of the snake type. Do NOT try to kill the snake at the risk of further bites. And do NOT tie an arterial tourniquet above the wound.

Wrap a wide bandage directly over the bitten area, as firmly as if you were binding a sprained ankle. Extend the binding as high as you can—to the thigh if a foot or leg is bitten—and secure a splint to the whole leg. If the bite is on a hand or forearm, apply bandages and a splint as far as the elbow and place the arm in a sling.

Keep the victim warm and as still as possible.

Check regularly for breathing. If first aid comes too late and paralysis sets in, mouth-to-mouth resuscitation may be necessary. If the victim must be moved, it should be done gently—preferably on a stretcher.

Exactly the same pressure/immobilisation first aid works for funnelweb spider bites. It is not necessary for the bite of the redback spider, which has a slower-acting venom. Pressure on a redback bite only increases pain, and that can be eased by cooling the wound with a mixture of ice cubes and water in a plastic bag—but do NOT apply ice directly to a wound.

Warm water, on the other hand, is often a pain-reliever for the victims of stinging fish. Cone shell stings and blue-ringed octopus bites are dealt with by the pressure/immobilisation method. Jellyfish stings can be neutralised to some extent with vinegar—NOT methylated spirit or other alcohols. The main risk of marine stingings is for a person to collapse and drown—but be as gentle as possible in removing a victim from the water.

PART 4

Discovering the coast

Faced with the immensity of the seaboard, travellers must be selective. For every person who seeks reassuring surroundings and familiar activities at journey's end, there is another who hopes for surprise and challenge.

Fascination may lie in landscapes and wildlife, or the ocean itself may be the lure.

Coastal towns can command attention in their own right, or be seen as mere resting places. Choice is a matter of personal taste and circumstances.

In this part of the book the options are left open. With the widest range of interests in mind, priority is given to solid, serviceable information about scores of localities.

Most of the places described are illustrated with aerial photographs, and wherever possible these have been joined together to give the broadest possible view, even if there is a shift in colour.

These sweeping panoramas could otherwise be photographed only from a great altitude, where atmospheric haze reduces clarity.

The photographs provide a remarkable new perspective of even familiar areas. Mysteries of local topography, access, vegetation and waterways all become clear.

Even individual houses can be easily identified.

Evening clouds gather over a coastal mountain range

Aerial photography A bird's eye view of the shore

Nearly all of the illustrations in the following guide sections are reproduced from specially commissioned vertical aerial photographs. The technique of taking them is a demanding one, calling for exceptional precision in navigation and timing. But nothing else is so effective in showing the positions of ground features in relation to one another. The pictures work as living maps. And some incidental points of information emerging from them could not be conveyed even in the most elaborate formal mapping.

Aerial cameras work the same way as those used in conventional photography. But they are exceptionally big. They take rolls of film on which each frame is more than 225 mm square—almost the size of this page—and each roll has room for more than 100 frames. The film magazine alone is bigger than a typewriter and almost as bulky. High-performance light aircraft are modified—their hydraulic systems and electrical wiring may have to be shifted—so that the camera can be mounted in the belly of the fuselage with a lens cone protruding downwards through the hull. Normal or wide-angle lenses may be fitted. The mounting allows the camera to be swung out of line with the heading of the aircraft, or to be tilted if the aircraft is not in level flight.

The requirements of the picture—always a compromise between the detail that can be shown and the area that can be covered—determine the shooting altitude. Reader's Digest decided on 3000 metres, giving a ground spread of about 4.5 km in each full frame. Each area was plotted on detailed maps, allowing for overlaps where it was intended that pictures be joined up. Then it was up to navigator-cameramen to direct pilots over exactly the right spot while maintaining the right height. Taking their bearings from the most prominent ground features, they set a course to the centre of the plotted area. Sighting instruments enabled them not only to trigger their cameras with split-second timing, but also to

Only the centre of an aerial photograph is a truly vertical view—features at the edges lean outwards

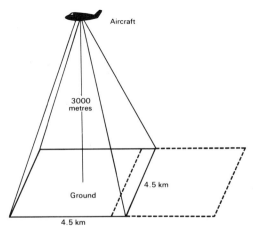

A normal lens used at an altitude of 3000 metres covers a ground area of 20.25 sq km. Pictures are overlapped to reduce the contrast in angles when they are joined

observe wind-drifting or tilting so that camera angles could be adjusted. The precision achieved far excels that of wartime bomb-aiming.

Because the distance between the camera and the ground is greater at the edges of each picture, angles are created that slightly distort the image. Tall features appear to lean out at all sides of a picture—most noticeably in city shots. Angling at the edges may also affect coloration, so that pictures that are joined with a considerable overlap do not match well. Readers will see some pictures that are much more obviously mis-matched: the hues of water and sometimes of vegetation seem to change completely. That is because they were not taken on the same aerial run. Flight plans are subject to sudden change for many reasons—for example, the requirements of air traffic control. And a delay even of minutes means a change in sun angle and perhaps in light intensity. If the delay is extended to days or weeks by bad weather, then water conditions and vegetation will almost certainly be different.

Given that pictures are taken in the desired place, the only yardstick of success in aerial photography is the sharpness of ground details. Good definition requires very strong sunlight. A picture taken in poor light will come out, but ground features do not stand out starkly enough for it to be of much use. So aerial photographers are much more subject to weather limitations than most other aviators, whose only concern is getting safely from place to place. Overcast conditions, even if the air is perfectly calm, mean no work can be done. Just a thin layer of light cirrus cloud above the aircraft softens the details in a picture. Isolated, fluffy cumulus clouds cast shadows that may obscure important features, interrupting or spoiling a run at the last moment. Clouds scattered below the plane may be less of a problem because their positions are more easily observed. But haze or extensive smoke—conditions that other fliers could avoid or ignore —rule out photography altogether.

Angling of the sun shortens an aerial photographer's productive hours, even in totally clear weather. The light cast below the plane is inadequate if the sun is within 30 degrees of the horizon—within three hours, say, of dawn or dusk around the latitude of Adelaide in mid-spring. Mid-winter work is scarcely worth attempting in the far south, not simply because of bad weather but also because the sun passes so far to the north that it is at a poor angle nearly all day.

The time of year is also important if the purpose is to assemble knowledge of vegetation, or to record slight contour variations that could be obscured by vegetation—for example, a flush of tall grass in late spring. In areas such as the far north, where there are big tide ranges and tidal flats kilometres wide, a set of pictures makes little sense unless the tide level is consistent. In that case the photographer can only work on certain days, regardless of weather and light conditions.

What the guide sections do

Information on virtually every place on the coast where travellers are likely to stay has been compiled from on-the-spot reports. In the descriptive material, every attempt has been made to bring out the points that give each place its own character, whether they be aspects of scenery, activity or historical interest. But the guide entries are not intended to amount to recommendations. Personal tastes vary as widely as the places. It is for readers to weigh up their own preferences and judge—from the pictures, from the descriptions and from the details of facilities and access—where the effort and expense of travel may produce the greatest reward.

Key maps are included with all entries. They place each locality in the context of its surrounding district, to assist travellers to find their bearings and to make sure that they do not overlook nearby points of possible interest. Minor roads, except for those essential to reach destinations discussed in the text, are omitted for the sake of

Key to town facilities

Hotel or motel — Holiday letting — Caravan park — Camping ground — Petrol — Chemist — Cinema — Public bar — Licensed club — Restaurant — Takeaway food — Boat hire — Bait — Swimming pool — Golf — Tennis — Bowls — Launching ramp

clarity. All key maps are designed with north to the top of the page. Shaded parts represent the areas covered in the accompanying aerial photographs. Some variation in the scale of the photographs has been dictated by space restrictions. The white northward arrow appearing on each picture indicates not only its alignment with grid north but also its scale: the arrow's length represents an actual ground span of about 250 metres.

Secrets unlocked from above

AERIAL pictures speak volumes to scientists. Botanists use them to classify vegetation—not only the dominant land plants but also seagrass beds and seaweeds. Zoologists can tell what animal life is likely to be found. Geologists are able to distinguish rock types, and by picking out ancient dunes and beach ridges they trace changes in sea level. Oceanographers discern currents, and 'fronts' of different water temperature. From wave patterns they can read the contours of the sea bed.

Laymen, too, can learn more—even of their home shores. Bushwalkers can spot unknown tracks, surfers can note unusual wave breaks, and boat owners can see the twists and turns of channels. Submerged reefs and bars and tricky currents show up. So do flood-prone areas.

Right: Contrasting colours of river and tidal waters at Burnett Heads, Qld, mark a 'front' where fish feed intensively

Travelling sand bars off Busselton, WA, go westward in storms, averaging a few metres each year. Beach sands move with them, perpetually altering the shoreline

Details of motoring access and of public transport availability are not exhaustive. They are based on the usual travel routes and practical requirements of most people. Other routes and services may be found, particularly from inland centres. Some hotels and motels operate pick-up services for booked guests arriving at railway or coach stations and airports. And once in a seaside township, visitors may find that they can avail themselves of local transport arrangements that are too variable to be listed.

Hours stated for surf club patrols, and for some other institutions such as museums and historic buildings, are subject to change, in most cases from year to year but sometimes at shorter notice. Weekday lifeguards, paid from council grants or business donations, may augment the part-time protection afforded by surf club volunteers in some beach towns. The financial basis of such services was considered too uncertain for them to be included in a book which it is hoped readers will use for many years.

Coastal conditions are subject to change, both gradual and sudden. References to the popularity of certain beaches for swimming, or to the suitability of certain spots for boating or fishing, should not be taken as absolute assurances as to their safety. It is always advisable for visitors to take every opportunity to borrow local knowledge, not only to avoid hazards but also to gain the maximum enjoyment from their stay.

The metropolitan sections do not include listings of transport details and other localised information. It can be presumed that all facilities will be found within a reasonable distance of the places dealt with in the text and that ample information on access and public transport will be easily obtainable by visitors.

The introduction to each regional section includes some discussion of general climatic factors, especially those that bear on the times of year when visits are likely to be most enjoyable. Charts showing the year-round averages of meteorological readings are included with some individual entries. They give a guide to seasonal trends in temperature, sunshine, rainfall and 3 p.m. relative humidity. But they have a most limited application. Actual weather conditions vary widely at any time, and quite small differences in distance or altitude from the site of the weather station could produce a markedly different climatic pattern. Figures are given only where they are of some relevance because the weather station is nearby.

Mallacoota to Melbourne

The coast of eastern Victoria offers a variety of great escapes for Melbourne residents and other holidaymakers with its manifold recreational opportunities—notably around the complex and extensive Gippsland Lakes system, the sandy straights of Ninety Mile Beach and the rugged terrain of Wilsons Promontory.

The world's southernmost mangroves grow at the margins of Corner Inlet, in the shelter of Wilsons Promontory

Cape Conran is a mecca for abalone divers

Mallacoota Inlet: a boat is essential

NEW SOUTH WALES

Snowy River

Cape Howe
Mallacoota

Marlo
Lakes Entrance **Lake Tyers**
Paynesville **Wingan Inlet**
Point Hicks

•**Melbourne**

Gippsland Lakes

VICTORIA

Ninety Mile Beach

Golden Beach•

•**Seaspray**

Somers• **French Island**

Shoreham• •**Flinders**
Phillip Island

•**Inverloch**
Cape Paterson **Venus**
Bay

•**Sandy Point**

BASS STRAIT

Waratah
Bay **Wilsons Promontory**

SOUTHERN OCEAN

The doctor who courted danger

LIFE ashore at Sydney Cove bored navy doctor George Bass (left). He revelled in taking risks. So he resolved to find out whether Tasmania was an island or part of the mainland—still a mystery 10 years after the First Fleet arrived.

Bass, 26, set out in December 1797 in a 9-metre whaleboat with six volunteer oarsmen. Storms forced them to land for a miserable Christmas at Cape Howe. But at New Year they passed James Cook's landfall at Cape Everard—called Point Hicks now—and entered the unknown.

In a gale-lashed attempt to salvage stores from a Furneaux Islands shipwreck, the boat sprang a leak. But Bass pressed on, westward out of the shelter of Wilsons Promontory. He met high seas and a huge swell that he knew could come only from the Southern Ocean. Tasmania had to be an island. Bass had found a passage cutting a week or more off sailing times from England.

Two days farther into the strait that bears his name, Bass halted for repairs at Western Port and decided that he had learned enough. His 11-week expedition was more than a masterpiece of seamanship, keeping his crew safe in a storm-tossed open boat. He also produced charts, sketches and notes of 1000 km of new territory. Bass's information, vital to mariners, played an important part in shaping the southward expansion of the colony.

Havens of calm on a wild strait

WESTERLY gales of the Southern Ocean, funnelled through Bass Strait, are thwarted by the high granite bastion of Wilsons Promontory. So Victoria's eastern coastline is shielded from most winds —but not from the power of the sea. Heavy swells are bent around the promontory so that they push directly in at the shores beyond. Strong wave action, virtually constant for 6000 years, has produced a freakish sand barrier system along Ninety Mile Beach, backed by a maze of boating lagoons—the Gippsland Lakes.

Capes to the west of the promontory guard deeply indented bays where long-established fishing and boating resorts enjoy similar shelter. Summer temperatures throughout the region are usually warm by day and mild at night; winters are cool to cold but frost-free. A low rainfall is spread fairly evenly year-round except near NSW, where the summer months may be wetter.

Croajingolong National Park, adjoining the no-man's-land where the border was marked last century, preserves the greatest variety of landforms and plant life to be found in Victoria. It also offers the best opportunities for solitude on this coast. Resorts from Lakes Entrance to Western Port are under heavy holiday pressure. Even the bush trails of 'the Prom' are over-used: camping and walking have to be rationed.

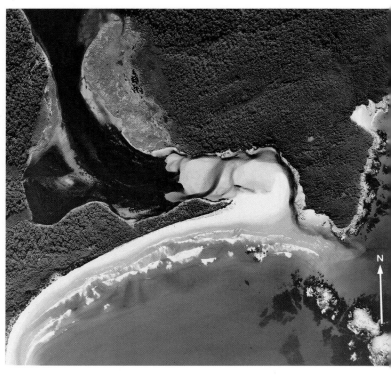

Seals breed on the Skerries, off the sand-barred mouth of Wingan Inlet

Croajingolong National Park

Like Mallacoota's early settlers, visitors spending much time in Croajingolong National Park find a boat indispensable. Until a road was cleared to the township in 1918, residents—mainly fishermen and their families—had to row downstream from Genoa or Gypsy Point, 20 km away. Most of the inlet's eastern shoreline remains inaccessible to cars, but boats can tie up at jetties. Nearby picnic grounds have barbecues and firewood, and walking tracks lead around gentle, wooded slopes. Boats can be hired at Mallacoota or Gypsy Point, and ramps are available for private craft. Ruins of the Spotted Dog mine, a reminder of a short-lived gold-rush in the 1890s,

are a little more than 1 km from the jetty at Allen Head, along a walking track which passes a pioneer cemetery and returns to the inlet at Cemetery Bight. The bight is regarded as the safest swimming spot on shores which otherwise drop steeply into deep water. For surfers Betka Beach and Bastion Point provide fine sandy stretches.

Short, easy walking tracks fringe the western shores of Mallacoota Inlet, while unmarked trails strike out into remote, rugged regions through dense rainforest, open woodlands and low, windswept heath. The 489-metre summit of Genoa Peak is reached by a steep 1 km climb from the picnic area at its base, reached along a turn-off

from Princes Highway 1 km west of Genoa. Popular long walks link the camping grounds at Mallacoota, Wingan Inlet and Thurra River. With maps and advice from the park rangers, enterprising hikers can plan other routes to take advantage of the best bush camping areas and seasonal water sources. Camping grounds at Wingan Inlet and the mouth of the Thurra River have pit lavatories, fireplaces and fresh water. The sites are reached off Princes Highway along all-weather gravel roads which are rough in patches and unsuitable for caravans. Camping permits are required and bookings can be made over summer school holidays and Easter. Campers at Wingan Inlet fish in the estuary or paddle upstream in canoes to bathe in clear rock pools. Small boats can be launched over sand near the camp jetty.

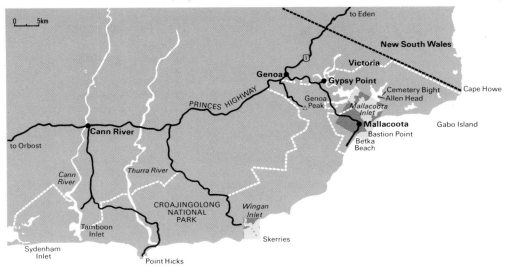

Upstream of a cramped entrance, Mallacoota Inlet has spacious boating waters and safe beaches

MALLACOOTA (pop. 725) south of Princes Highway 520 km from Melbourne, 574 km from Sydney (turn off at Genoa).

TRANSPORT: train Melbourne-Bairnsdale most days (4½ hrs); bus Bairnsdale-Orbost, Orbost-Mallacoota (6 hrs) daily; coach Sydney-Orbost daily (11 hrs).

YOUTH HOSTEL: 5 km north, open year-round.

	POINT HICKS											
	Jan	Feb	Mar	Apr	May	Jun	Jul	Aug	Sep	Oct	Nov	Dec
Maximum C°	23	24	22	20	16	14	14	15	16	18	19	22
Minimum C°	16	16	15	13	10	8	8	8	9	11	12	14
Rainfall mm	61	78	68	62	118	97	92	101	68	76	83	84
Humidity %	74	73	77	70	74	78	72	75	66	77	78	71
Rain days	9	8	9	10	14	13	13	15	13	14	12	10
Sunshine hrs	Summer 8 +			Autumn 7 +			Winter 5 +			Spring 6 +		

Marlo and the Snowy River

Strangers to eastern Victoria are incredulous when told that the gentle waterway flowing sluggishly past Marlo is the Snowy River. The ice-fed torrent that spills from the flanks of Mount Kosciusko, 2000 metres up and 140 km away, peters out meekly beside the pine trees and old weatherboard cottages of this little holiday settlement. Power boats scoot over the smooth waters of its last straight reach, so that water-skiers can perform their tricks for strollers on the township's Esplanade. Beyond a tiny ocean exit channel that twists around shifting sand banks, the great river dies in the shallow arm of French Narrows. Early on its winding course of more than 400 km, the Snowy is tamed

and tunnelled, diverted and depleted. Between the late 1940s and early 1970s, in the most ambitious engineering project undertaken in Australia, its flow was channelled to hydro-electric stations which supply a major part of the power needs of New South Wales and Victoria. Much of the water is not returned to the Snowy: it goes instead into the Murray and Murrumbidgee Rivers to augment their capacity to provide irrigation for agriculture in their valleys. The Snowy loses 2.35 million million litres a year—enough water to raise the level of Port Jackson, Sydney, by 45 metres.

Regulation of the Snowy works in Marlo's favour. With the lower reaches less prone not

only to flooding but also to drought, the township now has a year-round popularity among anglers and boating enthusiasts who cruise the peaceful river channels, creeks and lakes to the north. Shore-based anglers throw lines from the jetties near boat ramps at Marlo or on the Brodribb River, 2 km to the north, reached along Old Marlo Road through an avenue of eucalypts, their branches interlocking overhead. Sheltered beaches line the river banks east of the Marlo jetty, and a short boat trip across the river takes board-riders and surf casters to a long stretch of secluded surf beach. Walking access to the ocean coast is 4 km east of the town, across a narrow plank bridge spanning French Narrows. The

Dunes bar the depleted flow of the Snowy River opposite the boating town of Marlo, allowing only a trickle into the ocean; much of the water stagnates in the blind arm of French Narrows (right)

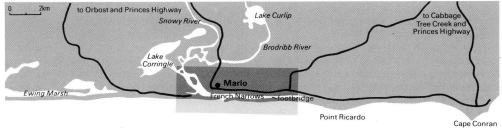

beach, backed by scrub-covered dunes, continues unbroken past a popular surfing spot at Point Ricardo to a big caravan park and camping ground near Cape Conran. A small jetty and boat ramp to the west of the cape's 150-metre-high lookout point give crayfishermen and abalone divers access to offshore waters.

Visitors to Marlo are often surprised to find the small town supports a well-patronised cinema, the only one within more than 100 km. Screenings on Friday, Saturday and Sunday nights attract holidaymakers and residents from the surrounding country towns.

MARLO (pop. 316) south of Princes Highway 375 km from Melbourne, 671 km from Sydney (turn off at Orbost eastbound, Cabbage Tree Creek westbound). **TRANSPORT**: train Melbourne-Bairnsdale most days (4½ hrs); bus Bairnsdale-Orbost daily (1½ hrs); none beyond Orbost, 15 km away.

	MARLO											
	Jan	Feb	Mar	Apr	May	Jun	Jul	Aug	Sep	Oct	Nov	Dec
Rainfall mm	63	58	69	68	76	68	63	55	65	73	61	61
Rain days	6	6	7	9	9	10	9	9	9	11	8	8
Sunshine hrs	Summer 8 +			Autumn 6 +			Winter 4 +			Spring 6 +		

Lakes Entrance

Tourist cruisers plying the waters of the Gippsland Lakes have forerunners dating back to 18 June 1889, the day jubilant lakeside residents and holidaymakers crowded aboard steam-powered tugs to inspect the lakes' new outlet to Bass Strait. The night before, a storm-driven high tide had broken through the sand bar of Ninety Mile Beach, sweeping aside a dredge at work on a channel. Nature did what 20 years of engineering had not yet achieved, giving fishermen and coastal shipping a permanent entrance to the interconnecting chain of lagoons reaching west towards Bairnsdale. Fishermen now share the channel and inland waters with fleets of yachts, hired boats and cabin cruisers based at the many thriving summer holiday settlements dotted around the lake shores.

A footbridge across Cunninghame Arm connects Lakes Entrance with the scrub-covered dunes of Ninety Mile Beach. The waves here and at nearby Eastern Beach break on a sand bottom with a shape and power which makes them popular with board-riders. During the summer months fast, tube-like waves provide exhilarating conditions for the sport. Experienced surfers tackle steeper and stronger waves breaking into shallow water at Shelly Beach—also known as Red Bluff—near Lake Tyers.

Lake Bunga foreshore reserve, east of the Lakes Entrance golf course, was formed from

sand banks which soon accumulated at the old, impermanent entrance after the breakthrough to the west in 1889. It offers pleasant, shady picnic grounds, lake bathing only 100 metres from the surf, and an easy, clearly marked nature trail which takes about 30 minutes to walk.

Lake Tyers is not a sand-barriered lagoon, like those to its west, but a conjunction of flooded valleys. Its arms reach far inland, penetrating the wooded slopes of Lake Tyers Forest Park. The western section of the park is easily accessible by sealed roads off Princes Highway. Picnic areas and lavatories are provided in two spots at the water's edge, and trails lead to remote ridges and

gullies. Separating the two sections of the park is Lake Tyers Aboriginal Reserve, which had its origins in a mission station founded in 1863. Now it is a flourishing agricultural community, owned and managed by its people.

Lake Tyers township, a small settlement whose summer population is swollen by an influx of caravans to its three camps, is a popular boating base for prawning and fishing. Two launching ramps lead into sheltered waters near the lake entrance, and a jetty and another ramp are sited to the north-west at Fishermans Landing. Cruises of the lake and its long, twisting arms start from the jetty.

Lakes Entrance township covers a long finger of land separating Cunninghame Arm and North Arm

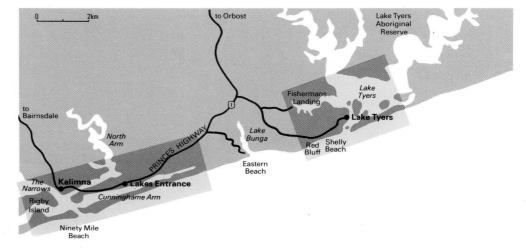

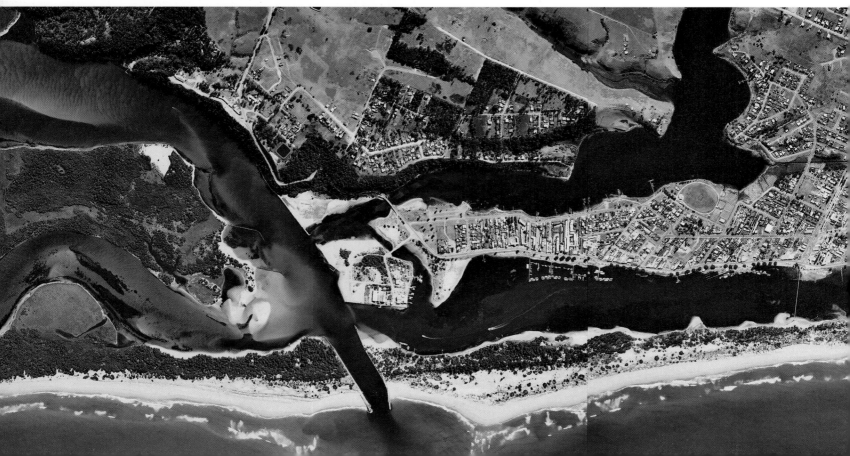

Spacious waterways behind Lake Tyers settlement reach Aboriginal farmlands and a forest park

LAKES ENTRANCE												
	Jan	Feb	Mar	Apr	May	Jun	Jul	Aug	Sep	Oct	Nov	Dec
Maximum C°	24	24	22	20	16	15	14	15	17	19	20	21
Minimum C°	14	15	13	11	8	6	5	6	7	9	10	12
Rainfall mm	54	54	51	44	68	47	34	61	40	54	84	69
Humidity %	69	62	71	65	66	69	59	61	66	65	67	67
Rain days	8	8	9	10	12	11	9	14	12	13	13	10
Sunshine hrs	Summer 8 +			Autumn 6 +			Winter 5 +			Spring 6 +		

LAKES ENTRANCE (pop. 3414) on Princes Highway 314 km from Melbourne, 732 km from Sydney.
TRANSPORT: train Melbourne-Bairnsdale most days (4½ hrs); bus Bairnsdale-Lakes Entrance most days; coach Sydney-Lakes Entrance daily (11¾ hrs).
SURF CLUB PATROL: December-March, Saturday 13.00-18.00, Sunday and public holidays 09.30-18.00.

🛄 🏠 📷 ⛺ 🛏 ☺ ✳ 🚑 🍴 🍽 🍴 🚌 🦐 🐟 〰 ⚓ 🪝 ⛽

LAKE TYERS 12 km east of Lakes Entrance.
TRANSPORT: none beyond Lakes Entrance.

🏠 📷 ⛺ 🍴 🚌 🐟 ⚓

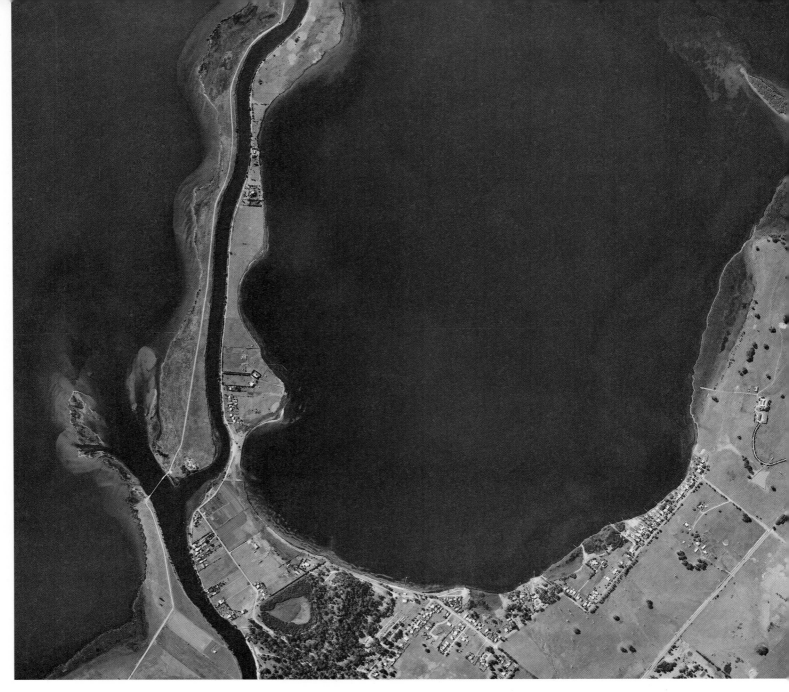

Gippsland Lakes west

From the narrows off Shaving Point at Metung, the channels of the Gippsland Lakes' lower reaches open out to the wider and deeper waters of Lake King and Lake Victoria. The lakes' marshy, undeveloped shores are broken by small holiday settlements—favourite haunts of fishermen and boating enthusiasts, and hopping-off spots for bushwalkers and campers heading for the big national parks between Lake Victoria and the narrow, often dry, stretch of Lake Reeve.

Glimpses of graceful, tall-masted yachts and big cabin cruisers flash through an avenue of waterfront trees on the approaches to Metung. Below the town's camping grounds and bungalows, Bancroft Bay is lined with jetties and hiring depots offering launches, dinghies, canoes and catamarans. The Metung Hot Pools are found near the entrance to Chinamans Creek on the northern shores of the bay. Water bubbles up from a bore drilled into a hot artesian basin in the 1920s by a company searching for oil. Three pools, each about 3 metres across, are knee-deep and often muddy.

Jones Bay is almost separated from the northern reaches of Lake King by twin fingers of silt more than 9 km long, formed as the waters of the Mitchell River slow on entering the lake. The river channel between these 'silt jetties' is navigable by small craft and is a popular fishing spot. Houses are built to the muddy tip of the south jetty and land-based anglers drive along a gravel road, stopping off to cast from a rock wall built to protect the jetties from erosion. High cliffs overlook the mouth of the Mitchell River and give good views of the silt jetties, the lake's sandy swimming beaches and the ramps, man-made jetties, camping grounds and picnic areas of Eagle Point. Passenger cruises down the Mitchell River to Eagle Point from Bairnsdale depart at 14.15 during holiday seasons.

The larger resort town of Paynesville is located on the straits between Lake King and Lake Victoria, 3 km south of Eagle Point. Paynesville is a venue for yachting competitions and the home of a professional fishing fleet. It has ramps, slipways, public moorings and boat service

Finger-like natural jetties (left) in Lake King, just north of Paynesville, are formed from silt deposited by the Mitchell River; the build-up is high enough to carry dairy pastures and roads

facilities. A car and passenger ferry across McMillan Strait links Paynesville with Raymond Island, and boats can be hired for trips to Lakes National Park and Gippsland Lakes Coastal Park. Both parks have picnic spots with lavatories, tables and fireplaces, but fresh water may be scarce. Visitors should check with rangers or take their own supplies. Boat-based bush camping is available at Bunga Arm, east of Steamer Landing, and at sites west of Loch Sport. Cleared tracks through woodland, swamp and coastal scrub provide easy access to secluded areas in the parks, along Ninety Mile Beach or around the northern shores of Lake Reeve to Sperm Whale Head and a camping site at Point Wilson.

PAYNESVILLE (pop. 1597) south of Princes Highway 294 km from Melbourne, 782 km from Sydney (turn off at Bairnsdale).

TRANSPORT: train Melbourne-Bairnsdale most days (4½ hrs); bus Bairnsdale-Paynesville weekdays; coach Sydney-Bairnsdale daily (12¼ hrs).

METUNG (pop. 342) south of Princes Highway 307 km from Melbourne, 757 km from Sydney (turn off at Swan Reach eastbound, Kalimna West westbound).

TRANSPORT: train Melbourne-Bairnsdale most days (4½ hrs); coach Sydney-Bairnsdale daily (12¼ hrs); bus Bairnsdale-Swan Reach most days; none beyond Swan Reach, 8 km away.

The lure of the lakes

WATER sports to suit any taste draw hundreds of thousands of summer holidaymakers to the Gippsland Lakes. The lakes themselves—though not always the resort townships—absorb this annual onslaught without undue strain. Their interlinked system is easily Australia's biggest, covering nearly 400 square kilometres.

Pleasure craft and fishing boats of all descriptions ply the waterways. Ocean cruisers and a substantial commercial trawling fleet—boosted during the 1970s by a boom in scallop dredging—venture out into Bass Strait. The man-made passage at Lakes Entrance is the only breach in the phenomenal sand barrier known as Ninety Mile Beach.

The extent of the beach is a striking example of how the sea can build land, as well as destroy it. Until about 9000 years ago the lakes region was a vast, open bay. As the sea level rose with the passing of the last Ice Age, waves bending around Wilsons Promontory pushed persistently in towards the East Gippsland shore, carrying with them millions of tonnes of seabed sediments. Eventually a closed bay was formed, filled with fresh water from Snowy Mountains streams, and an ever-increasing amount of river silts. Sea water penetrates these days, because of the navigation cutting, so the lakes are partly brackish. But silting goes on. Unless there is a drastic change in ocean currents or climate, the whole of the old bay will one day become dry land.

Tourist authorities, anxious to ease summertime pressure on the East Gippsland coast, have taken to promoting its off-season advantages. They have dubbed it 'the Victorian Riviera', pointing out that average winter temperatures are markedly higher than Melbourne's. Nature supports their claim. Forests abounding in the region include a surprisingly wide range of subtropical rainforest species.

Longline fishing boats of the ocean-going commercial fleet tie up beside Cunninghame Arm, Lakes Entrance

Morning breezes ruffle Lake Wellington, behind Paradise Beach

At Metung boats negotiate a channel into Lake King

Ninety Mile Beach is a sand bar that turned an ancient bay into a chain of lakes

Ruler-straight beaches line the Gippsland coast. Tiny settlements at Seaspray (above) and Golden Beach provide some facilities

Ninety Mile Beach

Tents pepper the scrub-covered dunes between Seaspray and Paradise Beach in summer. By the Australia Day weekend, when surf casters compete for big cash prizes, there is scarcely a camping space to be found. Ninety Mile Beach runs all the way from Lakes Entrance to the inlets near Wilsons Promontory. But only along the 30 km stretch north of Seaspray is there a public coastal road giving highway vehicles easy access to the ocean shore. Seaspray and Paradise Beach have camping ground with full facilities, for which the Gippsland Lakes Coastal Park management charges a small fee. Bush camping is allowed without charge or permit along the dunes between the two settlements. The only store, apart from those at Seaspray, is at Golden Beach. There is fair surf in easterly conditions.

An alternative route to Golden Beach from Longford passes through low, flat pasture land and crosses the narrow arm of Lake Reeve. The lake has been mostly dry since Lakes Entrance was opened in 1889 and the level of the Gippsland Lakes dropped by about 50 cm. Even in the wettest seasons the lake rarely rises to the causeway, which is less than 1 metre high. Among the

prolific bird life on and around Lake Reeve, wild duck, quail and Japanese snipe may be hunted under licence during the autumn shooting season. A shorter season is open to hunters stalking hog deer, introduced from Sri Lanka in the late 1800s. Rabbits can be shot at any time in a limited area just east of Paradise Beach.

SEASPRAY south of Princes Highway 246 km from Melbourne, 870 km from Sydney (turn off at Sale) or east of South Gippsland Highway 315 km from Melbourne (turn off 4 km north of Darriman).
TRANSPORT: train Melbourne-Sale most days (3 hrs); coach Sydney-Sale daily (13½ hrs); none beyond Sale, 35 km away.
SURF CLUB PATROL: December-March, Saturday 13.00-16.30, Sunday and public holidays 09.30-16.30.

	SEASPRAY											
	Jan	Feb	Mar	Apr	May	Jun	Jul	Aug	Sep	Oct	Nov	Dec
Rainfall mm	43	41	55	48	49	50	42	46	47	55	55	54
Rain days	6	6	7	8	10	11	11	12	10	11	9	7
Sunshine hrs	Summer 7 +			Autumn 6 +			Winter 5 +			Spring 6 +		

Where oil flows beneath the surf

SUNBATHERS tan themselves on Golden Beach oblivious of rich streams of Bass Strait oil and gas flowing just 3 metres below them. Two trenches were jet-blasted from the shallows to bury pipes coming 25 km from Barracouta, Australia's first off-shore oil and gas well. It began production in 1969.

On a clear day the Barracouta platform is just visible from the backshore dunes. Other drilling sites, either in operation or under construction, are well beyond the horizon. Kingfish B, the farthest from land, is 77 km out.

From Golden Beach, and another pipe coming ashore near Loch Sport, oil and gas are relayed to a processing plant at Longford, just south of Sale. Two platforms, Marlin and Barracouta, supply natural gas to Victoria. Most oil in the 1970s came from Halibut and from Kingfish A and B, where production is now declining. Four new oil fields were developed in the early 1980s and an additional gas processing plant brought on stream at Longford.

The discovery of Bass Strait oil was no surprise to older residents around the Gippsland Lakes. Seepages were noticed early this century, and in the 1920s and 30s more than 50 bores were sunk in the area. Small quantities of low-grade oil were produced for use as a lubricant on Melbourne's trams.

Bass Strait production platforms

● OIL

● GAS

● OIL/GAS

1 Barracouta
2 Snapper
3 Marlin
4 Tuna
5 Flounder
6 Halibut
7 Fortescue
8 Mackerel
9 Cobia
10 Kingfish A
11 Kingfish B
12 West Kingfish

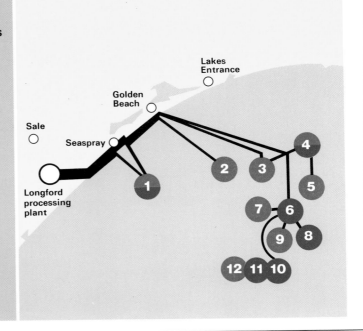

Wilsons Promontory

Terrain as rugged as any on the Australian coast is found in Wilsons Promontory National Park, on the southern tip of the mainland. Windswept dunes, long surf beaches, swamps and fern-filled gullies are towered over by heavily wooded slopes and the peaks of massive granite outcrops. Most of the 48 900-hectare park and its 160 km coastline can be reached only by walking trails to bush camping sites. The park headquarters settlement at Tidal River, however, offers a good many of the comforts of home: a store, butch-ery, laundry and cinema, and a doctor in resid-ence during holiday periods. The area between the shallow river and the popular surfing beach becomes a large, bustling resort during summer and at Easter. Five hundred tent sites—arranged in parallel curves along numbered avenues—and furnished cabins and flats are in heavy demand. The camp grew around the barracks of a World War II commando training base.

Leaflets available at the rangers' office at Tidal River describe more than 30 trails through the park, and explain its history, geography, flora and fauna. The Lilly Pilly Gully nature walk branches off from a car park on the road into Tidal River. It takes about three hours to com-plete and includes 16 identified stops showing the park's diverse plant and animal life, and the remarkable regeneration of the bush after disas-trous fires swept over the promontory in 1951.

The longest of the park's walks leads 18.4 km from Tidal River to South East Point. A light-house at the point, built in 1859, can be visited

A 'blow-out' of drifted sand behind the Oberon Bay beach may have been triggered by cattle grazing—the district was farmed in the 19th century

on Tuesdays and Thursdays by prior arrangement with the head keeper. This and many other of the walks in the southern section of the park link up, so hikers have no need to double back and can spend each night at a different camp close to freshwater creeks and fine swimming beaches, some with good surf. Many of the trails are rough and climbs are steep, but they are rewarded by superb scenery. Walks in the northern section of the park are over low, marsh-fringed ground with little shade and unreliable supplies of fresh water in summer. The beaches in the north-east are popular for surf casting but can be dangerous for swimming.

As a legacy of the bushfires of 1951—sparked by a billy fire not completely put out—regulations in the park are strict. Campers are encouraged to bring their own stoves, and during summer open fires may be totally banned. The popularity of the park leads to other restrictions during the heavy holiday season, when not only the cabins but also the walks must be booked.

TIDAL RIVER south of South Gippsland Highway 231 km from Melbourne, 1020 km from Sydney (turn off at Meeniyan eastbound, Foster westbound).
TRANSPORT: coach Melbourne-Foster daily (3 hrs); none beyond Foster, 62 km away.

🏠 🏕 ▲ ✴ 🍴 🚌 🐚

TIDAL RIVER												
	Jan	Feb	Mar	Apr	May	Jun	Jul	Aug	Sep	Oct	Nov	Dec
Maximum C°	21	21	19	17	14	13	12	12	14	16	17	19
Minimum C°	14	15	14	13	11	9	8	8	9	10	11	12
Rainfall mm	49	48	70	90	111	121	115	117	97	94	73	64
Humidity %	75	73	74	77	78	80	79	79	77	76	74	76
Rain days	9	9	11	15	18	19	19	19	17	16	13	11
Sunshine hrs	Summer 7 +			Autumn 4 +			Winter 3 +			Spring 5 +		

Coarse white sand, with grains the size of match heads, awaits walkers trekking to Waterloo Bay

Craggy shores to the east of Cape Paterson are relieved by a sandy bathing beach at Safety Bay

Waratah Bay and Venus Bay

Sparsely settled and largely inaccessible shores face the westerly gales and heavy seas of Bass Strait north of Wilsons Promontory. Cape Liptrap and Cape Paterson, however, give some shelter to wide embayments behind them. And each bay has an extensive, sand-barriered inlet—one is almost a mirror image of the other—making a haven for boats. Both areas became natural choices for the establishment of farming communities in the late 19th century, when dairy pastures were sown on the rich plains of south-west Gippsland. Now within an easy half-day drive of Melbourne, they are increasingly popular for weekends and summer holidays.

Sandy Point, on Waratah Bay, has a scattering of permanent residences and rows of weekend cottages along corrugated gravel roads. The township is buffered from the beach by the high hummocks of scrub-covered dunes. Behind, on the western shores of Shallow Inlet, boats are launched over firm, white sand below banks thick with ferns, tea-tree and banksia. The inlet is popular for fishing and prawning, although ebb tides expose wide mudbanks and shoals. A picnic ground is sited between the inlet and a caravan park with cattle grazing in the surrounding paddocks. From Sandy Point's shopping centre a track leads to a patrolled surfing beach. To the west the shoreline curves unbroken past Waratah Bay settlement and the little port of Walkerville. Cliffs rise behind Walkerville and reach round to Cape Liptrap. A dusty, rutted road to the cape offers exceptional views.

Sandy shores stretch north from Cape Liptrap to Point Smythe, facing across Anderson Inlet to the booming holiday town of Inverloch. A launching ramp, on the town side of the wide inlet entrance, leads into sheltered waters for sailing and fishing, and extends to the freshwater reaches of the Tarwin River. Shaded parkland, running along the inlet shores below the town, has picnic tables, electric barbecues and lavatories. West of Inverloch a coast road to Wonthaggi hugs rocky cliffs as far as Cape Paterson, where sandy beaches line two small bays. Wide rock platforms, popular with anglers, spread beside them. Grassy picnic grounds in a camping area slope down to the sheltered waters of Safety Bay, which has a natural tidal pool in the rocky outcrop in the middle of the beach. Danger Beach, farther east, does not enjoy the same protection from heavy seas and has a notorious rip, but is popular with board-riders.

SANDY POINT (pop. 122) south of South Gippsland Highway 197 km from Melbourne, 986 km from Sydney (turn off at Meeniyan eastbound, Foster westbound).
TRANSPORT: coach Melbourne-Foster daily (3 hrs); none beyond Foster, 28 km away.
SURF CLUB PATROL: December-March, Saturday 13.00-18.00, Sunday and public holidays 09.30-18.00.

🏠 🏕 ⛺ ⚓ 🚻 ⛵ ⚓

INVERLOCH (pop. 1523) on Bass Highway 150 km from Melbourne.
TRANSPORT: frequent trains Melbourne-Dandenong daily; bus Dandenong-Inverloch daily (2 hrs).
SURF CLUB PATROL: December-Easter, Saturday 13.00-17.50, Sunday and public holidays 09.00-17.50.

🏨 🏠 ⛺ ⚓ 🚻 🅿 🍴 ⛵ ⚓ ⛴ 🏌 ⚓

CAPE PATERSON (pop. 239) south of Bass Highway 145 km from Melbourne (turn off at Wonthaggi).
TRANSPORT: frequent trains Melbourne-Dandenong daily; bus Dandenong-Wonthaggi daily; none beyond Wonthaggi, 10 km away.
SURF CLUB PATROL: December-April, Saturday 12.30-17.00, Sunday and public holidays 09.30-17.00.

🏠 ⛺ ⚓ ⛵ ⚓ 🌊 ⚓

Hopefuls still hunt for Wiberg's gold

A FORTUNE in gold sovereigns lies hidden near Inverloch, some residents believe. If so, it has eluded discovery for a century. Visitors hearing the old story still poke about on the shores of Anderson Inlet or the banks of the Tarwin River, hoping for the clink or the glint of coins. Determined searchers come armed with metal detectors—and find the ring-tops off beer cans.

In 1877 a ship's carpenter, Martin Wiberg, pillaged a case of sovereigns sent from the Sydney mint to Melbourne for trans-shipment to England. In the weeks before his crime was detected, he lived at Inverloch. Eventually he was tracked down and convicted of the theft of 15 000 coins, none of which were recovered.

After three years in prison Wiberg offered to give up the gold in exchange for his release. He asked to be taken to the Tarwin River, where he and his two police escorts obtained a boat. Upriver, according to the policemen, he attacked one of them and capsized the boat. He was never seen again.

One theory has it that the police took the booty for themselves and disposed of Wiberg. Another holds that Wiberg recovered his hoard —perhaps splitting it with the police—and fled the country. An Inverloch woman claimed to have seen him later in Germany, running an inn. Then again, the coins may never have been at Inverloch: if Wiberg had planned an escape all along, he would not have led the police anywhere near the gold.

Some people, however, cling to the view that Wiberg's stolen sovereigns remain in the district. At 1980s prices, the cache could be worth $3-5 million. But it would be claimed by the federal government.

Both Inverloch (left) and Sandy Point (below) boast quiet boating waters as well as good surf

Phillip Island east

Pleasure boat jetties spike the shallows north of the bridge at Newhaven, the motorists' gateway to Phillip Island. From San Remo, on the mainland side of Eastern Passage, commercial craft ply the Narrows in summer on their way to trawling grounds in Bass Strait. Gourmets recoil when they learn that more than 90 per cent of the professional fleet's catch is shark. But more highly regarded species are available to anglers and divers from the island's rocks.

Cleeland Bight, east of the Woolamai isthmus, has sheltered swimming. Long, straight lines of surf break consistently on to Woolamai Beach on the opposite side. From the lifesaving clubhouse a gentle walking track extends 3 km to mottled granite cliffs and to the mound of Cape Woolamai—the highest point, at 109 metres, on an island that is mostly flat. A slightly longer track on the Cleeland Bight side leads to a granite quarry which in the 1890s drew 300 people to live at the cape—now an unpopulated coastal reserve. The cliffs of the peninsula are pitted with the nesting burrows of hundreds of thousands of muttonbirds—short-tailed shearwaters —which breed here in summer and autumn but spend the rest of their year in the northern Pacific. They have survived in spite of large-scale slaughtering last century for food and oil. Even their eggs were collected at the rate of 20 000 a year in the early 1900s, and sent to Melbourne for cake manufacture.

On the road west from Newhaven, just past the island's main information centre, milking herds graze next to the Dairy Centre of Australia. It has the country's most comprehensive collection of early dairy farming and factory relics and working models, and includes small cheese and confectionery plants. The displays are on view 10.00-17.00 daily from Christmas to Easter and during all school holidays. Directly north, Churchill Island is reached by a footbridge or a tidal causeway. It supports abundant birdlife and is being restored as a conservation area, but has picnic facilities. Seeds for Victoria's first European food crops were sown here in 1801, and the island was farmed continuously from 1857 to 1976. Near an 1860s homestead, there is a cannon presented to a mayor of Melbourne during the American Civil War, in thanks for the city's hospitality to the Confederate raider *Shenandoah*. This assistance strained relations with the recognised Union government of the northern states, and Britain was obliged to pay a heavy cash compensation for the indiscretion of its colonial capital.

Picnic grounds on Fishermen's Point, at Rhyll, surround a monument commemorating Phillip Island's discovery by George Bass in 1798. It also records later visits by British and French mariners and the founding in 1826—to beat a possible French claim—of a temporary British post called Fort Dumaresq. The site by then had long been occupied informally by sealers and whalers, sharing their shanties with Aboriginal women abducted from Tasmania or the mainland. Legit-imate settlement by farmers got under way in 1842. A curiosity of Phillip Island is the unusual suitability of its loamy, frost-free soil for the cultivation of chicory. Under the name endive, the leaves of this beet-like vegetable are used in salads. More importantly, the roots can be kiln-dried and ground to make a coffee substitute or additive. Late last century more than 30 farms on the island grew chicory. Two families remain in the business. The McFees, east of Rhyll Road towards Pleasant Point, offer a film screening explaining the industry and inspections of their farm and kiln at 10.30 daily during school holidays and on public holidays.

The Woolamai isthmus, just south of Newhaven, catches consistent surf from Southern Ocean swells

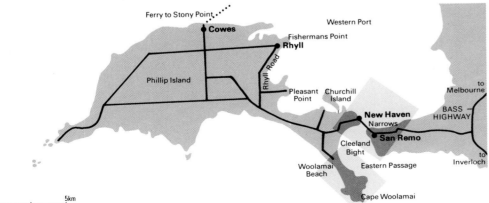

Phillip Island Bridge, spanning the Narrows from
San Remo on the mainland to Newhaven, was built
in the 1970s from 640 metres of pre-cast sections

NEWHAVEN (pop. 279) west of Bass Highway 127 km
from Melbourne (turn off at Anderson).
TRANSPORT: frequent trains Melbourne-Dandenong
daily; bus Dandenong-Newhaven-Cowes daily.
SURF CLUB PATROL: Woolamai December-Easter, Saturday 12.30-18.00, Sunday and public holidays 09.00-
18.00.

RHYLL 13 km north-west of Newhaven.
TRANSPORT: none beyond Newhaven.

Summerland Beach, to the east of the rocky peninsula of the Nobbies, has good surf and is the nightly venue of Phillip Island's celebrated 'penguin parade'

Phillip Island west

Western Port's quiet waters lap a matched set of little scalloped beaches each side of the ferry jetty at Cowes. Trim, tree-shaded lawns slope back to symmetrical town blocks. Boats rest in neat rows by their launching ramp. All is orderly and gentle—still in character with the upper-class tastes of the 1870s, when truly Victorian Victorians started a resort here. They called it Cowes, and its western extension Ventnor, in imitation of towns on southern England's genteel, royally patronised Isle of Wight. Surfing was unheard of then: Cowes is remote from the livelier Bass Strait seas on Phillip Island's southern shores. And since the 1940s, when the first road bridge brought in cars through San Remo and Newhaven, Cowes has ceased to be the main entry point. However, the ferry ride from Stony Point is still popular with holiday-makers as well as day trippers. Cowes retains nearly all the island's tourist accommodation, shopping and dining, and is the starting point for coach tours by visitors who come without cars.

Summerland Beach to the south-west has a moderate surf. But most of its visitors come at sundown to see the daily 'penguin parade'. Chattering international crowds arrange themselves each evening on miniature grandstands each side of a strip of sand leading from the waterline to shrubs and tussocks on the dunes. Among them are the nesting burrows of the little penguin, *Eudyptula minor*—Australia's only indigenous species and at 300-350 mm in height, the world's smallest penguin. Spotlights are turned on precisely at sunset. Within a minute the first penguins flop from the surf and stagger in the backwash. They wait in the shallows until all members of a group—perhaps 30 birds—have arrived. Then they waddle together to their burrows, where in summer their waiting chicks set up a squealing demand for regurgitated fish and squid. Compared with the never-failing, close-up view of the penguins, the sighting of fur seals offered to the west at the Nobbies is a disappointment. They are nearly 2 km away on Seal Rocks, and can be seen only through coin-in-the-slot binoculars or from tourist launches plying from Cowes. When a heavy swell is running, a blowhole on the south side of Point Grant may give spectacular displays. But signs warn of freak waves sweeping the rocks.

From Kitty Miller Bay, just east of Summer-

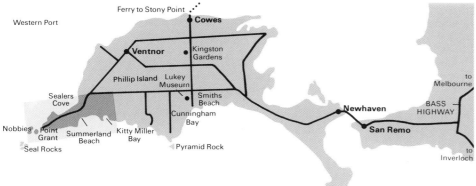

Koala sanctuary

PHILLIP ISLAND has been the salvation of koalas in Victoria—though it was not their natural home. So many of the sleepy, slow-moving 'native bears' used to be shot or trapped for their fur, or starved to death by the destruction of eucalypt forests, that in the 1930s there were only about 800 left in the whole state. Nearly all of those were on Phillip Island, where their ancestors had been introduced in about 1870. The island became the breeding ground for a successful mainland restocking programme after World War II.

Reserves south-east and south-west of Cowes are the easiest places in Australia to see koalas out of captivity. They are often sighted in trees elsewhere, and occasionally even in the town shopping centre. Drivers on the island are urged to take special care at night, when koalas are at their most active.

The koala is a common sight around Cowes

racing circuit are the Len Lukey Memorial Museum and Gardens, designed by a former champion driver and opened in 1980 after his death. The gardens are stocked with native and introduced birds and animals, and include a food kiosk, picnic grounds and swimming pool. The museum displays distinguished old cars, furniture, ornaments and Aboriginal artefacts. Hours are 12.00-17.00 on Saturdays and 10.00-17.00 on all other days. Kingston Gardens, a picnic park and zoo in mid-island between the racetrack and Cowes, is open daily from 10.00 to sunset.

COWES (pop. 1563) on Western Port 142 km by road from Melbourne (turn off Bass Highway at Anderson), 9 km by sea from Stony Point.
TRANSPORT: train Melbourne-Stony Point daily; ferry or hydrofoil Stony Point-Cowes; bus Dandenong-Cowes daily.

land, to Pyramid Rock, cliffed bluffs are interspersed with small beaches. Access is difficult, however. Farther east, roads lead to Cunningham Bay and a white curve of sand at Smiths Beach. Behind the bay's blood-red, broken cliffs is a 5 km motor racing track. The first Australian Grand Prix championships were conducted on Phillip Island from 1928 to 1935, though not on this track—the races then were over 16 km of closed public roads. The present track, built in 1956 and now privately owned, draws good crowds to about four meetings a season. Near the

COWES												
	Jan	Feb	Mar	Apr	May	Jun	Jul	Aug	Sep	Oct	Nov	Dec
Rainfall mm	44	43	57	69	76	78	75	74	70	68	58	52
Rain days	8	7	10	13	15	16	17	17	15	14	12	9
Sunshine hrs	Summer 8 +			Autumn 5 +			Winter 3 +			Spring 6 +		

Persistent westerly swells, snagged by Point Leo, have built a roomy beach at Shoreham and produce surfing waves on the farmland coast to the north

Western Port

In the embrace of the Royal Australian Navy, between the closed areas of Flinders naval depot and a gunnery range on bleak West Head, lies a haven of surprising peace. The Western Port coast is little known to travellers, and little frequented even by Melbourne people who make the opposite side of Mornington Peninsula a crowded, bustling summertime playground. Fine beaches, strung for 25 km between Somers and Flinders township, have somehow escaped intensive development. Holiday settlements remain scattered and quiet, sandwiched between rolling farmland and an almost continuous foreshore reserve. The most hectic activity is likely to be in preparation for races from the yacht clubs dotted along the bay, their moorings sheltered from the heavy westerly winds and seas of Bass Strait.

Recent attention has been focused on the eastern part of the district by the opening in 1980 of Coolart, a historic homestead in grounds which have been turned into a nature reserve. The 87.5-hectare property, halfway between Somers and Balnarring Beach, is especially interesting to birdlovers and bushwalkers. A lagoon near the homestead buildings commonly has about 30 species of waterfowl. A hide seating more than 20 people provides cover from which to watch birds building nests in spring and feeding their young in summer. To the south, a short bush track leads to Merricks Creek, crossed by a footbridge to the beach. A marked, 1.5 km woodland walk along the shallow creek takes about an hour.

The main building at Coolart, a two-storey, 24-room mansion of brick and slate surmounted by an observation tower, dates from 1895. An earlier house, built of clay bricks in the 1860s, has been restored to show the elegant lines of an old verandah. Stables and other outbuildings surround formal gardens which offer a half-hour walk among handsome trees, many of them exotic. Visitors can picnic in the grounds, and

teas are served in the mansion dining room. Coolart is open 11.00-17.00 every Sunday.

Somers is a pleasant township of curving avenues and crescents behind a generous bush reserve, with sandy clearings for secluded picnics. A narrow belt of sand slopes gently into quiet waters suitable for family swimming. Balnarring and Merricks Beaches are similar. Point Leo Beach, however, boasts year-round surf. Its caravan park, camping grounds and picnic areas occupy prime spots in the foreshore reserve which runs all the way from Balnarring to Flinders. There is further foreshore camping under shady trees at Shoreham.

Flinders has good barbecue and boating facilities, and superbly sited golf links at the base of West Head. Behind a white beach in Kennon Cove, a hilltop lookout has a cairn commemorating the bay's discovery by George Bass in 1798. He called it Western Port because of its bearing from Sydney, not suspecting that Port Phillip

Shelter-belt trees and hedges pattern the pastures behind Balnarring Beach and Somers; the most prominent avenue of trees (centre) leads from the main road to the homestead and gardens of Coolart

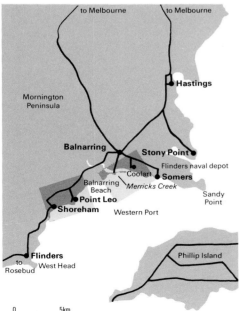

Bay lay just beyond. The lookout commands views along the coast and out to Phillip Island, with a glimpse of French Island between.

Passenger and vehicle ferries to French Island run from Stony Point, between the rambling naval base and the heavily industrialised inner shore of Western Port. From 1916 to 1975, farmers on French Island shared it with a prison settlement. Now a 7 700-hectare state park has been developed, with campsites and walking trails provided among the most extensive natural heath and woodland remaining in the Western Port district. The island's abundant wildlife includes a species of potoroo or rat kangaroo, *Potorous apicalus*, which was thought to be extinct until rediscovered here.

SOMERS (pop. 607) south of Nepean Highway 81 km from Melbourne (turn off at Frankston).
TRANSPORT: frequent trains Melbourne-Frankston daily; buses from Frankston to Somers, Shoreham and Flinders daily.

🏠 ⌂ ▲ 🛏 🚽 ⋈ ⚓

SHOREHAM on Frankston-Flinders road 17 km south-west of Somers.
TRANSPORT: as for Somers.
SURF CLUB PATROL: Point Leo Beach December-Easter, Saturday 13.00-17.00; Sunday and public holidays 09.30-17.00

⌂ ▲ 🛏 🚽 ⋈ ⚓

FLINDERS (pop. 380) 25 km south-west of Somers.
TRANSPORT: as for Somers.

🍴 ⌂ ▲ 🛏 🚩 🍽 🚽 ⋈ 👣 ⚓ ⛵

HMAS CERBERUS												
	Jan	Feb	Mar	Apr	May	Jun	Jul	Aug	Sep	Oct	Nov	Dec
Rainfall mm	39	47	54	76	80	72	88	78	77	79	62	56
Rain days	7	8	9	13	15	15	16	16	15	15	12	10
Sunshine hrs	Summer 8+			Autumn 5+			Winter 3+			Spring 6+		

Melbourne

Port Phillip Bay offers the residents of Melbourne and Geelong enormous scope for recreation. In summer thousands of people flock to the sandy beaches that line the bay's heavily populated eastern shore. Beyond Melbourne's southern limits, powerful ocean swells pound the rocky coast of Mornington Peninsula.

Bayside suburbs reaching south from Brighton to Mornington Peninsula

Lonely Cape Schanck juts into Bass Strait

City offices crowd the head of Port Phillip Bay

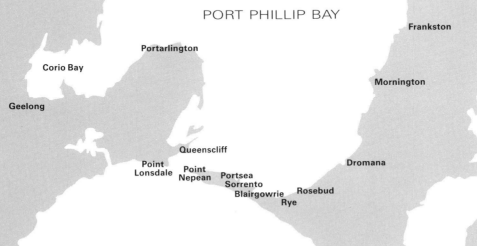

Yarra River

Melbourne

Port
Melbourne

Williamstown

St Kilda

Hobsons
Bay

Brighton

VICTORIA

Sandringham

Black Rock

Mordialloc

PORT PHILLIP BAY

Frankston

Portarlington

Corio Bay

Mornington

Geelong

Queenscliff

Point
Lonsdale

Point
Nepean

Portsea
Sorrento

Dromana

Rosebud

Blairgowrie

Rye

Cape Schanck

BASS STRAIT

Cities embracing a capricious bay

FROM Port Phillip Bay's low-lying shores, the expanse of water seems endless. Only from a higher vantage point—a Melbourne tower block, or the hills of Mornington Peninsula, for example—does the visible horizon recede beyond the meeting of sea and sky to indicate the limits of more than 1800 sq km of enclosed waters. Victoria's two biggest cities, Melbourne and Geelong, share the bay. Along with their suburbs and sprawling industrial estates there is still room for pasture lands, and for resorts where holidaymakers, anglers and water sports enthusiasts find ample scope.

Most of Port Phillip Bay's eastern shore is easily accessible to the public. Close to the central business area of Melbourne, promenades backed by parks and gardens run south-east from the wharves and docks of Port Melbourne. Farther south, private residences occupy much of the beachfront, but they give way at intervals to clusters of shops facing popular suburban swimming spots. Each has its lifesaving club—surprising at first to strangers, who see no menace in the bay's quiet waters or its gently sloping, surfless beaches. When visitors see how quickly a storm can churn up these waters, however, they understand the need for patrols. Where the bay shore curves south-west from Mornington to Portsea, beyond the metropolitan limits, beachfront camping grounds lie dormant during the cooler months. In summer, as Victorians take to the seaside in tens of thousands, these generous reserves bristle with tents and caravans.

At the northernmost end of the bay, the sluggish Yarra River winds out to sea, spanned just upstream by the Westgate Bridge, which reaches high over the river's port facilities and surrounding freight yards and heavy industry. Boating around the headwaters is limited to a speed of 8 km/h and complicated by tugs pulling freighters upriver to docks and wharves just east of the maze of tracks at Spencer Street railway station. From Princes Bridge, near the city centre, a ferry plies to the Melbourne Botanic Gardens, passing popular picnic spots and rolling lawns on the banks of the Yarra. The ferry operates at weekends from September to May; weekday services are added from November to January.

Western shores of the bay are less intensively used by holidaymakers, and much of the bayside land south of Williamstown is closed to the public and used for industrial or military purposes. But not all of this coast is inaccessible. The low-lying industrial suburb of Altona and the smaller town of Werribee South are popular fishing spots lined with reserves, picnic grounds and narrow, sandy beaches crossed by boat launching ramps. Industry claims much of the coastline around Geelong's harbour on Corio Bay, and big salt-evaporation pans flank the city to the east, giving way to grazing land and scattered beach resorts on Bellarine Peninsula.

Average weather statistics indicate a temperate climate, but the region is subject to sudden changes. Summer winds can veer in minutes from hot, dusty northerlies to cold, foggy south-westerlies. Gales whip up the relatively shallow bay waters, spelling trouble for inexperienced swimmers and for boatmen who put to sea in light craft on what seemed like a millpond. Short, steep waves, confused in direction, can easily swamp small boats. And even in calm conditions, boating is tricky near the bay entrance. Tides are so narrowly channelled that they produce currents of up to 9 knots (16 km/h). Tidal pressure at the entrance has scoured the sea bed to more than 60 metres—four times the surrounding depth—creating a submarine waterfall. Extreme surface turbulence above this chasm, combined with the speed of the tide race, make a zone of frequent danger which sailors know as the Rip. Craft entering or leaving the bay need radio equipment so that contact can be maintained with a surveillance base at the Point Lonsdale lighthouse. Few small boats venture over the Rip—there is little need because plenty of good fishing and sailing is to be had within the bay. Shoals around the Mud Islands attract boat anglers, but they need to be fully familiar with tidal channels and currents: water depths may be as little as 200 mm.

Melbourne's office blocks seem only a short distance from the bay at St Kilda

Sunbathers at Albert Park can enjoy the sea without a distracting surf

Westgate Bridge soars 56 metres above the Yarra, ample clearance for ships moving to Port Melbourne

The man who held back Melbourne

DAVID COLLINS was the wrong man to start a colony on Port Phillip Bay. When he found parts of its shores inhospitable, he was all too ready to give up and go somewhere else. And he gave the bay such a bad name that official settlement was delayed for more than a generation.

Collins, a colonel of the Royal Marines, was designated as lieutenant-governor of a convict colony in 1803, a year after Port Phillip was discovered. His expeditionary party from Britain included 299 convicts, 50 Marines to guard them, 26 wives and children of his men, and 18 free settlers. In the warship HMS *Calcutta* and a chartered store ship, the *Ocean*, they reached the bay in October 1803.

Their settlement, at Sullivan Bay near modern Sorrento, lasted a mere seven months. Water was scarce and the soil poor. But Collins seems to have been easily discouraged from efforts to find a better site. A launch party, sent out for eight days to examine other shores, returned after five days with a pessimistic report—and alarming news of an encounter with hostile Aborigines near the Yarra mouth. Collins quickly dispatched a boat to Sydney to seek permission to shift his settlement to Tasmania. Governor King consented.

The colonists sailed to the River Derwent in two parties, in February and May 1804. Hobart Town was established and Port Phillip abandoned. No further attempt was made to settle the bay until 1835—and then it was by land-hungry Tasmanians. Led by John Batman, they negotiated with the Aborigines in defiance of the Sydney authorities, who took a year to recognise that a Port Phillip settlement could succeed after all. Collins, who did the site of Melbourne no credit, is nevertheless honoured in the name of the city's most famous street.

	MELBOURNE											
	Jan	Feb	Mar	Apr	May	Jun	Jul	Aug	Sep	Oct	Nov	Dec
Maximum C°	27	26	24	21	17	15	14	15	17	20	22	24
Minimum C°	15	15	14	11	9	7	6	7	8	10	11	13
Rainfall mm	48	50	53	59	57	50	49	49	59	67	59	58
Humidity %	43	45	47	50	60	62	62	57	52	50	47	45
Rain Days	8	8	9	12	14	14	15	16	15	14	12	11
Sunshine hrs	Summer 8 +			Autumn 8 +			Winter 3 +			Spring 6 +		

This protected corner of Hobsons Bay, between Williamstown and the Yarra River's mouth, is a refuge for scores of boats. The area has plenty of scope for recreation despite its industrial surroundings

Hobsons Bay

Heavy industry, freight yards and commercial shipping piers share the northern shores of Port Phillip Bay with wide stretches of sandy beach at Sandridge and Port Melbourne. Massive freighters lie at anchor just offshore while, only a stone's throw from the busy docks, light catamarans are carried over the beach to a gently shelving coast which is busy enough in summer to support two lifesaving clubs, a yacht club and a small-boat harbour.

As the bayside esplanade curves southward to St Kilda, tall apartment buildings break the beachfront skyline and promenades line grassy parks dotted with picnic tables. The Catani Gardens, a remnant of 19th-century seaside

planning, are based around expansive lawns crossed by paths planted with rows of evenly spaced exotic trees. The gardens overlook a large boat harbour created by the St Kilda Pier, a popular walkway with a kiosk and small-boat jetty at its offshore end. Neon-lit hoardings and a bright-pink discotheque decorate the buildings at the former entrance to the St Kilda Baths. The swimming enclosures have been demolished and the old pavilion, once the hub of resort life, is now just one of the commercial attractions off the Esplanade. Nearby are an amusement arcade, an ice-skating rink and Luna Park, a funfair crowned with the plunging tracks of a roller coaster. On Sundays the Esplanade becomes a

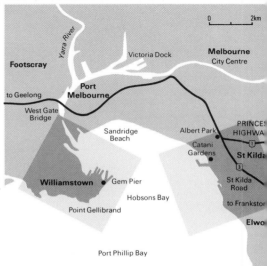

street market, crowded by stalls spilling over with displays of bric-a-brac and handicrafts.

South of St Kilda's beach and busy marina, where boats are stacked in three-storey sheds, playing fields, tennis courts, bowling greens and grassed picnic areas lie behind narrow Elwood Beach. Light sailing craft and sailboards are for hire on the beach during summer and a cycle track runs south along a rock revetment to Brighton. At Albert Park, just inland from St Kilda, an enclosed lake stretches for 2 km parallel with the coast, surrounded by two golf courses and more than 30 playing fields. Rowing boats,

canoes and sailing boats can be hired at the lake and there are restaurants and picnic grounds equipped with barbecues.

Facing St Kilda across Hobsons Bay are naval dockyards, commercial wharves and the anchorages of four yacht clubs at Williamstown, Melbourne's first port and once a proposed site for the capital of Victoria. Fine old bluestone homes, hotels and public buildings face the crammed waterfront, which gives way to a shaded reserve at Gem Pier. HMAS *Castlemaine*, a World War II minesweeper built at Williamstown, is permanently berthed at the pier. It houses a maritime

library and a museum of photographs, documents and relics from Australia's seafaring past. The ship is open for inspection at weekends, 10.00-18.00. At the southern end of Williamstown's port development, the crenellated Time Ball Tower is a link with the days of sail, when ships in the bay set their clocks by the position of a ball suspended from the tower. For townsfolk, the tower keeper fired a gun to advertise the coming time signal. Parklands stretch around the shores west of the tower, past neatly laid botanic gardens to picnic grounds adjoining a clean, sandy beach.

St Kilda pier partly encloses a small area of water at the head of Port Phillip Bay. Parkland fringes the shore to the north and south

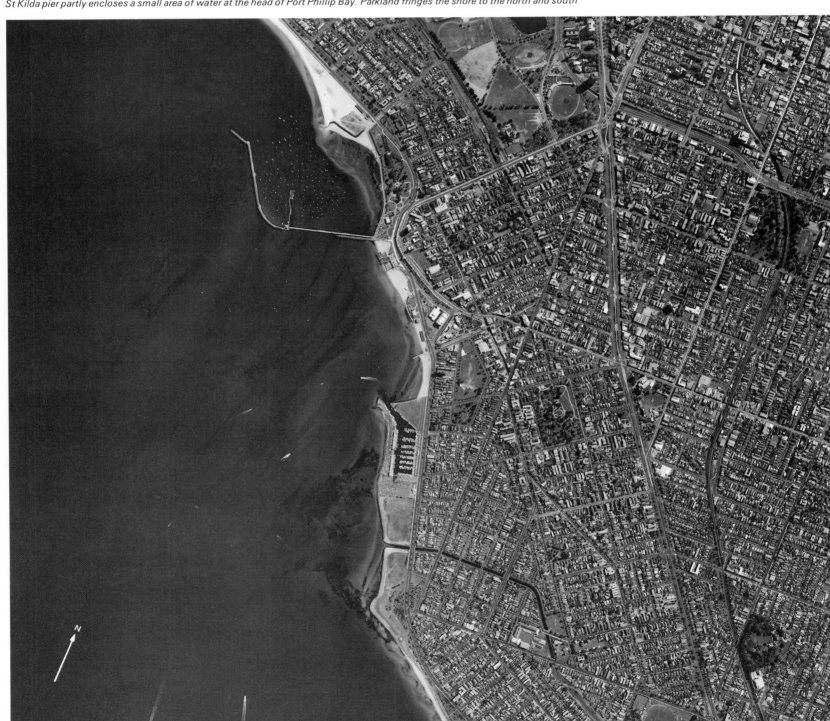

Map labels:
to Melbourne

0   1   2km

Brighton

Middle
Brighton Pier

NEPEAN

Beach Road

3

HIGHWAY

Hampton

Sandringham
Pier

Sandringham

to Frankston

Half Moon Bay

Black Rock

Port Phillip Bay

Beaumaris

Brighton to Black Rock

Extensive breakwaters shelter boat harbours and beaches at Brighton and Sandringham—a reminder of the capriciousness of Port Phillip Bay. Its wide waters normally provide calm, flat conditions for pleasure boating, and little more than ripples lap against its gently sloping beaches. But in bad weather the shores are washed by choppy waves which can wreak havoc among small craft and rip away the narrow strips of sand. Black

Rock's breakwater, protecting Half Moon Bay, is the rusted, graffiti-daubed hulk of a once-mighty warship, HMVS *Cerberus.* It was the pride of Victoria when the colonial government bought it in 1871 as Port Phillip Bay's watchdog, at a time when Australians were preoccupied by fears of a Russian invasion. Powered by steam as well as sails, *Cerberus* and its heavy guns guarded the bay for 50 years. In 1926 it was acquired by Sand-

Man-made breakwaters at Brighton (left) and Sandringham provide protection for boats on an otherwise exposed stretch of bay coast

Status symbols from a bygone era

BRIGHTLY PAINTED bathing boxes, strung along the Brighton backshore like a row of miniature houses, are prized possessions. They provide a place for changing clothes, storing beach equipment and even dining around collapsible tables for a small band of owners who pay a yearly site rental of $82. Most of the boxes have been passed down from generation to generation within the same family. On a rare occasion when one is sold, it may fetch as much as $3000. Similar boxes at other beaches around Port Phillip Bay are fast disappearing, due to opposition from conservationists and councils who blame them for damaging beaches and obstructing public access. The elements also take their toll—on average one box a year is destroyed by storms, and no new boxes can be built.

An unbroken line of bathing huts, shuttered for the winter, occupies most of Brighton's narrow beach

ringham Council, scuttled just offshore, and filled with concrete.

Beach Road runs south of Brighton to Black Rock along a coastline of sandy cliffs, surmounted at intervals by car parks near lifesaving clubs or boat sheds and launching ramps. For a fee of around $1, summer visitors can park and climb down to beaches hidden from the clifftop road by thick scrub. Boat-hire depots abound along this stretch of coast, offering sailboards, canoes and light sailing craft which are pulled up on to the foreshore. Patches of rocky shoreline extending from the beaches have small rock pools at low tide, and popular snorkelling and scuba-diving grounds in deeper water. Reserves line much of the clifftop stretch. Grassy, shaded parks are provided near the railway stations at Brighton and Sandringham, where sprawling residential development surrounds beach shops, restaurants and kiosks. Brighton also boasts the last remaining seawater baths on the eastern side of the bay. The shark-proof enclosure at Brighton Beach has been demolished, but one at Middle Brighton has been restored.

When Brighton's first baths were constructed in 1863, they were a highlight in the development of a beach resort which rivalled St Kilda with its entertainments and facilities. A writer of the 1880s, on a holiday jaunt around Port Phillip Bay by steamboat, saw Brighton as possessing 'all the conveniences of St Kilda with the super-added advantage of further removal from town. Here at intervals are held flower shows, bazaars, and morning concerts, where fashionable toilettes and pretty faces make havoc amongst the gilded youth of Victoria. Here, too, are the well-kept gardens and substantial villas which betoken wealthy ease'. During its heyday Brighton was the terminus of train travel from Melbourne south along the eastern shores of the bay. Travellers to Sandringham and Hampton connected with horse-drawn buses. Within a short walk of the station, holidaymakers had a hotel, refreshment stalls, merry-go-rounds and, until the construction of swimming enclosures, bathing machines which trundled down the beach allowing modest folk to enter the water unseen. By the 1890s a fully fledged summer carnival complete with roller-coaster was set up near the beach front, brass bands played and Italian street performers entertained the crowds.

Choosing sides: bay or breakers

TWO WORLDS share the slender toe of Mornington Peninsula, reaching from Rye to Point Nepean. One is cosy—almost quaint in its echoes of 19th-century gentility. The other, seldom more than 2 km away, is wild and demonstrably dangerous for the visitor.

At Sorrento and Portsea, ornamental trees from England shade old churches and houses facing Port Phillip Bay. Yachts and fishing dinghies bob in the usually tranquil waters of the bay, or at jetties strung along the shore. In summer the powerboat launching ramps draw a day long throng of cars and trailers. Toddlers build sand castles or paddle in the shallows with scarcely a glance from their mothers.

Unless a storm blows up, there is nothing to fear from the bay.

The ocean coast—the 'back beach', as they call it at Sorrento—could scarcely be more different. Struggling heaths and scrubs are windshorn by the westerly gales of Bass Straight. The limestone of ancient dunes is heavily wave-eroded, leaving craggy cliffs and weirdly-shaped offshore formations. Seas pounding at headlands fill the air with spray.

Boisterous swells and fast currents challenge the most adept surfers, and life-saving patrols are kept busy. Diamond Bay had a rescue organisation before the turn of the century—not for surfers then, but for shipwreck victims. The coastal walking track incorporates an old path cut into the cliffs so that rockets and lines could be carried to the shore. Cheviot Beach, near the tip of the peninsula, has a particular notoriety: Prime Minister Harold Holt, spearfishing in heavy seas there in 1967, failed to return.

Beaches and clifftops from Portsea to beyond Cape Schanck are protected for public recreation and plant regeneration in Cape Schanck Coastal Park. It is accessible from many points on the bay side and its whole length of more than 30 km can be walked in two or three days. To negotiate shoreline rock ledges and enjoy the natural pools that are formed, walkers plan sectional journeys to coincide with low tides.

Opulent holiday homes at Portsea give a dress-circle view of the annual Petersville Regatta on Port Phillip Bay

Surging seas at Cheviot Beach

Twilight tranquillity on the bay side at Sorrento

Wild shores of Cape Schanck Coastal Park can be walked at low tide in two or three days – but overnight camping is not allowed

Mordialloc to Mornington

Long, pleasant beaches stretch south from Beaumaris Bay, broken only by jetties and the mouths of small waterways. Melbourne's suburbia has sprawled over most of this flat southern region and concealed the seaside behind beachfront residential development. The coast attracts sufficient bathers, however, to support lifesaving clubs at Mordialloc, Aspendale, Edithvale, Chel-

sea, Bonbeach, Carrum and Seaford—beaches which correspond with railway stations and small shopping centres.

One residential development just off the coast has produced a point of interest for water-borne visitors. Up the Patterson River at Carrum, swamps 1 km inland have been converted into a canal and lake system, producing an attractive

marine housing enclave. Waterways, navigable by launches, link the river with two lakes, one with an inhabited island which is connected to the mainland by bridge. Around the lake shores there are private jetties, and the gardens of comfortable units and luxurious homes stretch down to the water's edge. In an aquatic version of the Sunday drive, visitors can cruise in from

Open farm land surrounds the township of Mornington at the southern end of Port Phillip Bay. Mornington is nearly 60 km from the centre of Melbourne

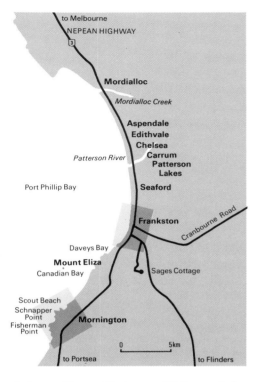

the bay and inspect the homes of Patterson Lakes from the water. The river itself is intensively used by boating enthusiasts. There are five launching ramps at marinas, several car parks on the banks and a championship water-skiing course 2 km upstream. Sailing clubs are dotted along the popular beach each side of the mouth of the Patterson River.

At Frankston a wide, sandy beach stretches along the city's shores to a deep-water jetty and the mouth of Kananook Creek. The creek runs parallel to the bay and is crossed by footways and a road bridge, providing access from the bustling shopping precinct to the beach. A launching ramp leads into the creek on the southern side of the mouth, and boats are for hire just upstream. Frankston, the gateway and service centre for Mornington Peninsula, has grown quickly since the early 1960s but remnants of a much earlier settlement have been preserved. Sages Cottage, built in 1853 6 km south of the business area, is a fine example of the old wooden slab homesteads of the Mornington region. Surrounded by extensive gardens, it is open 11.00-16.00 Wednesday to Saturday. Ballam Park on the Cranbourne road is a substantial brick building, also from the 1850s, still containing the furniture of its first occupants.

A short trip off the highway at Mount Eliza lie Canadian Bay and Daveys Bay, snug coves backed by sand cliffs. Both have boating clubs and Canadian Bay has a launching ramp. But there are no other public facilities and parking space is limited, so both areas are quiet and there are few swimmers and sunbathers.

Mornington township overlooks a small deep-water harbour flanked by a big jetty extending

A brown discharge from Kananook Creek stains the clear water beside Frankston pier

from Schnapper Point. Commercial scallop boats land their catches at the point for opening and packing at Mornington. In summer the fleet is joined by crowds of yachts and motorboats, and waters around Schnapper and Fisherman Points are popular with scuba divers and snorkellers. On shore, Scout Beach is backed by generous expanses of lawn overlooked by tall cypress trees shading picnic grounds in Mornington Park. Be-

sides its many old homes, Mornington boasts several historic public buildings. The still-functioning courthouse and prison, the Royal Hotel and the town's first post office all face the bay from a clifftop esplanade. The old post office is now a museum, open weekends and public holidays 14.00-17.00, with photographs from pioneer days and displays of postal and telegraphic equipment for inspection.

Dromana to Blairgowrie

Passengers on the Arthur's Seat chairlift, ascending 300 metres above Dromana, enjoy a unique view of Port Phillip Bay. Scenes of unbroken beaches and distant mountain ranges open up between spindly gum trees on the upper slopes of the peak, which was named after a hill in Edinburgh, Scotland. The summit, with its picnic grounds and lookouts, has been a popular tourist spot since a hairpin-bend road was opened in 1930. Seawinds, a 34-hectare park near the summit, is planted with formally landscaped flower gardens and exotic trees which produce colourful spring and autumn displays. Ornamental ponds, fountains and sculptures are set in well-shaded lawns with picnic tables and a short walking track. At the base of Arthur's Seat, Dromana spreads out along the Nepean Highway and merges with settlements lining a shallow embayment stretching for 24 km between Safety Beach and Blairgowrie. The gently sloping sea floor and sheltered offshore waters provide calm swimming and a superb area for canoeing, windsurfing and light craft sailing. Reserves backing the beach form an almost continuous camping ground south of Dromana. In summer holiday periods the strip between the beach and the highway is crowded with tents and caravans shaded by banksias and tea-tree. Away from the beachfront the coast is heavily settled with holiday houses and well served by shopping centres. Safety Beach, in the northern corner of Dromana Bay and by-passed by the highway, is less developed. Open, uncluttered shores provide uncrowded swimming water, boat ramps and easy access to the bay, though shade is scarce and picnic facilities are few.

Just south of Dromana is the MacCrae homestead, the first European dwelling on Mornington Peninsula. It was built in 1844 with timber-slab walls and a shingle roof. The building has been restored by the National Trust and is open daily 10.00-17.00 from December to Easter, and at weekends and on public and school holidays for the rest of the year. Much of the furniture is original and stands where it was more than a century ago, as shown in sketches contained in a small museum of family clothes and drawings.

The beachfront reserve at the busy commercial centre of Rosebud has ample beach parking, an aquarium and museum, bowling greens, a swimming pool and tennis courts. Day visitors, squeezed out of many other parts of this stretch of coast by campers in summer, find plenty of room to picnic. Boat ramps and jetties are scattered all along the beach, but the major boating facilities are at Rye, where big car parks serve a deep-water pier and a wide launching ramp. Roads branching south at Tootgarook and Rye lead to Cape Schanck Coastal Park, which occupies a narrow strip of land along the ocean coast of the peninsula. At Cape Schanck, the southernmost point, walking tracks give access to a lookout towering above the offshore stack of Pulpit Rock, and east around the scrub-covered clifftops of Bushrangers Bay. Pamphlets available at the Cape car park describe the geology, plants and wildlife of Bushrangers' Track, which turns inland at Burrabong Creek to follow a wooded corridor along Main Creek to Boneo Road. The Cape Schanck lighthouse can be visited on Tuesdays and Thursdays by prior booking with the head keeper.

Surf boils around the rocks of Cape Schanck, the southernmost point of a long coastal park

Ocean and bayside beaches draw closer together as Mornington Peninsula starts to narrow

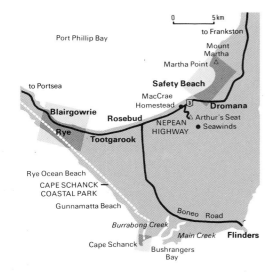

Houses line the shores of Dromana Bay. Behind the settlement at Safety Beach the wooded slopes of Mount Martha rise to a summit 166 metres high. Part of the mountain is a public park

Sorrento to Point Nepean

Portsea and Sorrento, on the narrow western tip of Mornington Peninsula, face long crescent beaches on the enclosed waters of Port Phillip Bay. Their ocean beaches, just 2 km away, front the open seas of Bass Strait. The towns' two aspects are vastly different: tranquil bayside shores on one side, shaded by long-established European trees, and wild, windswept beaches on the other side, broken by jagged rocky headlands and backed by dunes covered in stunted scrub.

George Coppin, a pioneer of Melbourne entertainment, introduced a steam tram from Sorrento to the ocean in 1890. In its best seasons it carried 20 000 passengers. Twenty years earlier, Coppin had begun promoting the area as a real-estate venture. He built a band rotunda on the beach, a hotel and swimming baths. In 1877 he

chartered a paddle-steamer to introduce Melbourne people to these delights. Many century-old buildings remain in use. The hotel, police station, post office, theatre, mechanics' institute, pharmacy and bakery face one another on Sorrento's short main street. Rambling holiday homes hide behind thick tea-tree hedges.

At Portsea Surf Beach, patrolled by a life-saving club at weekends and on public holidays in summer, a chairlift lowers surfers down steep dunes to water level. Walking tracks lead along the back beaches—part of Cape Schanck Coastal Park. They follow the foreshore, which may be impassable at high tide, or climb in and out of the dunes. Rock formations and natural pools attract walkers and swimmers to Sphinx Rock and the massive limestone arch of London Bridge. Off

Cheviot Beach, just north of London Bridge, Prime Minister Harold Holt disappeared while skindiving in heavy seas in 1967. But the area remains popular with scuba enthusiasts.

Long wooden jetties jutting out from the beaches at Portsea and Sorrento are favoured in the summer by anglers, and by bathers diving into sheltered, sandy depths. From the deep-water end of the piers, ferries embark passengers for trips across the entrance of Port Phillip Bay to Queenscliff. An aquarium, just north of the park adjoining Sorrento's pier, is open daily with displays of over 200 species of fish found in local waters. It also has seals, fed at 15.00. Less than 1 km past the picnic grounds behind Portsea's main bay beach, the Nepean Highway ends abruptly at the imposing gates of the Point Nepean

army officer cadet school. Two cannon there used to guard the entrance to Port Phillip Bay—and they fired the first shots on Britain's side in both world wars. In 1914 a shot was fired across the bow of the German freighter *Pfalz*, which had left its berth in Melbourne just before war was declared. It was forced to turn back and was captured. In 1939 the cannon were fired to warn an Australian ship to hoist identifying flags. Tours of Point Nepean, conducted by the Southern Peninsula Rescue Squad, leave from Sorrento police station several times daily between Boxing Day and early February. The route takes in the back beaches, London Bridge, the tip of Point Nepean and the cadet school's central core of buildings, erected in the 1850s.

Military occupation has protected the western end of Mornington Peninsula from development

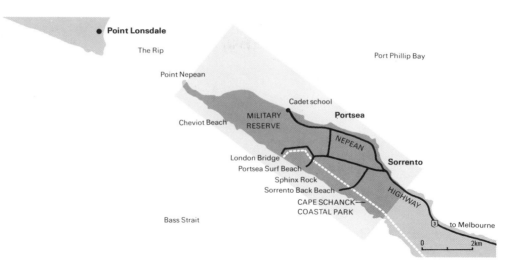

Geelong and Portarlington

With the advantage of hills rising gently away from Corio Bay, Geelong has a seaport atmosphere noticeably lacking in Melbourne. From thoroughfares leading down between the façades of historic buildings, visitors catch glimpses of wharves and of ships at anchor in the bay. In some ways Geelong was better placed than Melbourne to become Victoria's commercial and political capital. It was the gateway to the rich farming lands of the Western District, and was slightly nearer than Melbourne to the Ballarat goldfields. But a sand bar stretching across Corio Bay from Point Henry inhibited the port's growth until the Hopetoun Channel was dredged through it in 1893.

For an exploration of the city, a handy starting point is the old Telegraph Station in Ryrie Street.

Built in 1857, the station is now occupied by the Geelong Regional Tourist Authority, which has mapped a 5 km city walking tour. It takes about 90 minutes and passes 36 points of interest, including some of the more than 100 Geelong buildings classified by the National Trust. Eastward along the waterfront the tour passes old piers, bluestone wool stores, restaurants, a yacht club and fairground. Much of this stretch between the shore and city is given over to grassed and shady reserves. The Eastern Beach swimming enclosure, a short walk from the city centre, offers safe, sharkproof bathing for hundreds of swimmers. The bay beach is surrounded by a walkway and has brightly painted play equipment with a central raft surmounted by four slides. Lawns dotted with picnic tables and

a kiosk line the shores of the beach on the slopes rising to Eastern Park and the Geelong Botanical Gardens. Geelong's waterfront is currently subject to extensive redevelopment. Although an experimental breakwater formed of old car tyres towed into Corio Bay in 1982 was a failure, a new 220-berth marina which incorporates its own breakwater has been approved by the yacht club and port authority.

Bellarine Peninsula, the great thumb of land which extends into Port Phillip Bay south-east of Geelong, offers a variety of spots for safe swimming and boating on its northern shores. Chief among these is the fishing township of Portarlington, about 40 km from Geelong. Its camping grounds include a 1200-site park stretching more than 1 km along the beachfront. Shaded

parking and barbecue areas are found at the base of a long fishing jetty, with boat ramps and boat-hire depots nearby. Near the main Portarlington camping ground a four-storey mill, built in 1857, is now operated by the National Trust as a museum, open on Sundays 14.00-17.00. It has a comprehensive collection of Aboriginal artefacts found locally, for the area was a favourite camping spot long before Europeans came.

The stretch of coastline which bends southwards from Portarlington to Indented Head and St Leonards offers some of the better nearshore fishing found in Port Phillip Bay. Small camping grounds are situated between long, undeveloped swimming beaches buffered from the road by wide bands of parklands and picnic grounds.

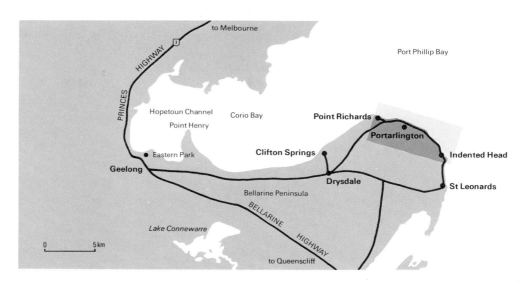

Sandy beaches line the uncluttered shores of Bellarine Peninsula. A jetty and marina mark the peninsula's major settlement at Portarlington

Queenscliff and Point Lonsdale

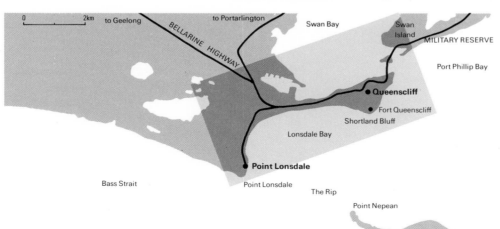

0 2km
to Geelong
BELLARINE HIGHWAY
to Portarlington
Swan Bay
Swan Island
MILITARY RESERVE
Port Phillip Bay
● **Queenscliff**
● Fort Queenscliff
Shortland Bluff
Lonsdale Bay
● **Point Lonsdale**
Bass Strait
Point Lonsdale
The Rip
Point Nepean

Australia's only black lighthouse, at Shortland Bluff, towers above the century-old buildings of Fort Queenscliff. Along with the light at Point Lonsdale, it forms a line to guide sailors through the treacherous waters of the Rip, at the entrance to Port Phillip Bay. The dark stone of the Queenscliff tower resembles the local bluestone used in many early buildings, but was quarried in Scotland, where it was also shaped and numbered before being shipped to Queenscliff for assembly. The fortifications at Shortland Bluff were a response to fears of Russian invasion during the 1870s and 80s. Since 1947, the red brick walls surrounding the fort have enclosed the army's senior officer training college. Guided tours of the buildings and grounds start at 14.30 at weekends and on public holidays. On the bay shores north of the fort, pieces salvaged from

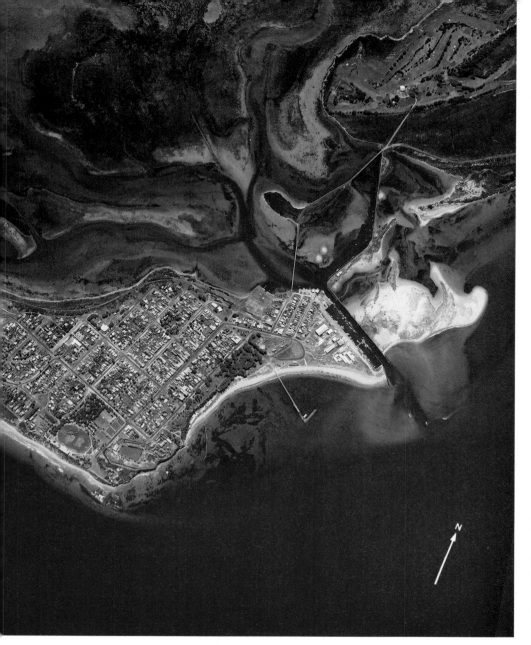

Quiet waters in Lonsdale Bay belie the peril to be found just to the south, where fierce tidal currents through the entrance to Port Phillip Bay create what seafarers know as the Rip; the headland settlements at Queenscliff and Point Lonsdale originated as light stations to protect Melbourne-bound shipping

The wild man of Bellarine Peninsula

JOHN BATMAN'S Tasmanians, preparing for the first permanent settlement on Port Phillip Bay in 1835, were staggered to find a European who had been there for more than 30 years. William Buckley, an English bricklayer and soldier convicted in 1802 of receiving stolen property and sentenced to transportation for life, had been sent to help found the original abortive settlement near Sorrento. He and three other convicts absconded, and only one returned before the colony was abandoned early in 1804.

When Batman's settlers were exploring Indented Head, north of Point Lonsdale, they were approached by a party of Aborigines. Among them was a man of unusual height—over 2 metres—with European features. His hair and beard were long and tangled, his skin was sun-blackened, and he wore kangaroo hides. One arm was tattooed with the initials WB.

Buckley could not speak to the newcomers at first, but managed the word 'bread' when given some to eat, and gradually recovered his use of English. However, his experiences during three decades alone or with the Aborigines went untold, or unrecorded. A cave in the cliffs of Point Lonsdale is said to have been his home.

Pardoned for his escape and original crime, Buckley was offered a post as a constable and interpreter. But he felt the mistrust of Port Phillip settlers and went to Tasmania, where he married at 57 and worked as a gatekeeper of a women's prison. He died in 1856, aged 76, after a road accident.

Buckley, restored to respectability in a suit

boats wrecked around the perilous heads are displayed on a grass reserve.

All camping at Queenscliff is away from the beachfront, leaving long stretches of uncrowded, open parkland along the bay. On the town's southern shores wide-spreading cypress trees shade picnic spots behind a deep-water jetty, where ferry passengers embark for Portsea on Mornington Peninsula. Pleasure boats, launched at a wide ramp just west of the Swan Island bridge, find their way out to Port Phillip Bay through a channel running alongside the boat harbour where Queenscliff's commercial fishing fleet is based. Swan Island is army property except for the golf links at its southern end. On the mainland, facing the golf links, is the terminus of the Bellarine Peninsula Railway, which used to run from Geelong. The station is now the head-

quarters of a volunteer organisation which operates a vintage steam train, pulling up to eight carriages on weekend trips around the shores of Swan Bay to Lakes Siding and Drysdale.

The lighthouse at Point Lonsdale overlooks the turbulent waters of the Rip and a superb surfing beach stretching west along Bass Strait. Calm bay beaches backed by steep sand cliffs sweep north of the point, past a jetty popular with walkers and fishermen. A rocky outcrop marks the southern end of a low-lying beach at Point Lonsdale's well-appointed holiday settlement. In a clearing among the tea-tree scrub surrounding the township's football oval, a stone cairn commemorates the first overseas radio transmission from the Australian mainland. The Marconi Company, founded by the inventor of radio, Guglielmo Marconi, set up stations at Point

Lonsdale and at Devonport, Tasmania, in an attempt to persuade the Australian government to adopt its system of wireless communication. In the presence of a crowd of VIPs and a Marconi representative—not the inventor himself, as the memorial's inscription suggests—successful messages were exchanged on 12 July 1906. But the government declined to buy the equipment, and three years passed before moves to set up permanent transmitters were initiated.

Melbourne to Adelaide

The limestone cliffs of southern Victoria have been sculpted into some of the coast's best-known natural features—the arches and rock stacks of Port Campbell National Park. Beyond the South Australian border, cliffs give way to a series of sand barriers that sweep up to the mouth of the Murray River and to the rocky shores of the Fleurieu Peninsula, south of Adelaide.

The Arch, west of Port Campbell

Whalers' Haven, Rosetta Harbour

Discovery Bay merits a detour when crossing between Victoria and South Australia

Rain clouds shroud the Great Ocean Road

SOUTH AUSTRALIA

●Adelaide

St Vincent
Gulf

Murray River

Aldinga Beach
Myponga Beach
Normanville
Rapid Bay
Kingscote
American River
Penneshaw
Kangaroo Island
Seal
Bay

Goolwa
Port Elliot
Victor Harbor
Cape Jervis

Lake
Alexandrina

The Coorong
Encounter Bay

●Kingston SE

●Robe

●Beachport
●Southend

VICTORIA

Melbourne●

●Mount Gambier

●Nelson

Port Phillip Bay

Barwon Heads ●Ocean Grove
Bells Beach ●Torquay
Aireys Inlet ●Anglesea

Portland● Port Fairy● ●Warrnambool

Peterborough●
Port Campbell

SOUTHERN OCEAN

●Lorne

Marengo●Apollo Bay

Cape Otway

BASS STRAIT

The Coorong extends 132 km along the coast behind Younghusband Peninsula

Towering cliffs and windswept dunes

MUCH more than a political division distinguishes the Victorian and South Australian sections of the Southern Ocean coast. They differ sharply in structure, presenting the traveller with clear-cut visual contrasts and varying ranges of activity.

On the Victorian side the coast is formed largely of cliffs. Often, particularly around Cape Otway, they drop vertically into the sea. Their soft limestone is easily cut back by wave action, and fallen rock disintegrates quickly. In the absence of headland shelves and boulders, protected sandy beaches are rare. But in scenic compensation, remnants of harder rock offshore provide an astonishing array of tall stacks, pinnacles and arches. Ranges just inland catch a high rainfall that promotes profuse forest growth. Last century, when timber-getters were denuding most of the east coast, their access to south-western Victoria was barred by the cliffs. Splendid hardwood rainforests remain, reaching close to the ocean and protected by the extensive declaration of national parks.

The Great Ocean Road, carved into steep rock faces for 320 km from Torquay to Peterborough, represents a notable triumph of pick-and-shovel toil. The project was launched at the end of World War I to make jobs for returning servicemen. It was completed in 1932, initially as a tollway costing a carload of five people 8s 6d—about a tenth of the basic weekly wage. Even at that price it was unsurfaced, and of single-car width in most parts. Only after World War II was it brought to its modern standard.

From east of Warrnambool almost to the South Australian border, a vast volcanic lava-flow plain sweeps from the north and east to meet the sea. The collapsed crater and scoria cones of Tower Hill, active not much more than 6000 years ago, represent the coastal outpost of a wide belt of old volcanoes reaching back towards Geelong. Where fine, wind-blown volcanic material accumulated above the lava layer, it has weathered into highly productive soil.

In South Australia, where the coastline veers north-west to Encounter Bay, it takes on an altogether different character. Parallel lines of dunes separate windswept, sandy beaches from lagoons or swamps just inland. Screened off from a barren, wave-battered shore, scrub grows densely and waterfowl abound. Rivers seldom reach the sea here: they are trapped behind the dune barrier, or farther inland by limestone ridges which represent old coastlines when the sea level was higher. Not even the mighty Murray, draining the sixth-biggest catchment area in the world, can often find the ocean. Behind its sand-clogged mouth, it forms the huge lagoon of Lake Alexandrina and the salty ribbon of the Coorong.

Cliffs loom beyond Encounter Bay, on the rugged southern flank of Fleurieu Peninsula. These are tough granite—not the soft limestone of Victoria. The ridges of the Mount Lofty Ranges twist westward and fall sharply to the sea at Cape Jervis, resuming more gently in Kangaroo Island. North towards Adelaide, facing the ocean swells that sweep into St Vincent Gulf, isolated sandy beaches are formed where river gullies run to the coast.

In spite of the contrast in landscapes, the whole Southern Ocean shore has a fairly uniform climate. Rainfall is moderate except on the Otway and Fleurieu coasts, and most of it occurs in winter. Prevailing south-westerly winds temper the midsummer heat that Melbourne and Adelaide suffer—and if the same winds can be avoided, off-season temperatures are usually mild.

The south coast of Kangaroo Island, a continuation of the Mt Lofty Ranges

The Twelve Apostles near Port Campbell, on one of Australia's most rugged coasts

The gentle hills of the Mt Lofty Ranges meet the sea at the tip of Fleurieu Peninsula, south of Adelaide, ending in both sharp cliffs and sandy pockets of beach

A ghost in the graveyard of ships

GALES have driven scores of sailing ships and even steamers to destruction on the wild Southern Ocean coast. Hundreds of mariners, convicts and immigrants lost their lives there last century. But the wreck that has excited the most lasting attention goes unrecorded in any chronicle of shipping.

Sandhills west of Warrnambool are said to hide the remains of an ancient 'mahogany ship'. Some people think it was a 16th-century caravel, supporting a theory that the coast as far east as Portland was secretly charted by a Portuguese flotilla in 1522.

At the time of European settlement, Aborigines in the district were said to have a tradition of 'yellow men' having come among them in the past. Reports of a sizeable hull of exceptionally hard wood, well back from the sea almost opposite Tower Hill, started in the 1830s. They persisted for more than 40 years, though it is not certain that they all referred to the same wreck. Some descriptions suggested an antique building method.

The last sighting was in 1880—the year a farmer burned what he thought was an old whaling punt to obtain its metal fittings. Local timber, saturated with whale oil and weathered for decades, could have been mistaken for mahogany. But sand drifts obliterated roads in the same year: a wreck of greater significance may also have been buried.

After the ship vanished, stories emerged of parts of it having been used for flooring or refashioned as furniture. If there is foreign timber of great age in the district, none has been offered for radio-activity dating. Penholders, said to have been carved from 'mahogany ship' wood in 1876, turned out to be made of Australian eucalypt. Excavation of the supposed site in 1890 yielded only a bronze spike, a stove latch and some rusted ironwork. Unsuccessful digs were made in 1955 and 1969. Searches were conducted with National Trust backing twice in the mid-1970s and again in 1981.

The last excavation uncovered pebbles from outside the district—perhaps ship's ballast—and a piece of wood. It is eucalypt, but it dates from the late 1600s. The same age is assigned to a piece of foreign timber donated early this century to the National Library in Canberra, with a note that it came from the 'mahogany ship'. So although there may never have been a Portuguese intruder, the story of the wreck may have a factual basis in the 17th-century activities of Dutch traders to the East Indies (now Indonesia). Many of their ships, bound for Java from the Cape of Good Hope in South Africa, ran too far east and unwittingly entered Australian waters.

Ocean Grove and Barwon Heads

Camping and caravan grounds cover the entire riverside spit jutting from Ocean Grove to the mouth of the Barwon. More of them occupy reserves on the opposite bank. Together they form a densely packed summer holiday city, so heavily in demand that two football ovals by the river mouth are also turned over to campers at the height of the season. Local businessmen have estimated that the visiting population—including day-trippers as well as holidaymakers—reaches 15 000. Sheltered ocean and river beaches are within easy reach, and a patrolled surfing beach lies at the northern end of the Ocean Grove spit. South of Barwon Heads the surf rolls on to a narrow rocky foreshore below steep, replanted dunes and a beachfront road covered in drifts of wind-blown sand. Barwon Heads surf club members patrol 13th Beach, 4 km west, where the rocks give way to a safer stretch of sandy coastline. The beachfront road continues past the clubhouse to two patrolled beaches at Breamlea, 8 km farther west. Light boats are easily launched over low-lying beaches on the Barwon, and there are concrete ramps for heavier craft on both banks, just north of the bridge across the river mouth. Shallow-draught boats can be taken upstream to Lake Connewarre, a reed-lined game reserve popular for fishing and sailing, and for duck shooting in the autumn season.

To the north, past a small private zoo and donkey-breeding stud, the Ocean Grove Nature Reserve is open 10.00-17.00 at weekends and during school holidays. It is a rare example of original forest on the intensively farmed Bellarine Peninsula. Walking tracks of 0.5 to 3.5 km are signposted at points of interest. Fire trails provide a further 15 km of walks and take photographers and bird watchers to three observation hides overlooking waterholes on the fringes of the reserve. An information office and picnic grounds with barbecues are located near the car park. The reserve is the last known Victorian habitat of an unusual butterfly, the small ant blue (*Pseudodipsas myrmecophila*). It spends the larval stage of its life in the care of ants, which make a nest for it and lead it out every evening for food. In return, the ants enjoy a sweet secretion from the caterpillar's body. A colony can be seen on request to the reserve warden.

Twin towns astride the last reach of the Barwon River become holiday cities in summer

OCEAN GROVE-BARWON HEADS (pop. 6776) south of Bellarine Highway 97 km from Melbourne, 21 km from Geelong (turn off at Wallington).
TRANSPORT: train Melbourne-Geelong daily; bus Geelong-Ocean Grove-Barwon Heads most days.
SURF CLUB PATROL: December-March, at Ocean Grove Saturday 13.00-18.00, Sunday and public holidays 09.00-18.00; at 13th Beach Saturday 13.00-17.30, Sunday and public holidays 09.30-17.30.

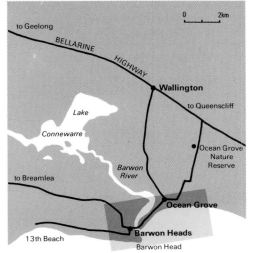

OCEAN GROVE												
	Jan	Feb	Mar	Apr	May	Jun	Jul	Aug	Sep	Oct	Nov	Dec
Rainfall mm	33	29	50	49	61	63	56	57	63	52	42	43
Rain days	6	5	8	10	12	14	14	14	13	11	8	7
Sunshine hrs	Summer 8 +			Autumn 5 +			Winter 3 +			Spring 6 +		

Town with no pub

OCEAN GROVE started as a 'dry' town, an exercise in temperance by two American Methodists who bought the land in the 1860s. They released town sites only on the condition that 'no malted, vinous or spirituous liquors shall be sold on the property'. The settlement failed to live up to its founders' puritan ideals and they returned to the United States. But even today, only the licensed bowling club and a solitary bottle shop have managed to breach the dry wall around the town—there is still no hotel. Ocean Grove's public drinkers go across the river to Barwon Heads.

Right: Instead of pubs and taverns, Ocean Grove in the 1880s rejoiced in a vast 'coffee palace'

Torquay and Bells Beach

Shop window displays, unusually dominated by surfboards, wetsuits and shorts, reveal the major role surfing plays in Torquay's commercial and holiday activities. Seven companies specialise in the design, manufacture and sale of surfing equipment and outfits. The stimulus is Bells Beach, 8 km south of Torquay and renowned among surfers for the size and reliability of its waves. Contestants at the 1981 national championships performed on and under rollers about 7 metres high—a great test of skill and daring and an amazing spectacle for onlookers.

Bells Beach has five separate surfing areas in the bays between its two small but well-defined headlands. Heavy swells rolling in from the Southern Ocean slow and steepen over the reef-strewn shallows to form waves that are consistent from week to week. If the bottom was sandier, shifting bars would keep changing the patterns and shapes of waves. But the breakers at Bells can be counted on for fast and challenging rides. The beach was the venue for the world amateur board-riding championships in 1970, and the annual Easter Open, inaugurated in 1962, is the longest-running major surfing contest in Australia. It started a year after surfers had pooled their own money to bulldoze a clifftop vehicle track from near Torquay. Before, they paddled their boards along the coast or risked getting bogged in pastures.

In spite of the fame of Bells Beach, there is not even a milk bar to serve the small army of board-riders who gather here at any time of year. The area was declared a nature reserve in 1971. The nearest shops and camping grounds are at Jan Juc, a surf beach with smaller waves 2 km south of Torquay. The surfers have their own names for the wild beaches below the sheer cliffs between Bells Beach and Jan Juc—'Steps', 'Boobs' and 'Evo's', for example. They are constantly moving in their search for the best waves.

Torquay itself is a well-equipped holiday

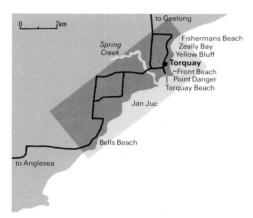

town surrounded by rich grazing land. It has been popular with people from Geelong and Melbourne since late last century. The town beaches were developed in the style of English seaside resorts, with neatly grassed parks shaded by tall trees where holidaymakers could stroll or relax after a paddle in the ocean. Near the boat ramp at Fishermans Beach, gently sloping lawns and picnic grounds with an electric barbecue dip from the road to the sheltered swimming waters of Zeally Bay, a popular spot for light sailing craft and fishing boats. Immediately south, past the picnic grounds and shady cypress trees of Yellow Bluff, Front Beach curves along the central Torquay beachfront to Point Danger. The point overlooks a patrolled beach at the mouth of

Spring Creek and has sweeping views along the coast from Point Impossible in the north to Bells Beach in the south.

TORQUAY (pop. 2879) south of Princes Highway 98 km from Melbourne, 22 km from Geelong (turn off at South Geelong).
TRANSPORT: train Melbourne-Geelong daily, bus Geelong-Torquay most days.
SURF CLUB PATROLS: Torquay Beach December-Easter, Saturday 13.00-18.00, Sunday and public holidays 09.00-18.00; Jan Juc December-Easter, Saturday 13.00-18.00, Sunday and public holidays 09.30-18.00.

Fine surfing beaches fringe a craggy, cliffed coast from Bells Beach (far left) to Jan Juc and Torquay

Anglesea to Aireys Inlet

Glimpes of the sea flash into view from wooded crests as the Great Ocean Road approaches Anglesea through the rolling forest hills and thick coastal scrub of the Otway Range. The highway, opened in 1932 to replace rough forest tracks, improved access to the isolated settlements between Torquay and Cape Otway. It soon brought an influx of tourists from the north. The towns, especially Anglesea, grew as popular holiday destinations. Anglesea was given a second boost in population and employment in 1959, when coal mining began from a deep open-cut basin in the hills north of the town. The tall chimney stacks near the mine belong to a power station which uses the coal to supply electricity to alumina smelters at Point Henry, near Geelong. In spite of the industry nearby, Anglesea remains a pleasant tourist centre. Camping and caravan reserves at the river mouth are surrounded by bowling greens, tennis courts and a playing field. The Scouts and the National Fitness Council have established two big campsites around the town, making the area accessible to hundreds of youngsters during school holidays.

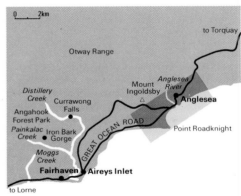

Point Roadknight and the forested foothills of the Otway Range give shelter to Anglesea's beaches

The Anglesea River is popular for fishing and swimming, and brightly painted paddle boats are for hire near the bridge. A patrolled surfing beach runs south of the river towards a boat ramp sheltered by Point Roadknight, where sheer red cliffs are topped with a car park lookout. The shores remain rocky south of the point before reaching an isolated stretch of sandy surf beach.

Dry-weather touring roads lead inland from Anglesea through low hills around the river valley. West of the town an all-weather road passes a track climbing to Mount Ingoldsby (121 metres) and 2 km farther on branches off to Angahook Forest Park. The road is an alternative route to Aireys Inlet, a small settlement above a patrolled surfing beach with a hotel and restaurants and caravan park, but no camping. Cleared trails take visitors on walks around Angahook Park from picnic grounds at the Distillery Creek entrance. An 11 km walk taking about four hours leads to the deep ravine of Iron Bark Gorge, the Currawong Falls across the higher reaches of Distillery Creek, before returning beside a tea-tree-bordered swamp. Walks also branch out to the Moggs Creek picnic ground at the southern entrance of the park.

ANGLESEA												
	Jan	Feb	Mar	Apr	May	Jun	Jul	Aug	Sep	Oct	Nov	Dec
Rainfall mm	32	52	40	58	62	54	64	71	59	61	56	45
Rain days	6	7	8	11	13	14	15	17	14	12	11	9
Sunshine hrs	Summer 8 +			Autumn 5 +			Winter 3 +			Spring 6 +		

ANGLESEA (pop. 1460) on Great Ocean Road 115 km from Melbourne.
TRANSPORT: bus Melbourne-Anglesea most days, Geelong-Anglesea daily.
SURF CLUB PATROL: December-March, Saturday 13.00-18.00, Sunday and public holidays 09.30-18.00.

Lorne to Mount Defiance

Mount St George and the lofty ridges of the Otway Range, catching the brunt of Southern Ocean storms, favour Lorne with more than its share of sunshine and warmth on a cold and cloudy coast. At the same time they trap a high rainfall, supporting forest trees and ferns in almost tropical profusion on the steep slopes behind the town. Surf rolls in reliably to the broad town beach, south of the Erskine River mouth. All the beachfront is reserved for recreation: there are picnic grounds, playgrounds, public tennis courts, amusement centres, a swimming pool and a bowling green. Behind, past take-

away bars and restaurants jammed with tourists in summer, spacious and expensive houses overlook Loutit Bay. Property values rose 500 per cent between 1967 and 1976. Most of that increase occurred in one year, after Lorne was declared a 'site of special significance' under a development planning order.

Picnic grounds at Allenvale, less than 4 km inland from the town centre, are the starting point for a web of bushwalks in Lorne Forest Park. Of varying length and steepness, they lead through soaring stands of eucalypts to rivers and waterfalls shaded by ferns and willows. Along

with common native mammals, there is a chance of sighting the rare tiger cat, *Dasyurops maculatus*. Weighing up to 3 kg and distinguished by a white-spotted back and tail, it is the biggest of the mainland native cats. If the thylacine—the Tasmanian 'tiger' or 'wolf'—is truly extinct, this distant relative is now the largest meat-eating marsupial in Australia.

South from Lorne, the Great Ocean Road skirts the cliff edge so closely that the surf seems to disappear beneath it. Spray rises like steam, drifting over cars on the snaking highway. Beaches are tiny if they can be found at all. On

the inland side of the road a naked rock face climbs vertically: slips can block this route after heavy rain. Past the Spit there is a generous wedge of sheltered beach at the Cumberland River mouth, backed by camping and caravan grounds and a picnic area. A walking track leads 3 km upriver, and a dry-weather road climbs south-west around the shoulder of Mount Defiance. South of the river, the forest park reaches right to the coast for about 6 km. Halfway along, the turreted walls of the clifftop Mount Defiance Lookout stand as a tribute to Howard Hitchcock, one of the initiators of the awesome Great Ocean

Road project. There is no access from the road to the sea until the Jamieson River, almost at the end of the park. The mouth has a pocket-handkerchief swimming beach, and fishermen can make their way along to Artillery Rocks—so named because the rocks shielding the road from the surging sea look as if they were shattered in a naval gunnery attack.

LORNE (pop. 893) on Great Ocean Road 146 km from Melbourne.
TRANSPORT: bus Melbourne-Lorne most days, Geelong-Lorne daily.

SURF CLUB PATROL: December-Easter, Saturday 13.00-18.00, Sunday and public holidays 09.30-18.00.

	LORNE											
	Jan	Feb	Mar	Apr	May	Jun	Jul	Aug	Sep	Oct	Nov	Dec
Maximum C°	23	24	22	20	17	14	14	14	16	18	19	21
Minimum C°	15	15	14	13	10	9	8	8	9	10	11	12
Rainfall mm	56	73	62	83	81	69	66	102	75	76	76	54
Rain days	11	9	11	12	18	18	18	21	17	17	14	10
Sunshine hrs	Summer 8 +			Autumn 5 +			Winter 3 +			Spring 5 +		

Beaches are rare below the cliff-hugging route south of Lorne—the toughest part of the pick-and-shovel Great Ocean Road project, completed in 1932

Apollo Bay and Marengo

Long green breakers bend around Point Bunbury and into Apollo Bay's sandy, cypress-lined beach. Behind, the township wedges into cattle and sheep paddocks on the slopes towards the Otway foothills. By the golf links on Point Bunbury, the Fishermen's Co-operative sells fresh fish seven days a week. Surf erupts higher than the rock breakwater, but inside it the fishing fleet is moored in mirror-calm water. Apollo Bay is a fishing, farming and tourist town, fully equipped to cope with a heavy flow of visitors. A variety of roads and tracks penetrate the forested hills, giving access to rivers, waterfalls and lookouts. One of the easiest picnic spots to reach, at Paradise by the Barham River, has a remarkable profusion of ferns.

Apollo Bay was named after a sloop which ran wool from Portland and Port Fairy to Melbourne in the 1840s. In those days whale oil and blood drenched the Point Bunbury backshore where the golf club's neat fairways are now formed. A whaling station operated intermittently until 1847, three years before timber cutters founded a settlement. Historical society members collect 'anything that comes our way' for their Folk Museum, open 14.00-17.00 on Sundays and public holidays, and daily during

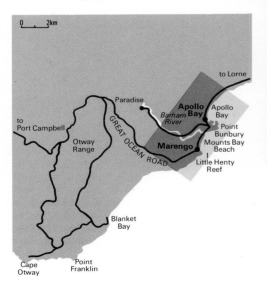

school holidays. Among a wide range of relics from the district's pioneering era, there are details of the coast's many shipwrecks. Not all were of sailing vessels, driven ashore in storms: the freighter *City of Rayville*, which struck a German mine off Cape Otway in November 1940, was the first United States ship to be sunk during World War II. All the crew except one were rescued by Apollo Bay fishermen. At Mar-

engo, parking bays off the Great Ocean Road give access to Mounts Bay Beach, its sand tightly bound with grass and dune shrubs. Surf climbs from Little Henty Reef in a year-round display of the power and persistence of the sea. In front of the point a flat rock platform, lined and patterned as if by an artist, runs to the bulging boulders which take the brunt of the surf 100 metres out. The highway veers inland after

Breakwaters in the hook of Point Bunbury enclose a capacious boat harbour for Apollo Bay fishermen

Marengo to avoid high ridges reaching to Cape Otway. The roundabout route to the cape is long and twisting, and no longer rewarded by the chance to see inside the oldest remaining lighthouse on the Australian mainland. It has been closed to visitors since one fell to his death in 1979. But the grounds, which give a better view than the tower itself, are open on Tuesdays and Thursdays.

APOLLO BAY (pop. 921) on Great Ocean Road 190 km from Melbourne.
TRANSPORT: bus Melbourne-Apollo Bay most days, Geelong-Apollo Bay daily.
SURF CLUB PATROL: December-March, Saturday 13.00-18.00, Sunday and public holidays 09.00-18.00.

APOLLO BAY												
	Jan	Feb	Mar	Apr	May	Jun	Jul	Aug	Sep	Oct	Nov	Dec
Rainfall mm	50	54	70	89	105	111	117	126	110	99	83	63
Rain days	8	8	9	13	15	16	18	19	15	15	12	10
Sunshine hrs	Summer 8 +			Autumn 4 +			Winter 3 +			Spring 6 +		

Port Campbell National Park

Relentless seas have carved gorges, arches, blow-holes and scores of towering, jagged nearshore columns out of the sheer limestone cliffs which border the coastal plains of Victoria's Western District. In Port Campbell National Park, along a 32 km strip of this coast, many of the more striking formations can be seen from signposted clifftop lookouts close to the Great Ocean Road. First to strike the eye, approaching from the east, are the Twelve Apostles—great stone stacks soaring from the ocean opposite 3 km of continuous cliffs. Early settlers cut steps above Gibson Beach, just east of the lookout, for access to one of the many popular surf-fishing beaches in the area. A tunnel joining Gibson Beach with the beach at the foot of the Apostles can be entered at low tide in calm water.

Mutton Bird Island is the biggest of the park's nearshore stacks. At dusk from September to April, short-tailed shearwaters fill the air as they return to their breeding grounds after the day's hunt for food. They can be watched, alighting at their burrows and feeding their chicks, from a lookout close by. Other lookouts on the same side road have views of the Blowhole, Thunder Cave and Loch Ard Gorge. A stairway on the gorge's eastern wall takes visitors down to the beach where the only two survivors of the wrecked *Loch Ard* were washed ashore in 1878. Tom Pearce, 18, showed extraordinary strength and courage in climbing out of the gorge to fetch help for Eva Carmichael, also 18. But their story had no fairytale ending; she went back to Ireland to marry someone else. From the end of the lookout road a steep path leads down past picnic grounds to a sheltered swimming spot in the estuary of the Sherbrook River. The sea at the river mouth may look calm enough but here, as at most beaches in the park, rapidly changing currents and tides make swimming extremely dangerous. The small bays at Port Campbell and Peterborough provide the safest bathing.

Two dry-weather tracks run off the Great Ocean Road near Sentinel Rock for anglers skilful enough to cast from the windswept clifftops. The gravel road to the gorge near the jagged, bald rock offers solitude, and impressive views of the high yellow cliffs. The highway lookout by Port Campbell Creek gives a sweeping view of Port Campbell Bay—its shores lined with pines, a camping ground and a spread of holiday houses on the slopes to the north. Reefs make the bay a sheltered harbour for small boats, though the town's crayfishing fleet must still be winched on to the jetty when heavy seas are running. A 2.5 km walking track, rough in places, runs west from Port Campbell Creek to Two Mile Bay. Dunes line the shore in contrast to the limestone cliffs of most of the park. The walk to the bay and back takes about 90 minutes. Numbered posts along the trail mark the features of land formation, vegetation, wildlife and history outlined in

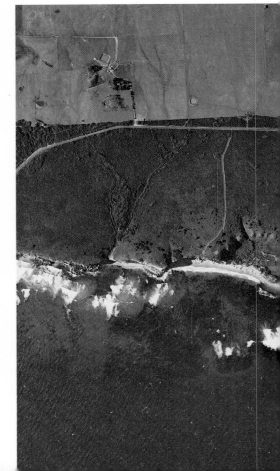

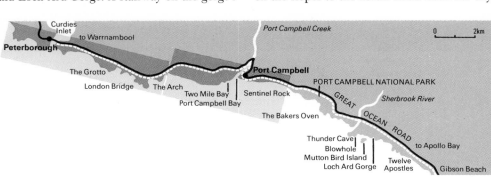

a guide brochure available from the park's information centre, open daily in Port Campbell.

At the western end of the park the coastal contours soften with dunes and a sandy beach on the approach to Curdies Inlet and the relaxed holiday centre of Peterborough—a town that is popular with fishermen.

Port Campbell township is at the centre of the narrow coastal national park that bears its name

PORT CAMPBELL on Great Ocean Road 287 km from Melbourne.
TRANSPORT: none beyond Warrnambool, next page.
SURF CLUB PATROL: December-Easter, Saturday 13.30-16.30, Sunday and public holidays 11.30-17.00.

PETERBOROUGH on Great Ocean Road 299 km from Melbourne.
TRANSPORT: as for Port Campbell.

Peterborough beach is one of the few places on this cliff-lined coast where it is safe to bathe

PORT CAMPBELL												
	Jan	Feb	Mar	Apr	May	Jun	Jul	Aug	Sep	Oct	Nov	Dec
Rainfall mm	41	41	53	79	96	98	108	108	91	84	62	53
Rain days	9	9	11	16	17	18	20	21	18	18	14	12
Sunshine hrs	Summer 7 +			Autumn 4 +			Winter 3 +			Spring 5 +		

Warrnambool and Port Fairy

Beaches to the south of Port Fairy are protected from the full force of southerly swells by a rocky barrier that lines the coast

Maritime links are cherished at Warrnambool and Port Fairy, 120 years after their heyday as wool and grain ports for Victoria's Western District. Two heavy cannon point over Lady Bay from the walls of Fort Warrnambool, built in 1887 when Australians feared a Russian invasion. Now the fort and a nearby lighthouse and keeper's cottage are part of Flagstaff Hill, a re-creation of a 19th-century port centred around original buildings, with restored sailing ships moored in a small lake. A ship's chandlery, blacksmith's shop, marine museum and other period buildings have artefacts and displays which illustrate the life and history of a shipping town. Flagstaff Hill is open daily, 09.30-16.30. The square, red-trimmed lighthouse looks over the island-dotted waters of Lake Pertobe Park, with its causeways, walking tracks, picnic sites and well-equipped adventure playground behind the sweeping surf beach of Lady Bay. Boat owners have the choice of launching into the breakwater harbour at the southern end of the bay, or into the wide lower reaches of the Hopkins River, beside which the settlement's first cattle grazed. From a lookout at the river mouth easy walking tracks lead back along the rocky bank or down to the sandy northern end of Lady Bay.

In contrast to the port at Warrnambool—little used since railways diverted its trade—Port Fairy's Moyne River harbour still bustles with the activity of a large fishing fleet. Much of the atmosphere of an old seaport is retained by the town's verandah-fronted streets and old houses, some dating from the 1840s. More than 50 buildings have been classified by the National Trust, including the bluestone cottage of a whaling skipper who came in the 1830s, and the Caledonian Hotel, continuously licensed since 1844. A Port Fairy Historical Society booklet guides visitors around and has notes on the architecture and history of many of the old buildings. The society opens its small museum in Bank Street during school holidays, 14.00-17.00.

East of the town a wooden footbridge crosses the Moyne River to the surfing beach of Port Fairy Bay. At the southern end of the bay a calm swimming beach, sheltered by Griffiths Island, is dominated by an old fort and signal station on Battery Hill. A short track leads up to a lookout with fine views of the town and coast. South Beach—locally known as Pea Soup Beach—is another popular surfing spot, with rock fishing ledges to the east and west. Griffiths Island, the site of an early whaling station, is now a wildlife reserve. It is riddled with the nesting burrows of short-tailed shearwaters, which crowd the island between September and April each year.

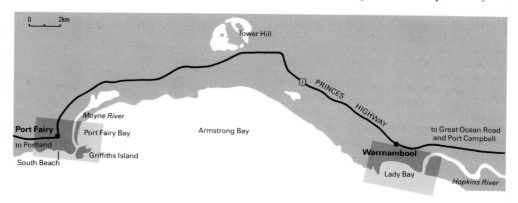

WARRNAMBOOL (pop. 21 415) on Princes Highway 262 km from Melbourne, 654 km from Adelaide.
TRANSPORT: train Melbourne-Warrnambool daily (3½ hrs); flights Melbourne-Warrnambool daily; coach Adelaide-Mount Gambier most days (6½ hrs), coach Mount Gambier-Warrnambool weekdays (3½ hrs).
SURF CLUB PATROL: December-Easter, Saturday 13.00-17.00, Sunday and public holidays 09.00-17.00.

🏛 🏠 ⛺ ▲ 🛎 ◎ ✶ 🎒 ♀ 🍴 ⊜ 🛶 ⚓ 〰 ♂ ✠

PORT FAIRY (pop. 2276) on Princes Highway 290 km from Melbourne, 626 km from Adelaide.
TRANSPORT: as for Warrnambool; bus Warrnambool-Port Fairy daily.
SURF CLUB PATROL: December-Easter, Saturday 13.00-17.00, Sunday and public holidays 10.00-17.00.

🏛 🏠 ⛺ ▲ 🛎 ◎ ✶ 🎒 ♀ 🍴 ⊜ 🛶 ⚓ ♂ ⛵ ✠

WARRNAMBOOL												
	Jan	Feb	Mar	Apr	May	Jun	Jul	Aug	Sep	Oct	Nov	Dec
Maximum C°	23	23	22	20	16	15	14	15	16	18	20	21
Minimum C°	13	13	12	10	9	7	6	6	7	9	10	12
Rainfall mm	32	36	47	60	77	75	84	83	71	64	53	44
Humidity %	60	63	63	61	69	72	72	67	65	66	63	64
Rain days	8	8	10	13	17	17	20	20	16	16	13	11
Sunshine hrs	Summer 8 +			Autumn 4 +			Winter 3 +			Spring 5 +		

Where nature has a second chance

TOWER HILL and its surrounding lake, beside the highway between Warrnambool and Port Fairy, are the remains of Victoria's most recent volcano. High crater walls collapsed inwards during its dying stages, 6000 years ago, and blocked the 3 km-wide crater. Rainwater filled the rest of the basin, around minor cones formed by the last eruptions.

Early European settlers saw Tower Hill thickly wooded and teeming with wildlife. But they wanted grazing land: the slopes were cleared of timber, and only grass and bracken grew. The area was declared a national park in 1892, but the quarrying of scoria for roadmaking went on until 1941. A programme of full re-afforestation did not start until the 1960s. About 250 000 trees have been planted.

With the restoration of natural habitats, some species of wildlife were brought back. Long-nose bandicoots, ducks, geese, black swans, koalas and emus have been established, and the reintroduction of more than 20 other species is intended.

Sealed roads lead to the main island, where bush-walks radiate from a natural history centre, open 08.30-16.30 daily. It has displays on the area's volcanic history and recent rehabilitation. The islands and lake are a game reserve where ducks can be shot in the autumn season.

Tower Hill's water-filled crater retains its volcanic appearance after 6000 years

A generous open space separates the beaches of Lady Bay from the bustling streets of Warrnambool

Turning the clock back

DEDICATION and craftsmanship of rare quality have gone into Flagstaff Hill, Warrnambool's re-creation of a little 19th-century seaport. Building materials and methods are authentic. Appropriate relics, lovingly restored, include old sailing craft in a man-made harbour. Sauntering down the slope overlooking the village's blue-stone-tiled rooftops, or poking about in its shops and storehouses on a quiet day, visitors require no great stretch of the imagination to feel they have stepped back in time.

Shipping movements were signalled from the hill in the 1850s. Twin lighthouses were built in 1871 and artillery fortifications in 1887. These remain as features of

the maritime village, which opened in 1975 and is still growing. The complex is more than just a tribute to Warrnambool's past. It salutes the role of seafaring in the early development of all of Australia, and it offers grim reminders of the risks mariners ran on the Southern Ocean coast.

Hundreds of articles salvaged from shipwrecks are on display at Flagstaff Hill. Divers are employed to gather more. They are credited with the discovery in 1982 of the barquentine *La Bella*, not seen since she went down just off Lady Bay in 1905. Relics from the *Loch Ard* disaster, which claimed 52 lives near Port Campbell in 1878, command major attention. Finds

include a lifesize pottery peacock, dating from 1851, and an exquisitely ornamented brass lamp bracket.

But the greatest of Flagstaff Hill's treasures sat there unrecognised for five years. In 1975 a metal lid was recovered from the wreck of the *Schomberg*, which hit a reef at Peterborough 120 years before. The lid, heavily encrusted with marine growths, was put on display with a collection of salvaged silverware. Not until 1980 did the village director find time for the slow and tricky task of cleaning it up. As part of the crust was dislodged, he found embedded in the lid a golden ring, set with a flawless Brazilian diamond.

The water is in a manmade lake and the buildings went up in the 1970s. But the effect is uncannily convincing

Fear of a Russian attack brought fortifications

Authentic goods stock the ship chandler's shop

Nineteenth-century sailing craft are skilfully restored

Unscathed survivor of the Loch Ard disaster

Portland

Cape Sir William Grant, breaking the fury of storms raging up from the Southern Ocean, creates a wide body of sheltered water along the western shores of Portland Bay. Crews of everything from sealing boats to supertankers have appreciated the protection of this massive promontory and of Portland Harbour's long breakwater walls, built of stone quarried from the 80-metre cliffs of the cape's eastern face. The harbour—Victoria's largest outside Port Phillip Bay—was the site of the state's earliest permanent European settlement. A 17-year-old, William Dutton, came ashore in 1828 to man a whaling station. He had a flourishing industry by the time the first squatters, the Henty family, arrived in 1834—a year before the official settlement of Melbourne.

Portland Harbour has grown to occupy all of the low-lying beach where Dutton built his hut and boiling-down works. The port is destined to expand even more to handle shipments to and from Alcoa's alumina-smelting plant, under construction 6 km to the south at Point Danger. The plant, estimated to cost $1500 million when site preparation started in 1981, will eventually employ 1200 people. Many more will be engaged indirectly in servicing the industry. But the town's expectation of an early economic fillip were dampened in 1982, when depressed world markets for aluminium and a shortage of cash forced Alcoa to defer the start-up of the first potline from the end of 1983 to late 1986. The company had already spent $250 million.

Headlands on the bay side of the smelter site are to be left undisturbed. Their rocky shores will remain accessible to surfers, anglers and skin-divers by sandy tracks off the quarry road from Blacknose Point to Point Danger. Crumpets Beach, tucked away below the high cliffs of Blacknose Point, is the closest surfing beach to Portland but is unpatrolled. The town's life-savers have established their club at a more popular beach almost 20 km to the west in Bridgewater Bay. Pleasant calm-water swimming spots are found near the centre of Portland. One is on what remains of the harbour beach between the marina and the commercial fishing wharf. A second, Nuns Beach, is immediately outside the harbour's northern breakwater. Motorists can drive out to the end of the breakwater for superb views of the city, and fishermen cast from the giant bluestone rocks.

In Cape Nelson State Park, 12 km south-west of Portland, high school students have helped make a walking trail through scrub and forest and around the cape's rocky western cliffs. The 3 km walk crosses some rough terrain: strong

footwear is needed and two hours should be allowed to complete it at an easy pace. The park and lighthouse are reached by a scenic road skirting high, sheer cliffs around Nelson Bay, past a popular surfing beach at Yellow Rock.

Travellers into South Australia need not rejoin Princes Highway immediately. From Portland a pleasant alternative route via Bridgewater leads north-west behind Discovery Bay Coastal Park, which has several lakeside campsites and swimming spots. The road meets the coast 5 km short of the border at Nelson, the favourite beach resort of Mount Gambier people. Fishermen rate Nelson highly, and there is sheltered swimming and boating in the Glenelg River. Interesting limestone formations are found in the nearby Princess Margaret Rose Caves.

Great scars on Point Danger mark the site of a planned alumina-smelting plant, only 6 km from busy Portland Harbour

PORTLAND (pop. 9353) on Henty Highway 262 km from Melbourne, 568 km from Adelaide.

TRANSPORT: train Melbourne-Warrnambool with connecting bus to Portland daily (4½ hrs); flights Melbourne-Portland daily; coach Adelaide-Mount Gambier daily (6½ hrs); coach Mount Gambier-Portland weekdays (1½ hrs).

SURF CLUB PATROL: Bridgewater Bay December-March, Saturday 13.00-16.30, Sunday and public holidays 11.00-16.30.

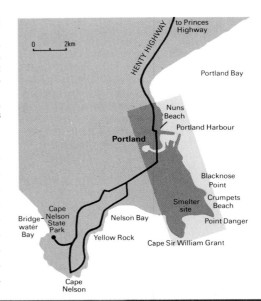

PORTLAND												
	Jan	Feb	Mar	Apr	May	Jun	Jul	Aug	Sep	Oct	Nov	Dec
Maximum C°	22	22	21	19	17	14	14	14	16	17	19	21
Minimum C°	13	14	12	11	9	8	6	7	8	9	10	11
Rainfall mm	28	24	35	59	78	89	133	123	95	88	66	48
Humidity %	70	69	74	72	75	79	77	74	76	73	70	69
Rain days	6	7	9	14	15	17	21	21	19	16	11	12
Sunshine hrs	Summer 8 +			Autumn 4 +			Winter 3 +			Spring 5 +		

Southend and Beachport

Beachport's Pool of Siloam, fed by underground springs and six times saltier than the sea, offers visitors the nearest thing to walking on water they are ever likely to experience. Practised bathers can stay upright with their heads and arms out of the water, simply by paddling their feet with a treading action. Some show-offs try reading a book. When the novelty of Siloam wears off, there is calm sea bathing from the town beach on Rivoli Bay, and surfing at the Blowhole, to the west near Pleasant Cove. A long pier spearing into the bay serves a prosperous crayfishing industry, which exports frozen tails to the United States under its own 'Beachport' brand. Crayfish around Cape Martin and Penguin Island are protected, but other rock fishing is available from the cape and off the little headlands west of town. The island is a sanctuary for penguins. Its shores are dangerous in most seas: a boat landing is best not attempted without local knowledge. Relics of Beachport's whaling and fishing past, along with artefacts of the district's Aborigines, are displayed in the town museum. It is in a century-old wool and grain store, open afternoons only during weekends and public holidays.

Beachport Conservation Park, a 710-hectare wilderness of shifting dunes and sparse coastal vegetation, is 2 km north-west of town by gravel road and sand track past the western shore of Lake George. Where the road meets the lake, a 300-metre stretch of enamel-smooth sand makes a natural launching ramp. Yachts can be hired here in summer. On the ocean side of the road, 'live' dunes snake into the scrub like giant yellow lizards, burying paperbark trees and the marram grass that is meant to stabilise the sand. The higher dunes give good views of the lake and its backdrop of inland hills, but the steeper sand tracks should not be attempted without four-wheel-drive.

Southend, tucked in the opposite corner of Rivoli Bay, still appears on some maps under its old name of Grey. Shifting dunes have been both the discoverers and the gravediggers of the district's history. A stone cottage of the late 1800s is buried on the township backshore, where the first settlers had their boat jetties. Elsewhere, dunes have moved and left exposed old Aboriginal campsites, with fireplaces and shell dumps. Many are to be seen in Canunda National Park, which has its entrance at Southend. The 9000-hectare park, extending more than 40 km along an uninhabited coast, has picnic areas with barbecues, but no fresh water or lavatories. Camping permits can be obtained from the ranger at

Southend. Walking trails have been developed and some tracks are negotiable by car. The wildlife to be seen may include the tall black-toed emu and the orange-bellied parrot. Sea lions, fur seals and leopard seals occasionally sun themselves on the park's rocky beaches.

BEACHPORT (pop. 357) west of Princes Highway 456 km from Melbourne, 371 km from Adelaide (turn off at Millicent westbound or 31 km before Millicent eastbound).
TRANSPORT: bus Adelaide-Millicent most days (5 hrs); coach Melbourne-Mount Gambier most days (6½ hrs); coach Mount Gambier-Millicent most days (1½ hrs); none beyond Millicent 35 km away.

SOUTHEND 21 km south-east of Beachport.
TRANSPORT: as for Beachport.

BEACHPORT												
	Jan	Feb	Mar	Apr	May	Jun	Jul	Aug	Sep	Oct	Nov	Dec
Rainfall mm	24	23	28	54	80	107	116	94	63	47	33	30
Rain days	5	5	6	11	15	18	19	19	15	11	8	7
Sunshine hrs	Summer 8 +			Autumn 5 +			Winter 3 +			Spring 5 +		

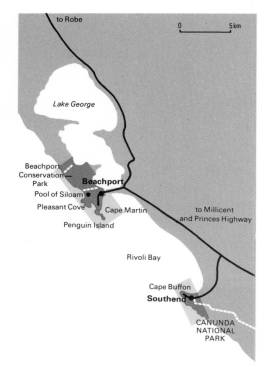

Barren coastal dunes and the shallow shores of Lake George create a striking landscape around the tiny fishing town of Beachport, in the remote south-eastern corner of South Australia

Southend is at the northern end of Canunda National Park which stretches 40 km along the coast

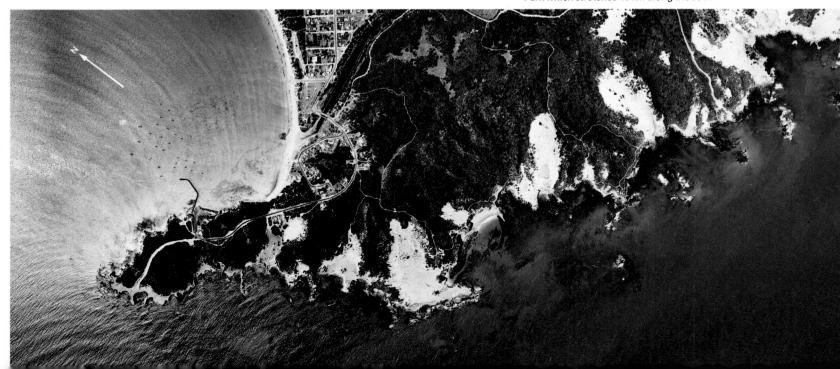

Robe to the Coorong

Cape Dombey and the deep scoop of Guichen Bay afford Robe unusual protection from the gales and boisterous seas of the Southern Ocean. Soon after its establishment in 1847, Robe vied with Port Adelaide as South Australia's leading port. Out of the limelight since railways changed the patterns of trade, the town now turns its favoured position to advantage as a summer holiday base. Its extent of sheltered swimming areas is more than generous. Along with three tidy little beaches on the town shore, the great sweep of Long Beach starts just to the east at the Outlet, where a canal spilling into the bay drains marshy ground for more than 50 km inland. Most of Lake Fellmongery is reserved for water-skiing, but swimmers have their own section marked off by floats. Fishermen can try all types of angling, and boating facilities are first class. The commercial fishing fleet is based at Lake Butler, in the heart of town. There is a good launching ramp by the lake's northern arm. Near the opposite shore is a receiving depot for crayfish: processing them for export is Robe's principal industry. The Lodge, a craft workshop on the way to Lake Fellmongery, was built as a butchery in 1850. At the Caledonian Inn, built in 1859, the publican's niece nursed the bush poet and champion horseman Adam Lindsay Gordon after he was injured in a racecourse fall in the 1860s. She later married him. The Customs House, built in 1863, is now a nautical museum, open 14.00-17.00 on Tuesdays and Saturdays.

Little Dip Conservation Park runs south of Robe along a narrow strip between the sea and a string of salt lakes. There are also freshwater pools and a picnic ground with fireplaces, but no lavatories. Camping permits may be obtained from the ranger at Robe.

North past Kingston South-East, a crayfishing port similar in character to Robe, another chain of salt lakes starts. The highway switches to the inland side of them, and 60 km from Robe the depression in which the lakes form becomes continuous. It is permanently filled with 'river' water, though it is usually brackish and sometimes completely salty. This is the Coorong, a blind arm of the Murray River trapped behind the thin sand barrier of Younghusband Peninsula. The Coorong, averaging only about 2 km in width, trails 100 km to the Murray's sand-clogged mouth. However, the highway veers north about halfway along it: the only vehicle access to the mouth is from the west. The Coorong and the peninsula form a national park. A 17 km section, centred on the park headquarters at Salt Creek, is a reserve for waterfowl. Hunting for foxes and rabbits is encouraged year-round, and some species of duck can be shot in season. Hunting permits include the right to camp.

ROBE (pop. 590) west of Princes Highway 503 km from Melbourne, 340 km from Adelaide (turn off 43 km north of Millicent northbound, at Kingston S.E. southbound).
TRANSPORT: bus Adelaide-Robe most days (4½ hrs); flights Adelaide-Mount Gambier daily, Melbourne-Mount Gambier most days; coach Melbourne-Mount Gambier most days (6½ hrs); coach Mount Gambier-Robe most days (1½ hrs).

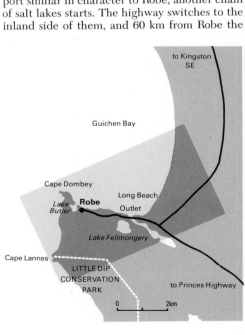

ROBE	Jan	Feb	Mar	Apr	May	Jun	Jul	Aug	Sep	Oct	Nov	Dec
Maximum C°	23	23	21	19	16	15	14	14	16	18	19	21
Minimum C°	14	14	13	12	10	9	8	8	9	10	11	12
Rainfall mm	21	20	25	47	76	96	104	82	58	44	29	28
Humidity %	58	60	62	67	71	75	74	71	70	66	62	60
Rain days	5	5	7	12	17	19	21	19	16	13	9	8
Sunshine hrs	Summer 8 +			Autumn 5 +			Winter 3 +			Spring 6 +		

Row upon row of parallel, scrub-covered dunes reveal the ancient shorelines of Guichen Bay. The town of Robe sits at the bay's far southern end

Gateway to the goldfields

A STONE cairn near Robe's boat harbour bears an intriguing inscription: 'During the years 1856 to 1858 16 500 Chinese landed near this spot and walked 200 miles to Ballarat and Bendigo in search of gold.' They did not do so by choice.

Rich Chinese masters to whom the goldfield's labourers were indentured refused to pay a £10-a-head landing tax imposed by the Victorian government. That was as much as it cost to ship a man all the way from Hong Kong. So the coolies were diverted to Robe. Their masters cared nothing that the overland journey was four times longer than from Melbourne, and the lonely trail more inviting to bushrangers. The travellers also found that in summer water was in short supply, and that the winter cold was severe enough to kill the weak.

Robe authorities made sure that the wretched migrants travelled in safety. Working for rations and a pittance, none of them made fortunes unless they smuggled gold out. But all contributed to Robe's prosperity. The town's gratitude is implied in the cairn, erected by its Chamber of Commerce.

Murray mouth to Victor Harbor

From Victor Harbor, linked to Granite Island by a causeway, a ribbon of houses runs around to Port Elliot

Australia's mightiest river expires in a feeble trickle half-way along Encounter Bay. The Murray mouth is no more than a drain for brackish lagoons and reed-choked channels behind the long sandspit barriers of Sir Richard and Younghusband Peninsulas. Sea water surges in, piling up against barrages in all the channels, more often than the river flows out. Only in seasons of phenomenal rain does the Murray carry down enough water to flush out the lagoons and force a convincing opening for itself. Cuts had to be bulldozed in 1981 and 1982 to prevent salt water from backing far upriver.

Seaports to the west, however, have easy land access to the last navigable channel of the Murray. If the first governor of South Australia, John Hindmarsh, had had his way in 1837, those ports—linked by canal with the river town of Goolwa—would have formed the nucleus of his capital city. He was overruled in London. Even so, a horse-drawn railway to Goolwa made Port Elliot the rival of Port Adelaide for a few years in the 1850s, until a spate of shipwrecks scared owners and insurers away. In the 1970s Goolwa boomed as the fastest-growing town in the south of the state. Housing and tourist facilities spread up the Murray bank, out to an ample bayside surf beach and across the river to Hindmarsh Island, connected by a cable-punt car ferry. Speedboat enthusiasts in particular are attracted to Goolwa, but every sort of water sport is catered for. As well as being the terminus for river cruising, Goolwa gives travellers their only access to the Murray mouth, by sightseeing boat or by the four-wheel-drive 'Coorong Express' bus along the Sir Richard Peninsula.

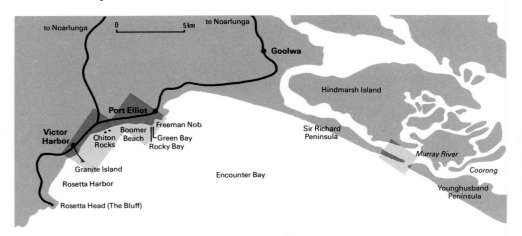

On Freeman Nob at Port Elliot, a popular cliff walk passes an obelisk built in 1852 to fly a warning flag when inshore seas were dangerous to shipping. Construction of the breakwater started at the same time, but funds were short and the job was incomplete in 1856 when four ships at anchor were driven ashore by gales. The port lost its trade to Victor Harbor. Heavy seas still pound Boomer Beach and foam among pearly grey boulders at Green Bay and Rocky Bay. But east of the Nob the breakwater, finished too late, protects Horseshoe Bay.

Victor Harbor is dominated by Granite Island —a tourist attraction since the 1880s, when a horse-drawn double-decker tram took families over the causeway for genteel afternoon teas. Now it is a wildlife reserve, frequented particularly by the little penguin, *Eudyptula minor*— Australia's only indigenous species. Visitors are still catered for. A Toytown-style train runs from town, and for the less nimble a chairlift scales the heights at weekends, and daily during school holidays. Grassy walking tracks criss-cross the island. Victor Harbor itself is a well-equipped holiday base with sheltered swimming and facilities for most recreation. To the south, on the Bluff (Rosetta Head), a plaque records the incident in 1802 which led the navigator Matthew Flinders to give Encounter Bay its name. He rounded the headland in HMS *Investigator* to find the French ship *Géographe*, captained by Nicolas Baudin, in the bay. Britain and France were on the verge of war, but the two men put exploration first and held a friendly meeting.

VICTOR HARBOR (pop. 4522) 89 km from Adelaide via Noarlunga.
TRANSPORT: bus Adelaide-Victor Harbor daily.
SURF CLUB PATROL: Chiton Rocks November-March, Saturday 13.00-17.00, Sunday and public holidays 12.00-17.00.

GOOLWA (pop. 1624) east of Noarlunga-Victor Harbor road 85 km from Adelaide (turn off 3 km south of Mt Compass).
TRANSPORT: bus Adelaide-Goolwa weekdays.

PORT ELLIOT (pop. 773) 8 km east of Victor Harbor.
TRANSPORT: bus Adelaide-Port Elliot daily.
SURF CLUB PATROLS: Boomer and Port Elliot Beaches November-March, Saturday 13.00-17.00, Sunday and public holidays 12.00-17.00.

VICTOR HARBOR												
	Jan	Feb	Mar	Apr	May	Jun	Jul	Aug	Sep	Oct	Nov	Dec
Maximum C°	24	24	23	22	18	16	15	16	17	20	21	23
Minimum C°	15	16	14	13	10	8	8	8	9	10	12	14
Rainfall mm	22	22	22	44	64	72	74	65	56	44	29	24
Humidity %	60	61	56	54	61	64	65	63	58	56	58	55
Rain days	4	4	6	10	14	15	16	16	13	11	7	6
Sunshine hrs	Summer 8 +			Autumn 5 +			Winter 3 +			Spring 7 +		

Tonnes of silt are carried out to sea as the Murray River completes its 2520 km journey. In recent years the river mouth has become blocked and has been opened with the help of bulldozers

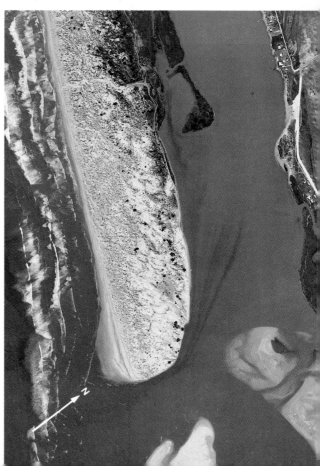

There is safe swimming beside the jetty in Vivonne Bay

A road winds down to Seal Bay (left) where visitors can see seals and sea lions. A long stretch of coast to the east of Seal Bay is part of a conservation park

Kangaroo Island

Sheer size enables Kangaroo Island to absorb tens of thousands of visitors a year with a minimum of disturbance to its natural blessings. At 4350 sq km it is Australia's third-biggest island, ranking behind only Tasmania and Melville Island. A central highway and more than 1000 km of gravel roads make nearly all parts accessible. Yet much of the 450 km coastline is untouched. Along with the immense wilderness of Flinders Chase National Park (59 000 hectares) there are 12 conservation parks on the main island and clusters of islet bird sanctuaries.

Kangaroo Island was discovered by Matthew Flinders in HMS *Investigator* in 1802, just before he met the French navigator Nicolas Baudin in Encounter Bay. Baudin in the *Géographe* charted the island's coastal features thoroughly, and many still bear French names. American sealers set up a station in 1803, and the first permanent European settlement was established as early as 1816—20 years before the South Aus-

tralian Company put official settlers ashore at Nepean Bay. There were no native people left: an early Aboriginal population seems to have died out about 4500 years ago.

Though fringed for the most part by steep limestone cliffs, Kangaroo Island is flat. Agriculture did not succeed, however, because of a shortage of fresh water and because of soil deficiencies which were not corrected until the 1930s. Fishing was the island's economic mainstay, and became one of its major attractions to visitors. Surf, rock and boat angling all produce good results, while big sharks cruising in deeper water provide sport for wealthy game fishermen.

Dangerous seas often pound the south and west coasts. The north is safer, but much of it is a day's journey from any harbour anchorage or ramp. So boating activity by visitors is largely confined to the sheltered bays of the north-east, facing the mainland. Kingscote, the principal town, and American River and Penneshaw, the

two other settlements with extensive tourist facilities, are in this area. All have beaches close by that are suitable for family swimming. Penneshaw often has good surf as well. Local advice should be sought about the safety of surf at remote beaches.

Kangaroo Island has no public transport, but coach tours leave daily from all three towns. Ferry travellers from Adelaide can bring their own cars, and other visitors can hire vehicles. Campers have a choice of eight remote sites but should check on permit requirements and facilities before leaving town. Perhaps the most rewarding of the shorter trips available is to Bale Beach, Seal Bay and Vivonne Bay, where the south coast road comes closest to the sea. Sheltered beaches are flanked by conservation parks, and sea lions are often to be seen out of the water on the rockier shores.

Flinders Chase National Park is a full day's outing from the tourist towns. It embraces the

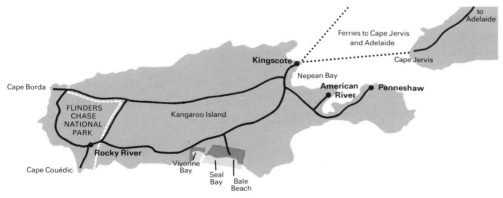

Cape Borda
FLINDERS CHASE NATIONAL PARK
Rocky River
Cape Couëdic
Vivonne Bay
Seal Bay
Bale Beach
Kangaroo Island
Nepean Bay
American River
Kingscote
Penneshaw
Ferries to Cape Jervis and Adelaide
Cape Jervis
to Adelaide

0   10   20km

KINGSCOTE (pop. 1236) on Nepean Bay 42 km from Cape Jervis, 140 km from Adelaide.
TRANSPORT: vehicle ferry from Adelaide most days (6½ hrs); passenger ferry from Cape Jervis some days in season; flights from Adelaide daily.

AMERICAN RIVER 38 km south-east of Kingscote.
TRANSPORT: none beyond Kingscote.

PENNESHAW 57 km east of Kingscote.
TRANSPORT: none beyond Kingscote.

	KINGSCOTE											
	Jan	Feb	Mar	Apr	May	Jun	Jul	Aug	Sep	Oct	Nov	Dec
Maximum C°	25	24	23	21	18	16	15	15	17	19	21	23
Minimum C°	15	15	14	12	10	9	8	8	9	10	12	13
Rainfall mm	15	18	18	37	60	74	79	65	46	36	24	19
Humidity %	55	57	59	62	66	71	71	70	67	60	58	56
Rain days	3	4	5	9	13	15	18	17	13	10	6	5
Sunshine hrs	Summer 8 +			Autumn 5 +			Winter 3 +			Spring 6 +		

whole wild western coastline from Cape Borda to Cape Couëdic, and extends in a huge triangle inland. There are fully developed camping and picnic areas at Rocky River. The island's own breed of kangaroo abounds there, tame enough to feed by hand. It is darker, stockier and slower-moving than the related western grey kangaroo of the mainland. Koalas are also numerous in the park's dense vegetation—but they are not native. They are one of the success stories of a 30-year programme, ending in the 1950s, to give a safer habitat to wildlife in danger of extinction on the mainland. The Cape Barren goose, now plentiful on the island, is another example.

Walking on the wild side

RESORT facilities on Kangaroo Island cluster around the eastern bays, within sight of the mainland across Backstairs Passage. Here they promise shelter from prevailing westerlies, and from the Southern Ocean swells that surge past the other side of the island.

Boat owners seldom venture far to the west. At least a dozen old shipwrecks testify to the savagery of the seas they could face along cliff-lined, reef-strewn shores. Many motorists, too, are discouraged. The only bitumen road to the west peters out in mid-island. After that, ironstone gravel loosely laid on dirt produces uncertain surfaces and clouds of summertime dust. Routes down to remote bays are often through sand.

Camping treks on horseback—and even a train of camels—take visitors to many coastal beauty spots and into the sugar gum forests and acacia woodlands of the interior, where in spring they see excellent displays of wildflowers. But for people with time and stamina to spare, the western coast of 'KI' is truly walkers' country.

A sandy vehicle track loops from the northwest to the Flinders Chase National Park headquarters at Rocky River. Walking trails leading off it descend the fern-lined gullies of streams that reach the coast in secluded coves. The hardest, but probably the most rewarding, is the trail down the Ravine des Casoars (Cassowary Gully), named by the French explorer Nicolas Baudin in 1802 after emus were seen there. Beside a delightful little beach, imposing limestone cliffs are pitted with big caverns that can be entered at low tide.

Shoreline walks near Cape Couëdic, in the southwest, are easily taken from the motor road. Limestone formations at the cape are contrasted to the east by extraordinary outcrops of ironstone, curiously eroded and very often coated with vividly-coloured lichens.

The Remarkable Rocks – eroded ironstone

Sea lions breed at Seal Bay

Kangaroos of the island – not hunted for thousands of years – are heavier and slower-moving than their mainland counterparts

Lichens add an orange coating to windswept rocks in the southwest. Heathland plants flower brilliantly in spring

Murray Lagoon, in Cape Ganthaume Conservation Park, is a haven for waterfowl

West Fleurieu Peninsula

A twice daily (three in peak season) car ferry service between Cape Jervis and Penneshaw on Kangaroo Island gives access to the more remote settlements of Fleurieu Peninsula. The quick journey across Backstairs Passage and the availability of packaged island excursions give travellers from Adelaide a new motive to tour south-westwards, instead of following the beaten track east to the long-established resorts on Encounter Bay. Cape Jervis itself is a quiet fishing village where public life revolves around a single store. Near a narrow wooden jetty and boat ramp, rocks form a natural breakwater and fishing platform. The cape has some beaches, but they are tiny and difficult to reach. The lighthouse, built in 1972 on a modernistic pyramid base, is automatically operated and not open to visitors. But a lookout behind it is higher, and commands better views.

Rapid Bay, marked by a T-shaped jetty jutting 500 metres into St Vincent Gulf, belongs to the Broken Hill Proprietary Co Ltd. Limestone is quarried here for use as a purifier in steelmaking. Visitors are welcome, however, and a beach

Caves pit the rocky shoreline between the beach at Rapid Bay and a tiny creek mouth at Second Valley

camping area is provided—though it will lack shade until newly planted Norfolk Island pines are mature. Swimmers make for the northern end of the beach, near a high, shallow cave. Caravans are catered for at Second Valley, only 2 km up the coast but 13 km by road. The little jetty there makes a pleasant fishing spot and skindivers comb the rocky shallows, but sandy-bottom bathing is limited to a narrow channel.

At Normanville a long, white beach stretches either side of the Bungala River mouth. A gravel road winds beside the river to a wooden boat ramp across the beach, where the sand is firm enough for cars. There is also a concrete ramp beside a little-used wooden jetty. As early as the 1850s, flour milled in Normanville and Yankalilla was shipped from a longer jetty on this site. With its old police station, lock-up and customs house, and modern tourist amenities such as tennis courts, a swimming pool, an 18-hole golf course and grass-skiing slopes, Normanville is bent on succeeding as a holiday town. Its ambition is shown in the new name being promoted for the developing area north of Carrickalinga Creek—'the Gold Coast'.

NORMANVILLE (pop. 290) on Noarlunga-Cape Jervis Road 87 km from Adelaide (turn off at Yankalilla).
TRANSPORT: bus Adelaide-Normanville some days.

RAPID BAY north of Cape Jervis road, 112 km from Adelaide (turn off at Delamere).
TRANSPORT: none beyond Normanville, 24 km away.
NEAREST SERVICES: Yankalilla.

NORMANVILLE												
	Jan	Feb	Mar	Apr	May	Jun	Jul	Aug	Sep	Oct	Nov	Dec
Rainfall mm	14	19	20	43	68	78	74	65	53	42	26	22
Rain days	3	2	4	8	12	14	15	14	12	8	6	4
Sunshine hrs	Summer 8 +			Autumn 5 +			Winter 3 +			Spring 7 +		

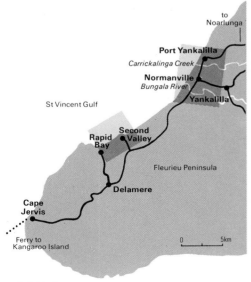

Resort developments are transforming old wheat fields and pastures at Normanville and Port Yankalilla

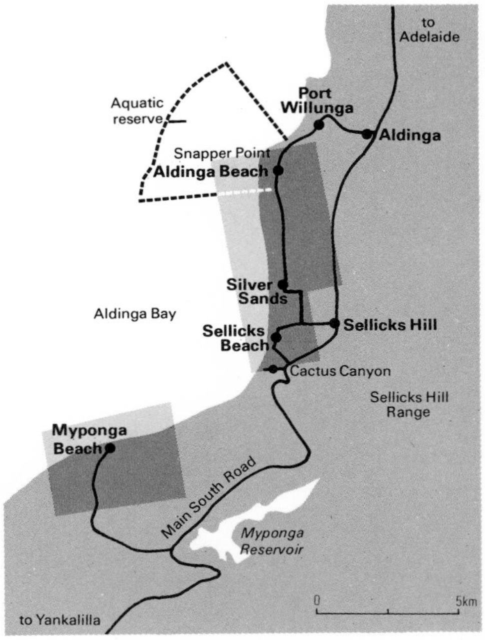

to
Adelaide

Aquatic
reserve

**Port
Willunga**

Aldinga

Snapper Point
Aldinga Beach

Aldinga Bay

**Silver
Sands**

**Sellicks
Beach**

Sellicks Hill

Cactus Canyon

Sellicks Hill
Range

**Myponga
Beach**

Main South Road

Myponga
Reservoir

to Yankalilla

0   5km

*Pioneer smallholders found heartbreak in the hills
behind Myponga Beach (below)*

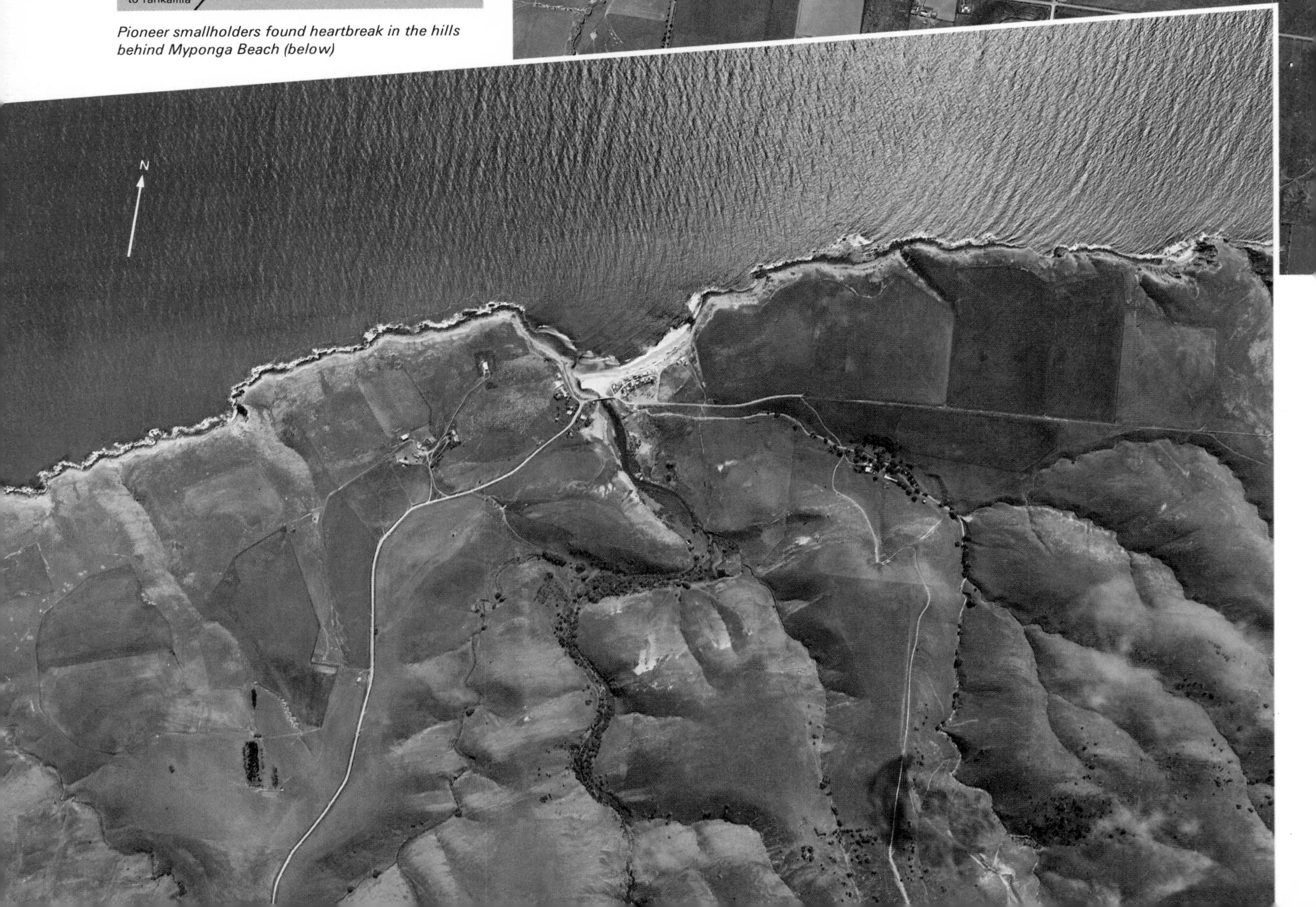

N

A near-straight stretch of sand, 5 km long, from Aldinga Beach to Cactus Canyon provides a highway for cars towing boat trailers

Aldinga Bay

Beach Speed Limit 25, a sign at the Silver Sands boat ramp warns. Tyre tracks carve unwavering trails north and south to other ramps at Aldinga Beach and Sellicks Beach. This long, straight northern reach beside Aldinga Bay takes cars and trailers easily, though there may be soft spots—every few days an unhappy driver has to call for the aid of a tractor. Motor-cycle racing at Sellicks Beach was a leading holiday attraction in the 1920s and 30s. A photograph from that period shows 10 machines lined across the sand. Motorcyclists as well as car drivers still take advantage of a natural freeway, though the days of roaring sprints for the chequered flag and a cash prize have long gone. The fanciful 1920s are also marked by a turreted wall in front of a holiday house on the Esplanade, built of colourful pebbles from the beach.

The shallow waters off Sellicks are lake-flat on still days, but waves are boisterous enough when the wind is up to attract body surfers and a few board-riders. Anglers and net fishermen make

good catches of mullet or salmon trout—which experienced locals are said to be able to spot in big schools from the clifftop of Cactus Canyon. This deep gorge, running from the bare heights of the Sellicks Hill Range, brings the 5 km stretch of beach to an abrupt end. The coast curving south-west to Myponga rises in high cliffs, presenting travellers with impressive views before the highway turns inland. Myponga Beach is a long side-journey from the Main South Road and offers little for visitors, other than a hint of the hardships suffered by smallholder farmers before pastoralists took over with sheep runs. Ruins of old stone farmhouses dot the hills behind the beach, which is uncomfortably pebbly and lacking in shade. A few grey piles and rotting beams are all that remain of a jetty built in 1860.

Off Snapper Point at Aldinga Beach, a wide sea-level reef extends to an aquatic reserve where fishing is prohibited. About 500 metres from the shore the reef has a limestone platform where people can walk and study shellfish and reef vegetation. At the outer edge, 1200 metres offshore, a 10-metre cliff is pitted with small underwater caves where seagrasses and sponges

grow profusely. Swimmers, snorkellers and scuba divers can see a variety of marine life rarely rivalled in southern waters. Reefs off Aldinga have a tragic history, however. In 1888 the grain ship *Star of Greece*, leaving Port Willunga with a cargo of 12 000 tonnes, was driven back by a gale and grounded less than 200 metres out. It broke up and 17 of the crew of 26 drowned. The failure of the townsfolk to observe the ship's plight and rescue any of the victims blackened Aldinga's name for many years.

ALDINGA BEACH-PORT WILLUNGA (pop. 2021) west of Main South Road 54 km from Adelaide (turn off at Aldinga).
TRANSPORT: train Adelaide-Noarlunga with connecting bus to Aldinga Beach weekdays.
SURF CLUB PATROL: November-Easter, Saturday 13.30-17.00, Sunday and public holidays 12.30-17.00.

SELLICKS BEACH (pop. 342) 4 km south of Aldinga Beach (turn off at Sellicks Hill).
TRANSPORT: none beyond Aldinga Beach.
SURF CLUB PATROL: as for Aldinga Beach.

Adelaide to the Bight

A continuous ribbon of broad, sandy beach fringes the urban shores of Adelaide from Largs Bay south. The partially enclosed upper reaches of St Vincent Gulf are not broad enough to generate a surf, but the calm, crystal-clear water is ideal for many sports. Surf-lovers can find waves on the more exposed beaches to the south, near the mouth of the gulf. To the west, around Yorke and Eyre Peninsulas and entering the Great Australian Bight, are numerous and varied opportunities for boating and fishing.

Innes National Park, Yorke Peninsula

At the Bunda Cliffs, harsh plains of the Nullarbor drop sharply to the Great Australian Bight

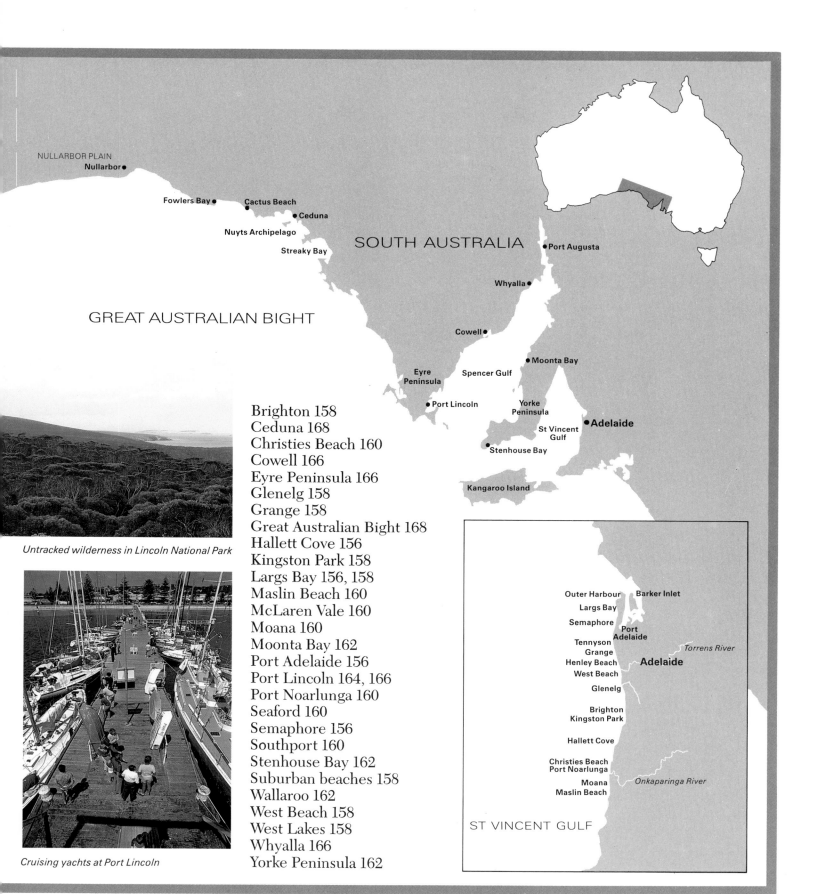

NULLARBOR PLAIN
Nullarbor●

Fowlers Bay ●
Cactus Beach
● Ceduna

Nuyts Archipelago

Streaky Bay

SOUTH AUSTRALIA

● Port Augusta

Whyalla ●

GREAT AUSTRALIAN BIGHT

Cowell ●

● Moonta Bay

Eyre
Peninsula

Spencer Gulf

Port Lincoln ●

Yorke
Peninsula

St Vincent
Gulf

● **Adelaide**

● Stenhouse Bay

Kangaroo Island

Untracked wilderness in Lincoln National Park

Cruising yachts at Port Lincoln

Outer Harbour   Barker Inlet

Largs Bay

Semaphore
Port
Adelaide

Tennyson
Grange   *Torrens River*
Henley Beach   **Adelaide**
West Beach

Glenelg

Brighton
Kingston Park

Hallett Cove

Christies Beach
Port Noarlunga

Moana   *Onkaparinga River*
Maslin Beach

ST VINCENT GULF

Unsung beaches of an inland capital

A twisted gum tree commemorates the event depicted on the right

IMAGES of park-girdled central Adelaide, with its gracious buildings on precisely gridded avenues ornamenting a dry inland plain, are so dominant that outsiders rarely know of the city's maritime heritage. When a broader view of the district is offered, it is usually of the scenically appealing Adelaide Hills and Mount Lofty Ranges to the east and south. Little attention is drawn to the 50 km sweep of metropolitan coastline, except where surf can be found off the southernmost beaches. But other beaches are less than 10 km from the city centre. Adelaide had its beginnings on these shores, and they remain rich in interest to visitors. Port Adelaide, separately settled and retaining an old identity all its own, is similarly neglected in publicity. No doubt the upright, affluent landholders of Australia's first free colony would have preferred that. The rough-and-ready style of a dockside community must have been offensive to their 19th-century sense of rectitude. Without the port settlement, however, their City of Churches could not have prospered. It might not even have been established.

History has vindicated the judgment of Colonel William Light, the brilliant surveyor who chose the site of central Adelaide and laid out its streets and parks. No more suitable place could have been found in the whole of South Australia. But Light's decision early in 1837 was bitterly opposed by many settlers and administrators, including Governor Hindmarsh. It meant a hot and dusty bush trek from the colonists' landing place at Glenelg. The port that Light proposed, on the inlet backing Lefevre Peninsula, was even farther from the city site and it had no fresh water. But he and some of his staff foresaw a time when Adelaide's expansion and industrial development would swallow the distance between the two. By promising to make an immediate survey of Port River building sites, Light won the support of merchants anxious to warehouse their deteriorating goods. They swung the balance in favour of his overall plan.

The port put Adelaide on its feet, but the limitations of a narrow inlet were fully exposed when bigger ships were built in the 20th century. Apparently roomier waterways to the east are clogged with mangroves and sandbanks; in the main their shores have proved useful only for salt evaporation and sewage treatment. Engineers have had to create additional ports artificially—at Outer Harbour for cruise liners and container ships, and at Port Stanvac, south of Hallett Cove, for oil tankers. But the old waterfront area remains busy, and many fine buildings from its mercantile heyday are preserved. Access is easy from the city centre or from the seaside suburbs to the west at Semaphore and Largs Bay. These districts developed as extensions of the port, and contain the military forts that were built to guard it. Semaphore also has the stately, century-old Customs House, with a gaily painted tower and flagstaff to serve as a landmark for ships making for the Port River entrance.

In the port itself, maritime relics are displayed in the Nautical Museum, open daily to the east of Birkenhead Bridge. The vehicle

Where the land reveals its past

ROCK LAYERS exposed north of Hallett Cove, 18 km from central Adelaide, have attracted worldwide scientific interest for more than a century. No other site offers a more comprehensive picture of the evolution of landforms. Its eroded cliffs are a geological sandwich in which evidence of ancient mountain-building, weathering, glaciation, submergence and re-emergence can be seen all at once. The timing of the earliest events corresponds with those of other continents, and the rock types match those of Antarctica west of the Ross Sea.

The basic rocks visible near the cove are sandstones and siltstones formed about 600 million years ago, and uplifted and folded about 100 million years later. Above them are grooved glacial pavements and sediments which were deposited in a major ice age around 270 million years ago. Higher up the cliffs, and in an inland recess called the Amphitheatre, can be seen a layer of fossil-bearing sandstone about 5 million years old. Higher still are clays washed down less than 2 million years ago.

Hallett Cove itself was almost overwhelmed by suburban development in the early 1970s, but most of the site important to scientists has been preserved. The National Trust of South Australia acquired the 4-hectare Sandison Reserve in the 1960s, and about 50 hectares adjoining it were bought by the state government and dedicated as a conservation park in 1976. Self-guided walks, on which 18 major points of interest are marked, cover about 3 km. Leaflets explaining the formations seen on the walks may be obtained from the National Parks and Wildlife Service office in Adelaide. Picnicking is allowed in the park, but it has no facilities.

The world's attention was first drawn to Hallett Cove in 1877. The rock formations just north of the area—some of which date from 600 million years ago—give powerful support to the now generally accepted theory of continental drift

Governor Hindmarsh proclaims South Australia to be a British Province on 28 December 1836

	Jan	Feb	Mar	Apr	May	Jun	Jul	Aug	Sep	Oct	Nov	Dec
ADELAIDE												
Maximum C°	28	28	25	22	18	16	15	16	18	21	24	25
Minimum C°	15	16	14	12	9	7	6	7	8	10	12	14
Rainfall mm	17	25	18	44	66	52	60	48	42	34	29	24
Humidity %	38	38	42	45	55	58	64	59	52	44	41	41
Rain days	5	3	5	11	15	13	16	17	13	10	7	7
Sunshine hrs	Summer 9 +			Autumn 6 +			Winter 4 +			Spring 7 +		

ferry to Kangaroo Island, *Troubridge*, berths at the other end of Gawler Reach. Nearby a former Sydney Harbour ferry, *Lady Chelmsford*, departs for sightseeing cruises to Outer Harbour. Snowden Beach, on the west bank of the inlet 1 km north of Port Adelaide, is a base for power boat racing and water-skiing. Fishermen's Wharf, where part of the day's commercial catch from St Vincent Gulf is sold direct to the public, faces Snowden Beach from just inside the entrance to North Arm. The city's proximity to water provides welcome relief, for Adelaide is the hottest of all Australian capitals in summer, with an average of 13 days exceeding 38°C and a peak temperature of 47.6, recorded in 1939. Summer humidity is extremely low, however. Coastal suburbs receive less than 500 mm of rain a year—less than half of the Sydney seaboard average—and most of it falls from May to August. Winters are cool but brief.

Calm, shallow water stretches for an extraordinary distance into St Vincent Gulf from the sands of Semaphore, one of Adelaide's popular city beaches

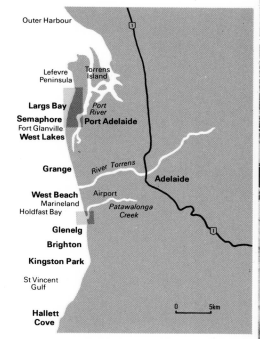

Suburban beaches

High-speed, off-road trams, running from the heart of Adelaide to Glenelg and decorated in turn-of-the-century style, keep alive an old attachment between the city and its beaches. The shores closest to central Adelaide lack surf, but their flat sands are remarkably spacious. From late Victorian times—when even to go paddling was adventurous—until the 1920s, when mass motoring made farther-flung surfing beaches popular, the 30 km stretch of sand from Largs Bay to Kingston Park was Adelaide's favourite playground. Trains and trams on a variety of lines fanning from the inner city were jammed with pleasure-seekers at weekends and during holidays. Now the old seaside resorts are solidly suburban, and the beaches are used mainly by local residents. But their calm waters still draw people from all over Adelaide for boating and fishing. This section of the St Vincent Gulf coast is studded every kilometre or so with jetties or ramps, and supports eight sailing clubs, a sea rescue squadron and nine lifesaving clubs.

Roads run along or close to the shore for 40 km, from the passenger ship and container terminals at Outer Harbour to the ancient rock formations of Hallett Cove. A third of this stretch, along the sandspit of Lefevre Peninsula, is backed by a narrow inlet winding south to a blind end only 200 metres from the beach at Grange. This is the Port River, though it no longer has a source. Once it drained swamps fed seasonally by the River Torrens, but in the 1930s the Torrens was channelled to the sea at West Beach. The port inlet has been further modified at West Lakes by swamp reclamation and the formation of an artificial lake and island—a prime housing area and a centre for water sports. On the beachfront nearby at Semaphore South is Fort Glanville, built in 1878 to protect the port behind it from a feared Russian invasion. Its restored ruins contain camping

Patawalonga Creek, in Glenelg, was the destination of South Australia's first colonists in 1836

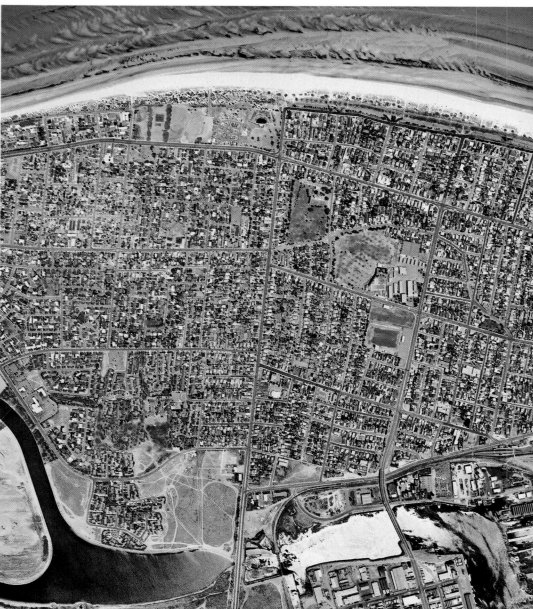

and caravan grounds in summer. Fort Largs, built 5 km to the north in 1882, now houses a police training school.

Near the jetty at Grange is a stone cottage occupied by the explorer Charles Sturt between 1841 and 1853, restored to its original condition and open 13.00-17.00 from Wednesday to Sunday and on public holidays. Marineland at West Beach claims to have the biggest roofed, all-weather display of marine life in Australia. Its picnic grounds include a children's zoo where Mr Percival, the tame pelican in the film *Storm Boy*, performs. West Beach Reserve has public golf links and a boating lake. Behind is Adelaide Airport, where a pioneer aviation display includes the Vickers Vimy flown from Britain in 1919 by Ross and Keith Smith.

Glenelg, the most intensively developed of the seaside suburbs, retains a notable living link with the earliest colonial days. A eucalypt in MacFarlane Street—so bowed that its top branches sweep the ground—looked exactly the same in December 1836, when it was the centre-piece of a ceremony to proclaim the founding of South Australia. The first colonists' ship, the *Buffalo*, anchored at Patawalonga Creek in Holdfast Bay—a name that became a bad joke to the settlers. They had to camp here for up to a year while arguments over the site of Adelaide were settled and surveys completed. In the meantime South Australia's first grapevines were planted by Richard Hamilton. A Moselle-style wine from his family's Ewell vineyards brought distinction to Glenelg until the end of the 1970s. But by then the estate, on land that was rated for its housing value, had shrunk to a few remnants around the winery—sandwiched between a school, a bus depot and a drive-in cinema complex. In mid-1982 nearly all the remaining vines, including some planted by Richard Hamilton himself, were bulldozed to make way for a housing project. Hamilton's, the last of many winemakers in the metropolitan area, has joined the others in a withdrawal to outlying districts. Efforts were made late in 1982 to preserve the family home-stead, near the intersection of Morphett and Oaklands Roads, but it was demolished in 1984.

Adelaide's straight beach strip narrows at Brighton and ends at Kingston Park, where recreation grounds surround a grand house, now closed, built in 1840 for George Kingston. He was deputy surveyor-general under William Light, who laid out the plan of central Adelaide. Kingston was sent back to London in 1838 to get staff for country survey work, but betrayed Light and returned with impossible demands from the colonial commissioners that forced his resignation. Kingston took over, and proved so incompetent that he lasted only four months. He fared better as a politician and land speculator, and was rewarded with a knighthood.

Adelaide's broad sandy beaches shelve gently into the calm, clear waters of St Vincent Gulf. The long jetties at Semaphore (left) and Largs Bay show how shallow the water is close inshore

Southern beaches

Suburban Adelaide points a long coastal finger down to Christies Beach and Port Noarlunga, putting them under intense pressure as family swimming and sunbathing spots. Their expanses of sand are generous, however, and accommodate big summertime crowds within a half-hour drive of the city centre. Southern Ocean swells, diverted into St Vincent Gulf by the granite tongue of Fleurieu Peninsula, have their last significant effects here. In combination with local winds they can produce interesting surf, on beaches so well frequented that three lifesaving clubs maintain patrols in a stretch of only 3 km from Christies Beach to the Onkaparinga River.

Christies Beach, lined by young Norfolk Island pines and facing the hooked white curve of Horseshoe Reef, is the main focus of seaside shopping and entertainment in the district. South around Witton Bluff, where the coast road climbs above rocks tinged with red and yellow ochre, a sandy shore resumes at the Port Noarlunga jetty. A rock platform at the end of the jetty is so straight and flat that at first glance it seems to be part of the construction. In fact it is a natural reef—one of a pair that form an aquatic reserve. Fishing of any sort is prohibited on the reefs or within 25 metres of them. The jetty reef is a learning ground for scuba divers, who tumble into clear green waters and practise their manoeuvres in close-range view of curious spectators. On the shore nearby is a cairn marking one of the landing places of Captain Collet Barker,

who was sent to explore the eastern side of St Vincent Gulf in 1831. He charted inlets, gorges and ranges from Cape Jervis to Port Adelaide. Then he took a party of soldiers to see if a better port, more accessible to the New South Wales colony, could be made at the Murray River mouth on Encounter Bay. To reach Younghusband Peninsula, Barker swam alone across the river mouth—then about 400 metres wide—only to be killed by Aborigines waiting on the other side.

A long spit of beach sand and sparsely vegetated dunes reaches south from Port Noarlunga, enclosing the last sluggish loops of the Onkaparinga River. Behind the Southport lifesaving clubhouse, a track leads to a footbridge over the river. Anglers line the steep banks while children

splash in shallow, sheltered waters just inside the mouth. The Onkaparinga was much deeper, and navigable by commercial craft to Old Noarlunga and beyond, until the 1930s. Then its flow was penned in Mount Bold Reservoir, 35 km upstream, to augment Adelaide's domestic water supply. Now only canoes can negotiate its silt-clogged shallows. They can penetrate about 15 km to the Onkaparinga Gorge, above which rapids and whirlpools bar their way. Beyond the reservoir, however, canoeists can paddle a further 15-20 km. Favourite spots for river anglers, seeking bream and mullet, are by the downstream footbridge and at Perry's Bend, about 3 km from the mouth.

Cliffs rise south of the river and line the coast

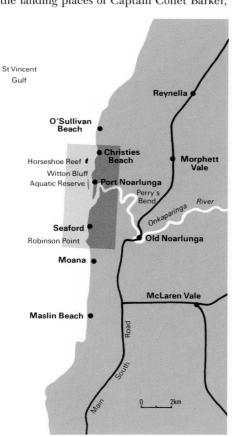

past Seaford to Moana. This is surfboard territory, and not much of it is for novices. Reefs screen almost all of the Seaford shore, except for a gap north of Robinson Point. Throughout the year the most practised surfers—wetsuited in winter against the chilling gulf winds—wait on the ocean side of the reef for waves that mount 100 metres from the beach and carry them in through the gap. The waves peak about 70 metres out, where less adventurous riders wait, and run in for 30-40 metres before breaking. Body surfers catch waves mounting inshore, farther north of the point. The cliffs, cut by angled vehicle tracks and railed footpaths from the coast road at Seaford, recede to the south at Moana and the water is clear of reefs. Since short surfboards became fashionable the waves bending into the little bay here have been regarded

as the best for competition in the Adelaide area. Moana was the venue for the national surf life-saving championships in 1982. It remains little developed, however, with only one store and a take-away food bar serving a caravan park.

Maslin Beach, the first in Australia where nudity was officially permitted, has an unpromising approach. The turn-off from the Main South Road is marked by a sand mining works, and the road as it nears the beach skirts Willunga Council's rubbish dump. A sign at the dump warns that the 'reserve for clad and unclad bathing' is not reached for a further 800 metres, and that 'unclad persons outside the reserve shall be prosecuted'. The warning is repeated at a car park 300 metres on. Would-be nudists trudge 500 metres more with their clothes on, until green marker posts signal their freedom to peel off.

Honeycombed cliffs of red, yellow, deep orange and dark brown rock shield the little beach, which draws big crowds in summer.

Only 7 km inland from Maslin Beach is McLaren Vale, the main centre of the Southern Vales winemaking district. Wineries and cellars concentrated here and at McLaren Flat, 5 km east, encourage tastings at almost any time of day. Many wineries also offer inspection tours at certain hours, or by appointment. Seaview, 6 km north of McLaren Vale, has an animal sanctuary opposite the entrance to keep children amused, and the winery interior is ornamented by fine paintings and wood carvings.

A network of roads and houses is gradually encroaching on farmland beside the Onkaparinga River, on the far southern fringe of Adelaide

Wheatfields surround the old copper-mining town of Moonta, just east of Port Hughes and the seaside resort of Moonta Bay; the bay shores curve north-west towards Wallaroo

Yorke Peninsula

South-westerly swells battering the toe-like extremity of Yorke Peninsula have fashioned the region's most arresting coastal scenery. Towering, sheer-sided limestone cliffs face Spencer Gulf and Investigator Strait. Wave-cut platforms and boulders of harder rock lie at the feet of rugged headlands, embracing unspoiled sandy beaches. Behind are low-lying dunes, salt marshes and saline lakes which for almost a century have been scraped to provide gypsum for plaster and cement manufacture. The coastline and more than 6000 hectares of the hinterland—excluding three lakes where gypsum mining continues—have been protected since 1970 by

the declaration of Innes National Park, principally to preserve the habitat of the rare western whipbird. Unsealed roads and tracks from Stenhouse Bay lead to three developed camping grounds and to bush camping sites. Expert surfers find good waves in Pondalowie and Formby Bays, but the beaches are unpatrolled and conditions are often too rough for novices. Sheltered anchorages and full boating facilities are available at Stenhouse Bay and Marion Bay.

Routes down each side of the peninsula, from Port Wakefield or Port Broughton, are sprinkled with resort townships, most of them based on old wheat-shipping or mining ports. Holiday facili-

ties at Ardrossan, where a deep-water wharf has been newly built for the bulk handling of dolomite ore and grain, are especially popular with gulf fishermen. Port Julia has a jetty and a quiet beach. Port Vincent, sprawling round a sheltered bay, is the biggest resort on the eastern shore and caters for every aquatic pastime. Other safe beaches and boating facilities are found at Stansbury, Coobowie and the clifftop town of Edithburgh, which also has a pleasant rock pool. Edithburgh is the start of a scenic drive to Stenhouse Bay and the national park.

The main road cuts across the 'ankle' of the peninsula, through Yorketown and Warooka to

Hardwicke Bay and the fishing village of Port Turton. Sandy swimming beaches lie to the west at Corny Point and north at Bluff Beach, where fishing boats hang on davits high above the tide level. Port Victoria, shielded by Wardang Island and a jumble of reefs and islets, is noted for good boat or jetty fishing, as are Port Hughes and Moonta Bay. The town of Moonta, 3 km inland, is the most historically interesting on the peninsula. A century ago, after the discovery of rich deposits of copper nearby, it was the second-biggest settlement in South Australia. The small triangle formed by Moonta, Wallaroo and Kadina had 20 000 people. Most were Cornish miners, recruited in England, and the district promotes its 'little Cornwall' heritage with a festival every second May.

A number of old buildings in Moonta, including a 14-room school which once had more than 1000 pupils, have been turned into museums. Some of the mine workings have been restored for inspection by visitors who can wander at will among dumps of tailings and ruins of pit-head buildings. Wallaroo, where the copper smelters were sited, is dominated now by grain silos and a fertiliser works. However an expansive beach and excellent boating facilities make it a leading holiday centre.

WALLAROO (pop. 2043) west of Highway 1, 159 km from Adelaide (turn off 3 km north of Port Wakefield).
TRANSPORT: coach from Adelaide most days (2½ hrs).

STANSBURY-EDITHBURGH (pop. 839) south of Highway 1, 218 km from Adelaide (turn off for Wallaroo, then Yorketown).
TRANSPORT: coach from Adelaide most days (4 hrs).

WALLAROO												
	Jan	Feb	Mar	Apr	May	Jun	Jul	Aug	Sep	Oct	Nov	Dec
Rainfall mm	15	18	20	33	47	48	42	40	33	30	21	16
Rain days	3	3	3	6	9	11	11	11	9	7	5	4
Sunshine hrs	Summer 10 +			Autumn 6 +			Winter 4 +			Spring 8 +		

Dry salt lakes, mined for gypsum, lie behind the little boating settlement of Stenhouse Bay

A salute to the sea

NO CITY owes more to the ocean. Port Lincoln's huge harbour gave it pre-eminence in the export of South Australian meat and grain. Its fishing fleet, the nation's biggest, fosters a vigorous industry. Water sport opportunities attract a flood of free-spending visitors through a long tourist season. The community acknowledges its debt happily, in a style all its own. Where else would beauty contestants vie to be called 'Miss Tunarama'?

Port Lincoln's permanent population of 12 000 is doubled during the late-January Australia Day weekend. The Tunarama Festival, established early in the 1960s, used to coincide with the start of the tuna fishing season, but that has now come forward to November. The Adelaide-Port Lincoln yacht race is timed to finish at the height of the festivities, which grow more varied and inventive by the year. A recent highlight has been the 'world championship of tuna tossing'. Beefy men compete to see who can hurl a frozen tuna the greatest distance. Fish are contributed by the family firm of the strongest man of all, 1984 Olympic weightlifting champion Dean Lukin.

Aside from its organised merriment and the high excitement of some excellent big-game fishing, the district offers a rare diversity of more quiet enjoyment. The vast expanse of Boston Bay allows safe boating under sail or power, and a big scenic cruise launch tours the harbour. It lands day-trippers on Boston Island, a sheep station since the 1840s, with a slab cottage of that era still standing. Holidaymakers can rent a more modern homestead and have the island to themselves.

Easy car excursions from the city take in arresting coastal scenery in Lincoln and Coffin Bay National Parks. Whalers' Way, skirting the very tip of Eyre Peninsula, passes through a flora and fauna reserve and also has remarkable shoreline formations including spectacular crevasses and blowholes.

Tuna come ashore by the tonne

Immortalisation on Japanese television awaits a Tunarama tossing entrant

Port Lincoln and the vast expanse of Boston Bay

Low, wind-rippled dunes fringe Sleaford Mere Conservation Park, one of the varied features of the Whalers' Way drive

Eroded limestone at Cape Wiles

Leisure centre, Lincoln Cove marina

Eyre Peninsula

Port Lincoln, the home base for Australia's biggest tuna-fishing fleet, is also a complete holiday city. Tourist facilities of all kinds are located close to the sheltered waters of Boston Bay—a harbour three times more spacious than Sydney's. Surfing beaches are less than 20 km away at Sleaford Bay, and nature-lovers are within a 20-minute drive of Lincoln National Park. Northern bays of the 17 000-hectare park are lightly wooded and grassy; for the more adventurous, the southern coastline presents a challenging terrain of exposed granite cliffs and slabs. A wide choice of campsites is offered, but no water. South-west of the park is Whalers' Way, a scenic drive along cliffs at the very tip of Eyre Peninsula. To the north-west, and quickly reached from Port Lincoln by Flinders Highway, is the slower-paced resort town of Coffin Bay. Beyond it is Coffin Bay National Park (29 000 hectares), which has car access to camping grounds and spectacular scenery at Yangie Bay, and to a good surfing beach next to Point Avoid. Coach tours from Port Lincoln include many unspoiled sections of the ocean coast, and a cruise boat shows visitors the sights of Boston Bay. The advantages of this harbour led to expectations that it would be the site of South Australia's capital, but doubts about the fertility of the semi-arid peninsula persuaded the colonisers to choose Adelaide. Port Lincoln was settled only three years later, in 1839, and eventually flourished on wool and grain exports. Now it is also a major outlet for frozen or canned fish, prawns and crayfish.

Whyalla, the leading city on the peninsula, is dominated by steelworks, shipyards—now defunct—and other heavy industry founded on iron ore quarried from the Middleback Ranges inland. But it has developed an extensive tourist industry to take advantage of its position at the eastern entrance to the region. Boating facilities and a pleasant beach lie within 10 minutes' walk

Port Lincoln's big commercial jetty spears into the glassy waters of Boston Bay, cut by the wakes of pleasure craft and busy tuna boats

of the city centre. The seafront reserve has a cara-van park, picnic grounds and a small zoo. Arid saltbush plains near the airport are occupied by a wildlife park including a reptile house and a walk-through aviary. Lincoln Highway next meets the coast at Cowell, behind the almost-landlocked waters of Franklin Harbour. The township, a quiet base for boating, fishing and safe swimming, is distinguished by having Aus-tralia's only jade factory, which visitors are wel-come to inspect. The jade is mined in the Mount Gerharty district, about 15 km to the north. Much of it is exported: some of New Zealand's Maori-style greenstone souvenirs, for example, are fashioned from Cowell jade. Farther south on Lincoln Highway, there are smaller seaside re-sorts at regular intervals. Arno Bay, Port Neill, Tumby Bay and Louth Bay all claim their share of holidaymakers, drawn by good boating and fishing opportunities.

Western shores of the peninsula, facing the Great Australian Bight, are virtually unpop-ulated between Coffin Bay and Elliston. Flinders Highway runs well inland to avoid a mountain-ous coast. Elliston enjoys some popularity among surfers. North to Venus Bay, a cliffed coastal plat-form is pitted with limestone caves. Among the most interesting are the Talia Caves, 6 km off the highway by a gravel road. A drive of about 50 km on unsealed roads, west through Calca or south from Streaky Bay, leads to Point Labatt and the only permanent colony of sea lions on the Aus-tralian mainland. Streaky Bay is a well-appointed holiday town, particularly favoured by boat fishermen for its deep, all-weather anchorage—the best between Port Lincoln and Albany, WA. Its port and harbour waters were used as locations for the film *Blue Fin*. Smoky Bay, a quieter resort also enjoyed by fishermen, has a camping and caravan ground on the water-front, next to a jetty and boat ramp.

WHYALLA (pop. 29 962) on Lincoln Highway 398 km from Adelaide.
TRANSPORT: coach Adelaide-Whyalla daily (6 hrs); flights daily.

COWELL (pop. 626) on Lincoln Highway 509 km from Adelaide.
TRANSPORT: coach Adelaide-Cowell daily (7½ hrs).

PORT LINCOLN (pop. 10 675) on Lincoln and Flin-ders Highways 675 km from Adelaide.
TRANSPORT: coach Adelaide-Port Lincoln daily (10 hrs); flights daily.

PORT LINCOLN												
	Jan	Feb	Mar	Apr	May	Jun	Jul	Aug	Sep	Oct	Nov	Dec
Maximum C°	26	25	24	22	19	17	16	16	18	20	22	23
Minimum C°	16	16	15	13	11	10	8	8	9	11	13	14
Rainfall mm	14	15	19	37	57	74	78	67	49	35	23	18
Humidity %	54	56	58	58	65	67	66	65	62	59	57	56
Rain days	4	4	5	10	14	16	18	18	13	11	7	5
Sunshine hrs	Summer 9+			Autumn 5+			Winter 3+			Spring 6+		

A jumble of low islands frame Franklin Harbour, giving perfect protection to Cowell's boating waters

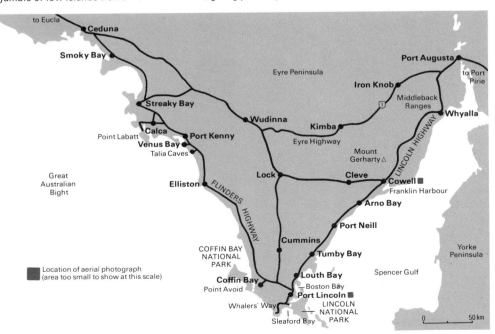

Location of aerial photograph
(area too small to show at this scale)

Gateway to the Nullarbor

EASTERN bays of the Great Australian Bight are more than mere resting places before or after a wearying journey across the Nullarbor Plain. Ceduna and its neighbouring seaside villages are establishing themselves as holiday destinations in their own right, with good opportunities for maritime pastimes and sightseeing.

The peak season is August-November, after chilly winter storms have ceased and before fierce summer heat arrives from the deserts inland. Sailboats and private fishing craft share sheltered waters with sizeable commercial fleets. Around Murat Bay at Ceduna, inviting lawns fringe the shores of peaceful bathing beaches. Port facilities for bulk-handling grain, salt and gypsum and for processing the fishing catch, are 3 km removed at Thevenard.

From Penong, an hour's drive west, an unsealed road leads about 20 km to Point Sinclair and Cactus Beach, where dedicated surfers carry in their supplies and camp in the dunes. They rate the three powerful 'breaks' off Cactus—two turning left and one right—as the best board-riding surf in Australia. However, huge white pointer sharks are often seen.

Farther west the vast shelf of the Nullarbor reaches all the way to the Bight. It ends with dramatic abruptness in vertical limestone cliffs up to 75 metres high, undercut and boulder-strewn at their bases. The coastal strip behind this forbidding shore is dry, but not a desert. Thick scrubs of mulga and stunted eucalypts are sustained by a rainfall that can be as high as Adelaide's. The reason for the dryness is a lack of surface water—the rain sinks quickly through the porous limestone.

Stockpiling gypsum at Ceduna

Thevenard's jetty takes deep-draught shipping

Expert board riders regard the surf off Cactus Beach as Australia's best, and make extraordinary pilgrimages to get to it

The Overseas Telecommunication Commission's satellite ground station, 34 km northwest of Ceduna, is open on weekdays

Dazzling dunes frame the Pink Lakes, near Penong

Lilliput lives on

WRITING *Gulliver's Travels* in 1717, Jonathan Swift put his amazing islands in the silliest place he could imagine—off the southern coast of 'New Holland'. No Englishman had seen the area, but Dutch navigators had charted it. Swift's book included a map showing two of the real islands of Nuyts Archipelago, off Ceduna. Their names are shown as St Pieter and St Francot. Now we call them St Peter and St Francis. It seems certain that Swift had these islands in mind for Lemuel Gulliver's adventures among the Lilliputians.

He placed Lilliput, where the people were less than a handspan tall, and Blefescu, the neighbouring island where Gulliver fled, northwest of Van Diemen's Land (Tasmania). That is the correct bearing for Nuyts Archipelago. But Swift mistook the latitude recorded by the Dutch—32° S. He made his figure 30° 2′. So he unwittingly put Lilliput on the fringe of the Great Victoria Desert, near the 1950s nuclear bomb testing site at Maralinga.

The chart from an early edition of Gulliver's Travels

Tasmanian coast

The stormy south and west coasts of Tasmania are part of one of the world's last great wildernesses— an area that is difficult to reach, but rewarding for those who make the effort to go there. Even those parts of the island's coast that are easier to visit remain largely unexploited, despite fine beaches and a challenging surf.

Looking west from over the Arthur Range in Southwest National Park, a maze of silent inlets reaches towards the sea

Table Cape, Wynyard

Maria Island tests bushwalkers

Dolerite clusters, Tasman Peninsula

King Island

Flinders Island

BASS STRAIT

Furneaux Group

Smithton
Marrawah
Stanley
Boat Harbour Beach
Wynyard
Burnie
Ulverstone
Devonport
Greens Beach
Port Dalrymple
Port Sorell
Bridport
Binalong Bay
Launceston
Scamander
Mersey River
River Tamar
Bicheno

TASMANIA

Strahan
Macquarie Harbour

Freycinet Peninsula

Maria Island

River Derwent

Hobart
Forestier Peninsula
Eaglehawk Neck
Tasman Peninsula
Port Arthur
Bruny Island
Adventure Bay

SOUTHERN OCEAN

Port Davey

Catamaran
Cox Bight
Cloudy Bay

TASMAN SEA

Contrasts of challenge and ease

AUSTRALIA'S smallest state is not one island, but a central island surrounded by more than 100 others, and bounded by a coastline which changes character with the points of the compass. The peaks of mountain ranges, once linking Tasmania to mainland Australia, became isolated pieces of land when water levels rose at the end of the last ice age, around 8000 years ago. In Bass Strait the islands remained separate, but in the south-east drifting sand built up narrow tombolos which joined islands and created peninsulas.

The state's biggest country towns—Burnie, Ulverstone, Devonport and George Town—share the north coast with smaller ports that thrived in the 19th century but lost their trade after the improvement of road transport and have become popular seaside resorts. Some are surrounded by extensive national parks. Inland, farming communities flourish on fertile plains, watered by rivers flowing from highlands 40 km or so away. The region is latticed with well-maintained roads for day trips through orchards and rolling pastures. From the foothills of the central plateau, steep roads wind up to mountain-top lookouts and parks stretching south into uninhabited sections of the island. The north coast, too, is a popular starting point.

The granite mass of The Hazards rises 300 m on Freycinet Peninsula

For many, the first experience of Tasmania is at Devonport, where the vehicle and passenger ferry *Empress of Australia* arrives three times a week after a 14-hour overnight crossing from Melbourne.

Devonport is Tasmania's largest seaside town—Hobart and Launceston are both river ports. Mersey Bluff, a promontory at the entrance to the wide Mersey River, is Devonport's popular waterfront recreation area with sheltered beaches, picnic grounds and a caravan park. Tasmania's surfing coast reaches east and west of Devonport, from Somerset to Low Head at the entrance to Port Dalrymple. Powerful westerly swells through Bass Strait produce fine board-riding waves. Lifesaving clubs patrol at Somerset, Burnie, Penguin, Ulverstone, Devonport and Low Head.

Tasmania's eastern shores are promoted as the Sunshine Coast by resort proprietors. This coast is screened from rain by the central highlands and has the lowest falls on the island. Its climate is also milder because it is reached by warm currents flowing down the east coast of the mainland. Their meeting with colder southern waters creates a feeding zone where fish are prolific. Most Tasmanian tourist literature highlights trout fishing in streams and mountain lakes, but saltwater anglers find plenty of scope from or near the shore, and some commercial fishing boats are available for deep-sea charters. A peculiarity of the eastern seaboard is its shore platforms, which make excellent casting positions with level ground to retreat over if freak waves threaten.

The proportion of the Tasmanian coast occupied by beaches increases from the south-western to the north-eastern corner. Small pocket beaches, caught between the high cliffs of the south-west, are replaced by long, deep sweeps of sand—the result of longshore movements influenced by strong southerly waves. The west coast has wide dune sheets but its ocean beaches have dangerous rips. Swimmers and anglers prefer sheltered waters at the mouths of rivers and around the old mining port of Strahan, on Macquarie Harbour. Remote fishing settlements scattered along the rest of the west coast are reached by rough tracks and have no facilities. Western Tasmania's exposure to the gales of the Roaring Forties, and the high rainfall trapped by its mountainous interior, have deterred settlement. But the great rivers of the highlands provide the state with one of its most exploitable assets—hydro-electricity.

Temperatures seldom reach extremes on any part of the coast because of the tempering effect of the surrounding oceans. Towards the end of a long hot spell, with northerly air masses heating further as they pass over the island, readings in the high 30s are sometimes recorded in the south-east. The same region is also the most exposed to the cold southerlies of winter depressions.

Mountains meet the sea on the coast to the east of Rocky Cape

Port Arthur on the Tasman Peninsula is a peaceful reminder of a brutal past

The Nut, a weathered volcanic plug, towers above the town of Stanley

The smooth white sands of Boat Harbour entice many summer visitors to Tasmania's north coast

The twilight of the first Tasmanians

TASMANIA's Aborigine population—perhaps 1200 before European settlement began in 1803—was reduced to fewer than 300 in 30 years. Government efforts to round them up and confine them in one area started in 1828, to encourage sales of farm land. This campaign quickly revealed that the native race was dying out. The 'Black Line' sweep of 1830, a costly two-month operation in which a cordon of troops and armed volunteers advanced on three fronts to drive east coast Aborigines on to Tasman Peninsula, had a farcical result. Instead of tribes numbering hundreds, only a man and a boy were flushed out—and the man escaped.

A bricklayer-turned-missionary, George Robinson, had more success with his own round-up methods. As superintendent of Aborigines on Bruny Island, he learned their language and customs. Year after year, Robinson took parties of Bruny Islanders to help him track mainland Aborigines and persuade them to go to his mission. There, with evangelistic zeal, he insisted on clothing people who had survived the rigors of the Tasmanian high country near-naked. His converts kept their garments on even when soaking wet, heightening their vulnerability to introduced diseases such as influenza, pneumonia and tuberculosis. The death rate was appalling, but Robinson continued recruitment.

In 1831 he chose Flinders Island as the future home for all Tasmanian Aborigines. The first families were moved there the following year, to a settlement called Wybalenna. Robinson took over as superintendent of a community of about 200 people in 1835, the year of his last round-up expedition. By 1847 only 44 of those people were alive, and all the females were past child-bearing age. Wybalenna was abandoned and the survivors were taken to Oyster Cove, south of Hobart. Sickly old men and women, the only known full-blooded representatives of their race, languished in convict-built barracks beside mudflats and salt marshes. The last to die, in 1876, was Truganini, a Bruny Island woman born in the first year of European settlement.

The last of Tasmania's full-blooded Aborigines languished and died in convict-built barracks

Stanley and Boat Harbour Beach

Circular Head, the massive round headland rising abruptly from the sea to the east of Stanley, is widely called the Nut. From the wharf and grey port sheds at the southern base of the Nut, the small farming and fishing settlement stretches across a narrow neck of land from Tatlows Beach to Godfreys Beach, a wide, flat foreshore backed by grassy picnic grounds, tyre swings and log see-saws. A track from opposite the post office takes a steep, winding course to the flat top of the headland, with sheep grazing on the slopes below its granite crown.

Stanley was founded in 1826, the first year of settlement in north-west Tasmania. It retains many fine old buildings, some of which are being restored. The Plough Inn, built in 1842, was a licensed hotel from 1854 to 1876. It is now privately occupied, but has a public section refurnished with period pieces and a cider bar, open 10.00-17.00 daily. Among the heavy bluestone buildings on the town's waterfront is a small weatherboard house, preserved as the birthplace

Circular Head (left) separates Stanley's two beaches; Sisters Beach (below) is reached from Boat Harbour through Rocky Cape National Park

of Joseph Lyons, Prime Minister of Australia from 1932 to 1939. Under the Nut's western face, an old stone building with a rusting iron roof was the general store of the Van Diemen's Land Company, formed in London in the 1820s. Its allocation of land, in an area previously untouched by Europeans, was parcelled out to tenant farmers. Smallholdings, now privately owned, are still characteristic of north-west Tasmania. The Van Diemen's Land Company retains one farm, Woolnorth, near Cape Grim,

where pioneer buildings stand among modern machinery. The property is open to visitors on guided coach tours leaving Burnie on Mondays from January to April.

The rugged section of coastline from Circular Head past Rocky Cape to Table Cape, near Wynyard, is most conveniently explored in small boats. The sheltered bays, with pockets of white sand and water-worn caves at sea level, are not easily accessible from land. Boats can be launched from ramps at Stanley, at Smithton to

the south-west of Circular Head, or at Wynyard. Firm sand for launching can usually be found at the resort settlement of Boat Harbour Beach. The road from Bass Highway to the beach snakes down a green cliff, overlooking Jacobs Boat Harbour and backed by rich sheep and cattle pastures. Private houses line the slopes of the bay, some having the brilliant white beach sand as their front yards. Orange, ochre and black rocks break up the beach into a variety of textures and colours. The resort is popular with divers and underwater photographers for the clarity of its water and the diversity of marine life close to shore. Equipment for scuba enthusiasts can be hired in the town. The main beach is protected by Shelter Point, a low projection enjoyed by fishermen and naturalists exploring the rock pools exposed at low tide.

Sisters Beach, 2 km long, is located in a valley between the hills of Rocky Cape National Park, a short drive west of Boat Harbour Beach. By the east bank of Sisters Creek is a spacious park with tall pine trees and paperbarks shading a gas barbecue and picnic grounds. In summer the creek mouth is a popular swimming spot for children and there is a constructed boat ramp at the northern end of the beach. Upstream the creek flows past Birdland Nature Park, where bushes and trees have been planted to attract native birds, particularly honeyeaters. Walking tracks lead through groves of banksias, ferns and coastal heath. The park's showroom has a superb display of bird photographs and there is an aviary housing Australian species. The park is open Monday to Saturday 10.00-17.00 and Sunday 14.00-17.00.

Three hours should be allowed for the walk from Sisters Beach to Rocky Cape, through untouched bush noted for its spring displays of wildflowers. Tracks branching off the main trail are well-defined and signposts give walking times to lookouts, a waterfall and caves along the coast, reached by paths worn by generations of anglers. There is no camping in the park, but a wealth of pleasant, shaded picnic spots.

STANLEY (pop. 603) on Stanley Highway 133 km from Devonport.
TRANSPORT: coach Hobart-Launceston-Devonport-Wynyard most days (5½ hrs); bus Wynyard-Boat Harbour-Stanley most days.

BOAT HARBOUR BEACH north of Bass Highway 86 km from Devonport (turn off 2 km west of Boat Harbour).
TRANSPORT: as for Stanley; none beyond Boat Harbour.

	STANLEY											
	Jan	Feb	Mar	Apr	May	Jun	Jul	Aug	Sep	Oct	Nov	Dec
Maximum C°	21	21	20	18	15	13	13	13	14	16	18	19
Minimum C°	13	13	12	10	8	7	6	6	7	8	10	11
Rainfall mm	42	46	49	75	93	107	115	104	84	87	66	61
Humidity %	63	65	67	72	74	78	78	75	72	69	66	66
Rain days	11	10	13	16	20	20	22	22	19	18	16	14
Sunshine hrs	Summer 7 +			Autumn 4 +			Winter 3 +			Spring 6 +		

Port Sorell and Asbestos Range Park

Port Sorell, founded in 1826, was the first centre of shipping on Tasmania's rugged and heavily timbered north coast. During the early days of settlement, when farming properties were most easily reached by water, small ports were established at some of the many river mouths along the coast, where protection was afforded from the rough seas of Bass Strait. Ports upriver, such as Ulverstone, George Town and particularly Devonport, have eclipsed them as commercial harbours and centres of population. As early as 1916, Port Sorell residents recognised the decline in the town's commercial importance and decided to promote the area as a resort, attracting tourists to its extensive sheltered inlet, sandy shores and wooded countryside.

On the north-west shores of the inlet, Port Sorell and its smaller satellite, Hawley Beach, are lined with narrow beaches shelving gently from deep boating channels. From Taroona Point to Port Sorell, wide expanses of shallow water lie off the beach and dry at low tide into hectares of rippled sand, strewn with groups of boulders covered with orange lichen. The concrete boat ramp at Taroona Point leads into a small, rocky bay opposite Griffiths Point in Asbestos Range National Park. The ramp at Port

Sorell is a pebbly road across more than 100 metres of beach sand, ending at a slope into the inlet, where tractors launch and retrieve trailer-towed boats. A short distance to the south is the town's jetty, an old plank structure popular for rod and handline fishing. A big pool dug in the tidal flats nearby provides a popular swimming hole for children, away from the danger of powerful tidal currents which flow through the channel just off the jetty beach. A second paddling pool has been constructed near the major boat-mooring area in Muddy Creek, on the town's southern border. At low tide yachts, motor launches and fishing boats sit on the creek's muddy bottom, supported by posts on either side, while birds feeding in the mud are joined by anglers searching for bait. Navigation upstream is hindered by a footbridge which

Most of Port Sorell's wide inlet is shallow; sands east of the little town beach dry out at low tide

crosses to holiday shacks on the south side of the creek and bushwalking tracks along the inlet shores to Squeaking Point.

Boating channels in Port Sorell are well-defined by buoys and marking posts, and many arms branch off the main body of water for cruising and fishing boats. Light craft can be taken about 5 km up the Rubicon River, to the south, or beached on the north-eastern shores of the inlet, close to picnic and camping grounds in Asbestos Range National Park. The park can also be reached by a good gravel road along the eastern shores of the port. The Asbestos Range extends into the park near Badger Head, but to the west falls away to low-lying, lightly wooded land which was farmed until 1974. Forester kangaroos, re-introduced to the area, have found good grazing on the former farm paddocks, which are being allowed to revegetate with natural bush. The homestead, Springlawn, is now the park rangers' headquarters, housing a visitor centre with displays on the park and its flora and fauna. Untouched areas of the park comprise a variety of habitats—tidal mudflats, woodland, heath and a lagoon—which support a diverse plant and animal population and provide plenty of scope for wildlife photography and bird watching. Bushwalkers have easy tracks in the low-lying parts of the park and a clearly marked trail climbing to Archers Knob and along to Badger Head, with sweeping coastal views from points atop the Asbestos Range.

PORT SORELL (pop. 859) north of Bass Highway 19 km from Devonport (turn off eastbound 4 km from Devonport, westbound at Sassafras) or 79 km from Launceston (turn off Frankford road at Harford).
TRANSPORT: coach Hobart-Launceston-Devonport most days (4 hrs); bus Devonport-Port Sorell Fridays.

Port Dalrymple and Bridport

Poor soils and wide bands of heath-covered dunes have discouraged agriculture along Tasmania'a north-eastern coast, leaving it sparsely populated except for a few fishing villages tucked into sheltered bays. Now their sandy beaches, protected from the heavy westerly winds and swells of Bass Strait, attract increasing holiday traffic. Only Bridport is highly developed as a resort, however. Other little settlements such as Weymouth, Beechford, Lulworth and Bellingham have little for visitors beyond basic shop supplies and petrol. Most holiday accommodation in the region is concentrated around Port Dalrymple, the wide estuary which funnels into the River Tamar. The river, navigable by pleasure craft, tourist cruisers and even ocean-going freighters and ferries, winds upstream to Launceston, the state's second-biggest city. Shores of the port and river are shared by fishing and boating resorts and residential townships, with pockets of heavy industry at Inspection Head and Bell Bay, where Australia's first aluminium smelter was built. George Town, founded in 1811, is the main commercial and residential centre. Beauty Point is the home port of the professional fishing fleet. To the south, Gravelly Beach and Windermere are popular for boat and jetty angling and Rosevears is a base for speedboat racing and water-skiing.

Holiday homes are strung along Port Dalrymple's eastern shores north of George Town to Low Head, where the Tamar pilot

West Head, at the entrance to Port Dalrymple, shields Greens Beach from Bass Strait gales

station has been manned since 1835. Photographers delight in the sparkling white building, set beside a stone-walled boat harbour. Low Head has patrolled surfing at East Beach and sheltered swimming in Lagoon Bay, but few facilities for tourists. They are better catered for across the estuary at Greens Beach. Its small resident population is swollen in summer by crowds who find the spot a pleasant retreat for holidays, or a day's swimming and picnicking on parkland between the golf links and the beach dunes. The West Head road runs north of the settlement to the boundary of Asbestos Range National Park, and continues through groves of casuarinas and paperbarks to shaded picnic grounds. A well-defined track leads downhill from the car park to a small, sheltered cove with

a patch of fine sand surrounded by massive grey boulders. Walking trails branch out through the park's heathland to the tip of West Head and the long stretch of Badger Beach. Great fingers of sand, reaching hundreds of metres inland and stripped of protective vegetation, indicate the power of winds to which the beach is exposed. There is no camping at West Head, but sites are available at three serviced areas near picnic grounds and popular beaches in the western section of the park, reached by good gravel roads from Port Sorell or from 4 km south of Kelso.

North of Bridport a narrow, wooded seafront park, the Granite Point Coastal Reserve, lines rocky shores. Picnic areas with barbecues overlook Lades Beach, a popular swimming spot which often produces waves suitable for board-

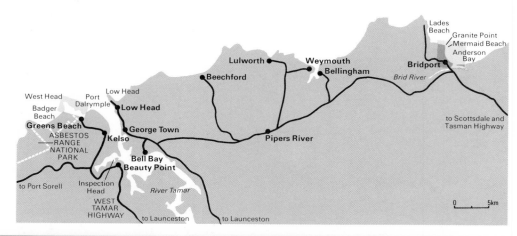

Bridport has expanded from its boat harbour, inside the shallow Brid River, north to Granite Point and a wooded reserve strip backing Lades Beach

riders. South Eastman Beach, at the centre of town, is a pretty little bay with a wide rock platform, a sheltered rotunda and a mass of casuarinas above shores strewn with smooth boulders. To the north, fishing boats moor near a long line of posts which once held a jetty. Bridport's caravan park occupies the entire strip of beachfront land between the mouth of the Brid River and the Granite Point Coastal Reserve, with a series of pocket beaches breaking the rocky coast. At Mermaid Beach a clear pool surrounded by smooth folds of rock catches the swells at high tide and provides shallow water for children. A launching ramp gives access to the sheltered waters of Anderson Bay and restoration of the deep-water jetty is proposed. Com-

mercial fishing is centred around a boat harbour on the southern banks of the Brid River, where a factory processes crayfish for export. A nearby trout hatchery produces eggs and fry for mainland rivers, and also exports fully grown fish. Sea and river fishing are popular sports around Bridport. Blackmans Lagoon, Waterhouse Lake and Little Forester River, all within easy reach, are natural feeding grounds for trout.

GREENS BEACH north of West Tamar Highway 101 km from Devonport, 58 km from Launceston (turn off at Beaconsfield).
TRANSPORT: bus Launceston-Beaconsfield weekdays; bus Beaconsfield-Greens Beach weekdays.

🏠 🏤 ▲ 🛢 🚽 🐚 ⚓ 🛥 🛝

BRIDPORT (pop. 885) north of Tasman Highway 91 km from Launceston (turn off at Scottsdale).
TRANSPORT: bus Launceston-Scottsdale with connecting bus Scottsdale-Bridport most days.

🏕 🏠 🏤 ▲ 🛢 🚽 🍴 🍽 🐚 ⚓ 🛥 🛝

	BRIDPORT											
	Jan	Feb	Mar	Apr	May	Jun	Jul	Aug	Sep	Oct	Nov	Dec
Maximum C°	22	23	21	19	16	14	13	14	14	17	19	20
Minimum C°	13	13	11	10	7	5	4	5	6	7	10	10
Rainfall mm	43	47	38	68	81	87	89	86	67	71	53	53
Humidity %	69	74	62	69	74	74	76	73	69	67	69	68
Rain days	7	7	8	11	13	14	16	16	14	13	10	9
Sunshine hrs	Summer 8 +			Autumn 5 +			Winter 3 +			Spring 6 +		

Forested hills surround Grants Lagoon, behind the little beach settlement of Binalong Bay

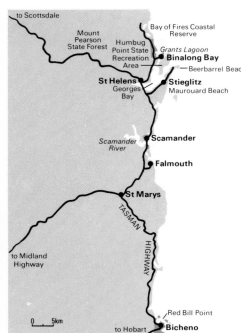

Scamander's surf beach bars a fine boating river

Binalong Bay to Bicheno

From the scrub-covered summit of Humbug Point State Recreation Area, a roadside lookout commands views over the neck of Georges Bay, with St Helens, the well-appointed hub of east coast resort activity, at its head. Coastal reserves surround Binalong Bay in the north and stretch beyond Scamander in the south. The small settlement at Binalong Bay, backed by the hills of Mount Pearson State Forest, is tucked between rocky shores and the sandy sweep of its beach. Below a cluster of holiday cottages the beach is

cut by a concrete jetty, a public boat ramp and the outlet of Grants Lagoon. Shallow-draught boats find enough clearance for sailing and canoeing on the lagoon, and the uncluttered waters are suitable for swimming. A good gravel road leads north around camping grounds on the western shores of the lagoon and skirts the narrow Bay of Fires Coastal Reserve, passing beachfront camping areas and dune-sheltered lagoons in the park's northern section.

On the southern shores of Georges Bay, St

Helens Point State Recreation Area has a launching ramp and camping grounds beneath the towering headland lighthouse and lookout point. Unsealed roads and walking tracks reach around the point's rocky shores to surfing spots at Beerbarrel Beach and the northern section of Maurouard Beach, which curves southward below the bare, sandy Peron Dunes. An authorised dune buggy course takes up 4 sq km of the dunes just east of Stieglitz.

At Scamander, the river estuary dividing the holiday settlement becomes a wide wading pool as it spreads over the shallow flats on the ocean side of the highway bridge. Children play in the clear water and anglers cast into the river channel from banks in the shadow of the bridge, while the noise of overhead traffic competes with the continuous roar of nearby surf. The Scamander River is navigable by shallow-draught boats

Boats shelter in the Gulch, a channel between the Bicheno headland and rocky nearshore islands

from a launching ramp near the town to trout-fishing waters in its upper reaches.

Resort motels sprawling around swimming pools and restaurants are the mainstay of Bicheno's tourist trade, while commercial fishing thrives on the lucrative crayfish market. Two processing plants deal with the catch of about 20 boats based in a snug, all-weather port at the Gulch, where a ramp and ample parking space also cater for pleasure boats. Using pots, rings or hand nets, amateurs can catch crays in nearshore waters or from the rocky foreshores around Bicheno. The limit is ten a day, with a licence obtained from any Fisheries Department office or the local police station. The town's professional fishermen often take visitors on early-morning runs to haul in pots set the previous day, and two launches offer game-fishing charters. Small coves with strips of sandy beach north and south of Bicheno's boating harbours are enclosed by rocky promontories and are popular with surfers and sunbathers. Walks around the rocks, from Red Bill Point past the Blowhole to steeply shelving Rice Beach, are easy at low tide.

The Sea Life Centre, open daily on the shores of Waubs Bay, has 28 tanks displaying species found in local waters. A prized exhibit is a deep-water crab of the biggest-bodied species in the world, *Pseudocarcinus gigas*. The carapace of the one on show is 450 mm wide, and specimens have been found up to 600 mm. Only the Japanese majid spider crab, which has extraordinarily long legs, is bigger overall.

BINALONG BAY east of Tasman Highway 179 km from Launceston, 275 km from Hobart (turn off at St Helens).
TRANSPORT: coach Launceston-St Helens most days (3 hrs); coach Hobart-St Helens daily (6 hrs); none beyond St Helens, 11 km away.

SCAMANDER on Tasman Highway 185 km from Launceston, 247 km from Hobart.
TRANSPORT: coach Hobart-Scamander daily (6 hrs); coach Launceston-Scamander most days (3 hrs).
YOUTH HOSTEL: 1 km north of river, open year-round.

BICHENO (pop. 674) on Tasman Highway 250 km from Launceston, 182 km from Hobart.
TRANSPORT: coach Launceston-St Marys most days (5 hrs); bus St Marys-Bicheno most days; bus Hobart-Swansea connecting with Bicheno bus most days (6½ hrs).
YOUTH HOSTEL: 3 km north, open year-round.

BICHENO												
	Jan	Feb	Mar	Apr	May	Jun	Jul	Aug	Sep	Oct	Nov	Dec
Maximum C°	21	22	21	19	16	14	14	14	16	18	18	20
Minimum C°	12	13	12	11	9	7	6	7	7	8	10	11
Rainfall mm	47	62	59	64	63	67	54	50	41	57	55	65
Humidity %	69	69	66	60	64	68	65	66	63	68	66	68
Rain days	7	7	7	8	9	9	9	9	7	9	9	9
Sunshine hrs	Summer 8 +			Autumn 5 +			Winter 4 +			Spring 7 +		

Where all hell broke loose

TASMANIA has coastal rock forms never seen on the mainland. It is more than a matter of climate, or the behaviour of the sea. The differences stem from events far in the past. Geologically this is another country —with a history of awesome violence.

For hundreds of millions of years, the Australian land mass seems to have been one of the least disturbed in the world. Continental drift altered its position on the globe, and warping of the earth's crust pushed up mountain chains here and there. But the movements were gradual and gentle. If there were any changes on a truly cataclysmic scale, they happened too long ago to be traced.

Not so in Tasmania. Here, about 165 million years ago, there was a sudden, immense upheaval. Many geologists suppose that this literally earth-shattering event was linked with the start of the break-up of 'Gondwanaland', the southern supercontinent. Molten material from under the crust—magma—burst up into beds of sedimentary rock, wrenching

them in all directions. Lava flooded the central plateau and spilled down to what are now the southeastern shores.

Mainland volcanic eruptions, relatively small and isolated, came much later— within the past 25 million years. Cooling lava turned into basalt. But at the time of Tasmania's transformation, the chemical composition of magma was different. The lava became an exceptionally hard rock called dolerite. As it solidified in deep beds it shrank into columns. Seen today on the coast, most notably at the capes of the Tasman Peninsula, they jut from the ocean like clusters of giant needles.

Elsewhere the older rocks are exposed, deeply fractured and sometimes tilted at absurd angles from their original bedding planes. Ancient ice ages are recorded, too. Only in Tasmania are the effects of glaciers easy to see. Among the layers of sediments showing in wave-eroded cliff faces, there is often a belt of boulders, carried long ago from the inland heights in slowly creeping rivers of ice.

Old marine sediments, high and dry

Sea caves form in vertically cracked limestone at Cape Maurouard

Quartzite beds at Rocky Cape tilted almost vertically

Needles of dolerite, from lava that flowed 165 million years ago, defy the elements at Cape Raoul

Cracked sandstone, its joints emphasised by tidal erosion, forms Eaglehawk Neck's famed Tessellated Pavements

Freycinet National Park

The flanks of the Hazards mountains rise massive and imposing to four summits of bare red granite above the marshy neck which connects the rugged ranges of Freycinet Peninsula with the Tasmanian mainland. North of the Hazards, the holiday township of Coles Bay sits at the doorstep of Freycinet National Park, offering a wide range of accommodation, supplies for campers and launching ramps and a jetty for boating enthusiasts and anglers. Scuba tanks and lessons in skin-diving are available near the sheltered fishing jetty and a narrow track leads to Richardsons Beach, its brown sand strewn with shells from century-old Aboriginal middens piled in the dunes.

Just inside the boundary of the 11 000-hectare park, beyond the bridge over Mosquito Creek, a shady caravan park is tucked between Richardsons Beach and Ranger Creek, near the park headquarters. Campsites along the beach face through a mass of casuarinas and eucalypts to Coles Bay and the shallow, muddy waters of the creek mouth. Toward the Chateau, a private hotel within the park, tracks branch off to barbecues just behind Richardsons Beach before the road forks east to Cape Tourville lighthouse and a car park above the steep slopes and rocky shores of Sleepy Bay, a spot popular with skin-divers, picnickers and rock fishermen. The southern fork leads to a cluster of holiday shacks at the Fisheries, named after a whaling station which operated nearby early last century. Car parks dotted about the Fisheries mark the beginnings of walking tracks around and into the Hazards. Several sites are suitable for bush camping, but water is scarce at some of them in summer, so it is advisable to check with a ranger. From the car park nearest the Fisheries, a track strikes up a stream between the granite peaks of Mount Amos and Mount Mayson. Bared tree roots give bushwalkers some purchase on the steep slope. A lookout 30 minutes along the track, perched above a chasm, commands views over the gleaming waters of Wineglass Bay, the

Steep ridges of the Hazards challenge walkers between Coles Bay and the sheltered waters of Wineglass Bay

towering peaks of Mount Graham and 620-metre Mount Freycinet, and the township of Coles Bay. The track descending to the swimming beach of Wineglass Bay is an easy stroll after the steep lookout climb. The walk from the Fisheries takes 4-5 hours, returning around the southern and western slopes of Mount Mayson.

A longer walk, suitable for overnight camping trips, follows the western shores to Cooks Beach, then crosses undulating country to a campsite at Bryans Beach. At the northern end of Cooks Beach a branch turns inland, skirting the slopes of Mount Freycinet, which can be climbed anywhere from the East Freycinet Saddle to the Graham Col. The trail steepens abruptly after a gradual climb before reaching the 579-metre summit of Mount Graham and heading downhill along Quartzite Ridge to Wineglass Bay. Eucalypts, casuarinas, banksias and wattles form the peninsula's main tree cover, with thickets of tea-tree making the going hard off the beaten track. In spring more than 100 species of native orchid bloom in the park and the low, scrubby heath-land explodes with colourful wildflowers.

Schouten Island, off the southern end of Freycinet Peninsula, is uninhabited and was added to the national park in 1967. It can be reached only by private boat or chartered fishing boat from Coles Bay. Campsites are grouped around a permanent creek at the western end of Crocketts Bay. An old homestead—a relic of the island's days as a sheep station—is also available for visitor accommodation. Walking tracks are not marked, but the gently rolling terrain makes for easy hiking. A clearly visible geological fault line splits the island between granite and dolerite zones. The fault is marked by a sudden change in vegetation, from tall, heavy timber in the west to sparse, stunted trees and thorny scrub in the east.

COLES BAY south of Tasman Highway 201 km from Hobart (turn off 11 km south of Bicheno).
TRANSPORT: as for Bicheno, previous page.

Maria Island and Eaglehawk Neck

Eaglehawk Neck's ocean beach on Pirates Bay runs north to the Tessellated Pavements

Cement silos tower above the jetty in Darlington Bay, where ferries from the mainland resort of Triabunna arrive at Maria Island National Park. Just east of the small harbour, visitors pass deserted mills where clinker was ground into cement in the 1920s, and a storehouse built by convicts almost a century before. Darlington's prison compound, east of the harbour along a creekside track, was first occupied in 1825. Outshone by the success of the convict settlement at Port Arthur, it was abandoned in 1832. The buildings and a reservoir, which still supplies the town's water needs, remained unused until 1842, when convicts returned to the island under a probation scheme. The prison buildings were refurbished and new barracks built, but by the late 1840s the flow of convicts to Van Diemen's Land had begun to slacken and in 1850 Maria Island was once more abandoned. For two periods between 1884 and 1930 the island again came to life under the hand of an Italian business entrepreneur, Diego Bernacchi. Buildings were renovated for a second and third time, and the township bustled with a variety of optimistic industrial and rural activities.

Today's visitors to Maria Island can explore and picnic around the old township and follow short walking trails to Cape Boullanger, the Fossil Cliffs, and lookout points atop the twin rocky outcrops of Bishop and Clerk. Many of the old buildings, so often renovated, remain in good repair—unlike the neglected buildings of the younger and more famous Port Arthur. Others have been restored and turned to new uses. Convict barracks and kitchens are used by campers and groups of schoolchildren; rangers have converted the mess hall into a workshop and the commissariat houses a small museum. Camping grounds are found at Darlington and around Chinamans Bay, an 11 km walk to the south along a vehicle track which is also suitable for bicycles. The track is an easy walk through patches of dense scrub and open grassland once grazed by sheep. Low cliffs indented by small pocket beaches line the seaward part of a walk from Chinamans Bay across McRaes Isthmus to the rugged southern section of the island.

Eaglehawk Neck joins Forestier and Tasman Peninsulas, which have been cut from the mainland by a canal at Dunally to shorten the voyage to east coast waters for Hobart's fishing fleet. A chain of guard dogs tethered from shore to shore—and rumours of shark-infested waters put about by the colonial administration to deter escapes—gained the narrow isthmus a sinister repution during the convict occupation of Port Arthur. But there is no special threat of shark attack in the waters of Pirates Bay and the beach has become a popular haunt for surfers and swimmers. Most travellers to Port Arthur stop at Eaglehawk Neck to see the Tessellated Pavements—vertically cracked sandstone beds with the appearance of an intricately tiled mosaic. At the southern end of the bay the coast curves to form a sheltered haven for fishing and pleasure boats. In summer, commercial fishermen take offshore game-fishing charters from the haven's deep-water jetty. On the seaward side of the bay's southern hook, sandstone has been worn into the gigantic Tasman Arch; nearby, the sea thunders into the long tunnel of the Blowhole.

TRIABUNNA (pop. 924) on Tasman Highway 89 km from Hobart.
TRANSPORT: bus Hobart-Triabunna most days (2 hrs).

🛏 🏠 🍴 ⛺ ⛽ 🏪 🍴 🚉 ⛵ 〰 ⚓

MARIA ISLAND 20 km east of Triabunna.
TRANSPORT: launch Triabunna-Darlington daily October-May, other times by charter.

🏠 ⛺

EAGLEHAWK NECK on Arthur Highway 79 km from Hobart.
TRANSPORT: bus Hobart-Eaglehawk Neck daily.

🛏 🏪 🍴 ⚓

DARLINGTON												
	Jan	Feb	Mar	Apr	May	Jun	Jul	Aug	Sep	Oct	Nov	Dec
Rainfall mm	45	55	49	59	59	67	59	50	45	56	57	70
Rain days	8	8	9	10	10	11	11	12	10	11	11	10
Sunshine hrs	Summer 8 +			Autumn 5 +			Winter 4 +			Spring 7 +		

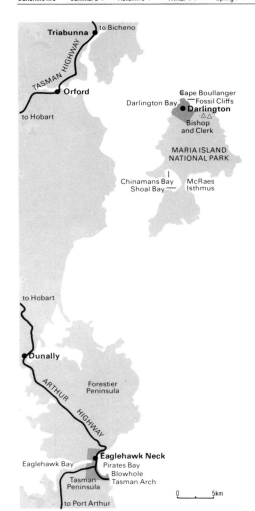

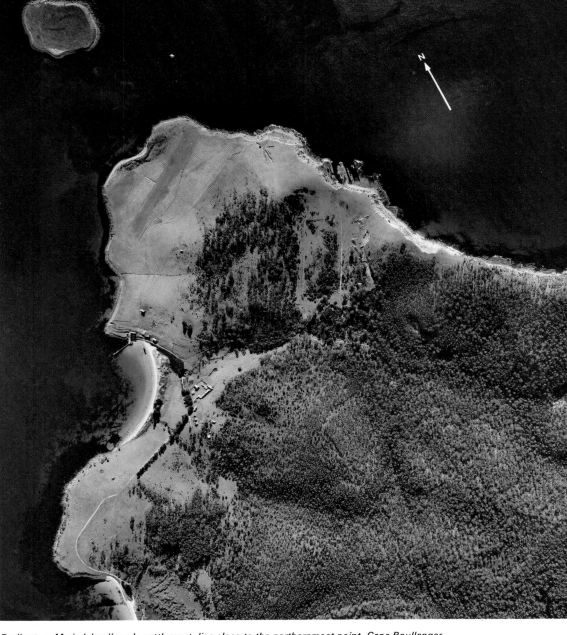

Darlington, Maria Island's only settlement, lies close to the northernmost point, Cape Boullanger

The island of broken dreams

PEACH TREES in fruit greeted Diego Bernacchi on his first visit to Maria Island in 1884. Flourishing untended for 34 years since the closure of the island's second penal settlement, they were a promising sign of the type of land the adventurous Italian needed for the silk and wine industries he had come to set up. On extensive land grants from the Tasmanian government, 50 000 vines from Victoria were planted, old convict buildings were renovated and the town of Darlington—renamed San Diego—supported a new population of 250 by 1888. At that year's Melbourne Exhibition, Bernacchi was able to display cement, marble, wine, fish, minerals and timber shipped from the small harbour in Darlington Bay. Business took a sharp turn for the worse in the depression of the 1890s. Bernacchi had over-reached himself financially and had to liquidate his Maria Island Company in 1892. By the end of the century Bernacchi had abandoned the island. It was not until after World War I that he returned—with an even more adventurous plan. In Melbourne and London he had floated a £600 000 company to set up a cement works, using limestone from Cape Boullanger and the Fossil Cliffs. Equipment was imported from Denmark and the works were opened in 1924, producing 30 000 tonnes in their first year. Output had to double for the enterprise to profit. Failing health forced Bernacchi away, and he died in Melbourne just over a year after the opening, leaving an estate valued at a mere £481 and a son who gained fame as an Antarctic explorer. The cement works, never viable, shut down in 1929.

Port Arthur

Port Arthur, once the centrepiece of the Van Diemen's Land convict system, is now the major crowd-puller of Tasmania's thriving tourist industry. At the height of the summer season as many as eight coaches travel daily between Hobart and the ill-famed penal settlement on Tasman Peninsula. They carry about 150 000 people each year—more than half of Tasmania's total number of visitors. Between 1830 and 1877 about 12 700 convicts passed through Port Arthur. It took habitual criminals, repeated offenders and those considered equally dangerous—educated prisoners. During the early 1840s more than 600 convicts occupied Port Arthur's prisons, and scores of other buildings were scattered around Mason Cove to house officers, soldiers and colonial administrators. Many

of the main thoroughfares of the old settlement have been maintained. Elsewhere, well-worn paths across wide lawns lead around the maze of imposing brick and stone ruins. A model of the township as it stood in the 1860s can be inspected at a visitor centre housed in a former insane asylum, with its clock tower and ornate brickwork intact. Maps and brochures are available to guide visitors around the buildings and a small museum displays tools and instruments used by and upon the convicts.

The asylum became the Tasman municipal town hall after the closure of the convict settlement, and was repaired after damage in bushfires which swept through the valley in 1895. Among the buildings which have fared less well is the partly restored model prison, where solitary confinement was introduced to replace the lash in 1852. The ravages of time and the elements have taken their toll on the settlement's main building, the penitentiary, originally constructed to

be a granary and mill. Weeds and saplings sprout from the top of its crumbling yellow brick walls, which dominate the shores of Mason Cove below the densely forested slopes of Mount Arthur. Steep, pointed roofs cap the small turrets decorating the shell of Port Arthur's ruined church, in the north of the settlement. The church was never consecrated because it was non-denominational—not, as legend would have it, because of supposed murders or a suicide during its construction by the convicts.

Port Arthur's residential and holiday houses cluster around the shores of Carnarvon Bay, overlooking jetties, sheltered moorings and the convict burial grounds on Dead Island. Towards Point Puer, golf links lie alongside a track leading to the scattered foundations which are all that remain of a boys' prison. Young masons trained at Point Puer shaped much of the sandstone used in buildings around Mason Cove. To the south a road skirts the crescent of Safety Cove and cuts

Mason Cove (top right), where convicts were landed to begin years of harsh servitude, faces across Carnarvon Bay to Dead Island, where many of them were buried

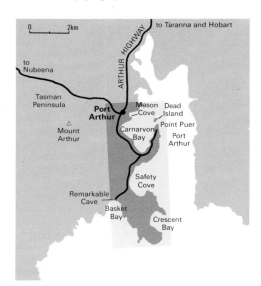

across a neck of land to a car park above the sheer red cliffs surrounding Basket Bay. A wooden walkway and stairs descend the cliff face to the floor of a deep, narrow inlet off the bay at the entrance to Remarkable Cave. The cave can be explored at low tide; looking seaward from inside it, the outline of its mouth bears some resemblance to the shape of Tasmania.

Ruins remain of timber mills at Premaydena and Koonya, and a coalmine at Slopen. Nubeena, an agricultural outstation during the convict period, has grown to replace Port Arthur as the centre of the peninsula's fruit-growing and fishing industries. It is a popular holiday resort, with facilities for fishing and boating enthusiasts. Taranna was the terminus of a wooden railway from Port Arthur which was powered by teams of convicts, hauling on ropes. The station building now houses paintings and historical relics; a

replica of an open carriage stands in the grounds. Nearby, a wildlife park beside a small stream displays native Tasmanian birds and mammals, including the bear-like Tasmanian devil, *Sarcophilus harrisii*, a carnivorous marsupial known for its fearsome snarl but easily tamed.

PORT ARTHUR on Arthur Highway 98 km from Hobart.
TRANSPORT: bus Hobart-Port Arthur daily.
YOUTH HOSTEL: open year-round.

	PORT ARTHUR											
	Jan	Feb	Mar	Apr	May	Jun	Jul	Aug	Sep	Oct	Nov	Dec
Rainfall mm	62	62	77	89	98	111	107	98	75	88	81	83
Rain days	11	10	12	13	15	16	16	16	14	15	14	12
Sunshine hrs	Summer 8+			Autumn 5+			Winter 4+			Spring 7+		

Bruny Island

Orchards scattered over Bruny Island had forerunners in trees planted by William Bligh of HMS *Bounty*, on the voyage that ended in mutiny. Bruny was sighted by Abel Tasman in 1642, but the first European navigator to go ashore was Tobias Furneaux of HMS *Adventure*, in 1773. Adventure Bay, east of the low, narrow isthmus that connects what are virtually two mountainous islands, was named for his ship. Its southern corner—now the main holiday area—offered a fine anchorage for ships rounding South East Cape and Tasman Head after a Roaring Forties crossing of the Southern Ocean. Mariners could find fresh water, food and timber on its sheltered shores. Bligh was first there in 1777, serving under Captain Cook. In anticipation of the founding of a New South Wales colony, which could make Adventure Bay a busy port of call, he was sent back in 1788 to augment its food sources. He planted fruit seedlings, strawberries, potatoes and watercress. Returning in 1792, he

Whalebone Point, jutting into the northern waters of Cloudy Bay, has good surf but rips are frequent; a big lagoon favoured by boat fishermen lies just north

Walking trails fan out from Adventure Bay, the landing place of many 18th-century navigators

found that only one apple tree had succeeded. But his cress was flourishing—it still grows along many of Bruny's creeks. Bligh made a last visit, as the newly ousted governor of NSW, in 1809. A museum at the bay, open 09.00-17.00 daily, is dedicated to him. It was built of stone from the ruins of a chapel at Variety Bay, constructed by convicts in the 1830s. Camping and caravan grounds border near the museum a creek from which the early navigators drew water.

Bruny Island has a resident population of less than 400, in small farming and fishing communities dotted around its many bays. Resort centres and groups of holiday cottages are clustered near white, sandy beaches at Dennes Point, Luna-wanna, Adventure Bay and Cookville. Alonnah is the administrative centre and boasts the island's only hotel, which overlooks d'Entrecasteaux Channel and the wide mouth of the Huon River. Patches of temperate rainforest, sheltered from the stiff south-westerlies which sweep across the southern tip of the island, occupy gullies on the slopes of Mount Mangana and surround the Waterfall Creek track to Mavista Falls. The walk is an easy hike of about an hour from a road branching south from the coast between Adventure Bay township and Cookville. Like most roads on the island it is unsealed and often deeply rutted, but safe at low speeds. The Fluted Cape State Reserve extends around the eastern shores of southern Bruny to East Cloudy Head. A short walking track from Cookville takes visitors through the reserve to Grass Point for views of Penguin Island, returning via Fluted Cape on a track above high cliffs. The route of an old railway leads from Cookville to abandoned granite quarries near Mangana Bluff and has become a popular walk through lightly forested country. Walks around Cloudy Bay are

rough and many maps currently available show tracks which have long been overgrown. A check with the island's ranger before beginning any extensive hiking in this area is advisable. The rocks and beaches of Cloudy Bay and its large lagoon are popular grounds for fishermen. Oysters are farmed commercially in the lagoon; large mud oysters, growing naturally, are also edible and may be taken by visitors. Strong rips off the bay's beaches make them unsafe for swimmers, but board-riders often find good waves around Whalebone Point. Colonies of little penguins, *Eudyptula minor*, have made their home around Bruny Island and are joined by flocks of 'mutton-bird' shearwaters, *Puffinus tenuirostris*, which breed in large rookeries between April and September. A sign alongside the isthmus road joining the two sections of the island warns that pen-

guins often use the strip as a crossing. Duck shooting in the autumn months is permitted in the Neck Game Reserve, an area of wetlands just north of the isthmus.

ADVENTURE BAY 73 km south of Hobart via Kettering and Barnes Bay.
TRANSPORT: bus Hobart-Kettering most days; vehicle and passenger ferry Kettering-Barnes Bay daily; bus Barnes Bay-Adventure Bay most days.

ADVENTURE BAY												
	Jan	Feb	Mar	Apr	May	Jun	Jul	Aug	Sep	Oct	Nov	Dec
Rainfall mm	68	56	92	93	90	103	102	109	86	99	80	86
Rain days	12	10	13	14	15	16	16	17	15	16	13	12
Sunshine hrs	Summer 7+			Autumn 5+			Winter 4+			Spring 6+		

Cox Bight, on Tasmania's remote southern coast, can be reached by aircraft which make beach landings

South and west coasts

The wilderness areas of Tasmania's rugged south-west confront visitors with a barrier of mountain ranges, river rapids, and dense rainforest—still unaltered and in parts unexplored. Overland contact from the east was impossible in the early days of settlement and even now few roads cross the central highlands. Those that do were stimulated by demand for minerals and hydro-electricity, and hard-won from an inhospitable terrain. Ports for the mineral-rich inland slopes around Queenstown, Zeehan and Dundas were the first settlements on the western coastline. The harbours were often in unsheltered gaps in the rocky shoreline, subject to the perpetual hazard of westerly gales from the Southern Ocean. When roads were cut through to the mines in the 1930s, shipping abandoned the west coast and the harbours fell into rapid decline. Trial Harbour, Granville Harbour and Temma are now no more than ghost towns or clusters of weekend fishing cottages with tank

water and no power. The rough tracks that reach them may be impassable to all but four-wheel-drive vehicles in wet weather.

Strahan, once the port for the Queenstown tin mines, is the largest west coast settlement. Fishing and tourism are now its economic mainstays, though some huon pine felled on remote river-banks is still floated down to mills on Macquarie Harbour. The wide, flat sands of Ocean Beach line 40 km of coast to the west. Picnic areas and camping grounds shelter on higher ground behind the beach, but strong rips discourage swimming. Protected bathing spots are found along the shores of Macquarie Harbour at West Strahan Beach and just inside the harbour entrance. Hells Gate, the narrow neck between the Southern Ocean and Macquarie Harbour, has a dangerously fast current at the turn of the tide, and even in the landlocked harbour steep, choppy waves can menace small craft. But the busy waterfront at Strahan indicates that there are still plenty of opportunities for cruising and fishing. Tourist launches cruise Macquarie Harbour most days, weather permitting, except during winter. Passengers are taken to the tiny, lighthouse-topped island caught in the mouth of

Hells Gate, the forested banks of the lower Gordon River and to Sarah Island (formerly Settlement Island), the site of the notorious convict establishment portrayed in Marcus Clark's novel *For The Term of His Natural Life*. The cancellation of the controversial hydro-electric scheme which would have flooded wilderness in the Gordon River's upper reaches was the greatest conservation victory in Australian history.

Port Davey, with its numerous small inlets and its sheltered inner haven, Bathurst Harbour, provides welcome protection for ships and yachts fleeing Southern Ocean storms. White, quartzite-studded hills tower above the wide inlet's button-grass wetlands, long deserted by bay whalers, huon pine sawyers, boatbuilders and prospectors who camped around its shores until the last decade of the 19th century. Now part of South West National Park (442 240 hectares), they are completely uninhabited. Walking tracks link them with Cockle Creek, south of Catamaran, 88 km from Hobart, and Scotts Peak Dam on Lake Pedder. The narrows between Port Davey and Bathurst Harbour are about half-way along the trail, which skirts Tasmania's southern coast before climbing inland. A landing strip on

Bathurst Harbour's Melaleuca Inlet allows walkers to fly in on aircraft chartered from Hobart, halving the 11-12 day walk. Dinghies pulled up on the shore are used for crossing Port Davey and New River Lagoon. Extra supplies must be carried because floods can swell rivers and creeks dangerously, causing long delays.

The Pieman River, north of the west coast mining towns, drains a big catchment area where the annual rainfall regularly reaches 2800 mm —not in sudden downpours, but steady falls, relentless drizzle and heavy mists which can continue for days on end. In a few hours floods can raise the river by as much as 15 metres in places where it is squeezed into gorges, overhung by dense, dripping rainforest. During summer a motor launch operated by the ranger of the Pieman River State Reserve descends the river's lower reaches from Corinna to headlands at its mouth. Boating and fishing enthusiasts can launch over a ramp at Corinna, where there are picnic areas and a bunkhouse for campers.

STRAHAN (pop. 402) west of Zeehan Highway 293 km from Hobart (turn off 4 km north of Queenstown).
TRANSPORT: coach Hobart-Queenstown most days (7 hrs); bus Queenstown-Strahan most days.

🖼 🏠 📷 ⛺ 🛏 💊 🍴 🖂 ⌚ ♿ ⛵

STRAHAN												
	Jan	Feb	Mar	Apr	May	Jun	Jul	Aug	Sep	Oct	Nov	Dec
Maximum C°	22	24	20	18	15	13	13	13	15	16	17	19
Minimum C°	10	11	9	9	7	5	5	5	7	7	7	9
Rainfall mm	88	96	92	169	176	158	168	194	188	148	104	115
Humidity %	61	60	65	71	77	79	73	70	68	66	67	63
Rain days	14	12	17	21	22	21	23	23	25	21	16	20
Sunshine hrs	Summer 7+			Autumn 3+			Winter 2+			Spring 5+		

Bass Strait islands

Between Tasmania and the Australian mainland more than 120 masses of land jut from the surface of Bass Strait. Some are mere outcrops of barren rock, and most are uninhabited. But the largest, Flinders and King Islands, support permanent populations of graziers, fishermen and miners. The islands and rocks are the peaks of mountains which towered over low-lying plains linking Tasmania with the Australian mainland before the sea level rose, about 8000 years ago. They still form a giant's causeway of stepping stones, never much more than 15 km apart, between Wilsons Promontory and north-west Tasmania. Rocks, reefs and shallow, stormy waters gave the strait a forbidding reputation last century. It was the graveyard of many ships, along with their passengers and crews. Modern charts continue to carry strong warnings of danger. Access to Flinders and King Islands is almost exclusively by air. Rental cars are available at the airstrips at Currie, on King Island, and Whitemark, on Flinders. Tracks take visitors to secluded coasts for walking, surfing, rock fishing and duck shooting. Scuba divers can explore more than 50 shipwrecks known to be scattered around King Island. Calm, reef-sheltered coves with clean shady beaches make for pleasant swimming and picnicking. Grassy, on the island's east coast, is a mining town employing about 300 people in big open-cut mines which extract scheelite, an ore which yields tungsten which is used for hardening steel and in lamp filaments.

Albatrosses, shearwaters, Cape Barren geese and little penguins are among the many sea birds which have permanent homes or breeding grounds in Bass Strait. Flinders Island's short-tailed shearwaters, known as muttonbirds, are the basis of its oldest surviving industry. Called 'birding', the annual harvest of thousands of chicks from rookery burrows supplies an export market in fat, oil, feathers and salted meat. In spite of that the breeding colonies remain crammed each year between September and April. Flinders' scenery—trackless hillside forests, flowering heathland and unspoilt beaches—attracts an increasing tourist traffic. The peaks of Strzelecki National Park (4215 hectares) provide challenging granite faces for rock climbers and bush trails for hikers and campers.

From Mount Strzelecki the view encompasses the shoals and island-studded channels of Franklin Sound and the mountain peaks on nearby Cape Barren Island. To the east the Logan Lagoon Wildlife Sanctuary protects a huge population of seabirds and waders.

Trefoil Island is typical of scores of tiny islets that dot the treacherous waters of Bass Strait

KING ISLAND (pop. 2592) 257 km north-west of Devonport.
TRANSPORT: flights from Melbourne, Launceston and Hobart most days.
YOUTH HOSTEL: 14 km from Currie, open year-round.

🖼 📷 🛏 ☎ ✈ 🅿 🍴 ⌚ 🌊 ♿ 🚤 ⚓

FLINDERS ISLAND (pop. 1039) 180 km north-east of Devonport.
TRANSPORT: flights from Launceston daily, from Melbourne some days.

🖼 🏠 📷 ⛺ 🛏 💊 🍴 🖂 ⌚ ♿ 🚤 ⚓

Calm days at Macquarie Harbour are rare, for this coast is notorious for its wild weather

Hobart

Australia's southernmost capital sits at the centre of a stretch of tortuous and rugged coast. Powerful South Tasman storms often push waves 20 km up the River Derwent to break against the sandy beaches that line Hobart's city shores. In winter the mountains overlooking the city are frequently cloaked in a mantle of snow.

Government House, sited beside the Derwent, gave up some of its grounds for the Botanic Gardens

Open-air shoppers throng Salamanca Place on Saturdays

Van Diemen's Land Folk Museum recaptures the 1830s

The Customs House brings grandeur to Constitution Dock

TASMANIA

River Derwent

Bridgewater

New Norfolk

Risdon Cove

Pitt Water

Carlton River

Dodges Ferry

Hobart

Bellerive

Carlton

Mount Wellington

Howrah

Frederick

Primrose Sands

Sandy Bay

Henry Bay

Cremorne

Kingston

Ralphs Bay

Blackmans Bay

Clifton Beach

South Arm

STORM BAY

Tasman Peninsula

D'Entrecasteaux Channel

Bruny Island

Hobart is internationally famous—for the yacht race from Sydney, and Australia's first casino in the foreground of the city as seen from Mt Nelson

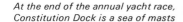

At the end of the annual yacht race, Constitution Dock is a sea of masts

Mountain flanks probed by the sea

FROM the crags atop Mount Wellington, 1270 metres above the wide River Derwent estuary, Hobart boasts the most spectacular coastal views of any Australian city. Streets from the port's busy waterfront climb into increasingly steep gullies and wooded slopes at the base of the mountain, and lookout points perch alongside the sole road to its summit. When the veils of cloud which often cover the windswept peak lift and winter snows allow access, the view embraces all points of the compass. At the mountain's foot the city spreads in ribbons along the Derwent banks, hemmed in by the high ridges of the Wellington and Meehan Ranges. To the south and east, patches of river and bay waters and the Tasman Sea gleam between the islands and peninsulas studded along the coast. To the west a belt of highlands stretches to the source of the Derwent in Tasmania's rugged central plateau.

Hobart's centre is 20 km upstream from the mouth of the Derwent, but anglers and boating enthusiasts are well acquainted with swells which can roll in from the open sea through Storm Bay to trouble the wide, shallow body of water. In calm weather the estuary makes a superb yachting basin, with easy access out to sea, into nearby bays and along d'Entrecasteaux Channel, a passage between the mainland and Bruny Island indented by coves sheltering fishing villages and small holiday settlements. Sandy beaches fringe much of the convoluted coastline near Hobart, with fine surfing waves forming in the more exposed sections of Storm Bay and Frederick Henry Bay. Wharves and jetties dotted along the shores provide the most popular casting positions for land-based anglers.

Saltwater reaches of the Derwent extend 36 km past Hobart to the river's head of navigation at New Norfolk. Rapids bar the narrowing waterway farther upstream. Salt and fresh waters mingle over a shallow river bottom at Bridgewater, but to the west the Derwent flows in two layers. Denser salt water sinks to the bottom and the strong current of fresh water flows on top, creating two fishing environments much to the enjoyment of sporting anglers. Lyell Highway skirts the southern Derwent banks as far as New Norfolk and boats can be hired in Hobart for cruising upriver past pasture

land and under tall river cliffs. Tasmania's abundant supply of hydro-electricity—some generated from dams in the upper reaches of the Derwent itself—has attracted heavy industries to the western shores of the Derwent north of the city's Tasman Bridge, including Australia's only producer of newsprint.

Spreading around Government House, near the western approaches to the bridge, the parklands and sports fields of Queens Domain reach towards the water's edge and act as a buffer between the city and the stretch of industrial installations. Adjacent to Government House are the Royal Tasmanian Botanic Gardens. A sixth of their area of more than 13 hectares was once part of the vice-regal grounds. During construction of the present Government House, George Arthur, governor of Tasmania from 1824 to 1836, oversaw the establishment of the gardens on land which had been farmed since the earliest years of the Van Diemen's Land colony. In 1828, a huge collection of plants from all over the world was founded with some 2000 vines and fruit trees imported by the gardens' first superintendent, William Davidson. Davidson's residence, which also housed the team of convicts who laboured to establish and maintain the gardens, now houses a botanic museum and education centre.

Downstream from Hobart the River Derwent makes its way out to sea, flowing past beach suburbs which hug the western banks at Taroona, Kingston Beach and Blackmans Bay. Research teams for the most far-flung section of coastline under Australian control, the Australian Antarctic Territory, use Hobart as their home port and have established headquarters at Kingston Beach. On weekdays their small museum exhibits equipment and photographs from past Australian polar expeditions, natural history displays and some of the specialised technology used at present-day bases. Scattered holiday settlements and orchards on the narrow peninsula of the South Arm district line the eastern banks of the Derwent near its mouth. Launches from Hobart cruise along the river's southern reaches on half-day tours which lead into d'Entrecasteaux Channel as far as the fishing village and Bruny Island ferry terminal at Kettering in Little Oyster Cove. Shorter cruises take in harbour sights around the city.

Second thoughts at Risdon Cove

AT RISDON COVE, 8 km upriver from Hobart's city centre, infra-red photography and geophysical surveys have helped archaeologists to uncover the scattered foundation and chimney ruins of Tasmania's first settlement, founded in September 1803. The cove is preserved as a historic site, where striking pyramid-shaped visitor centres present audiovisual displays covering its pioneer history, a collection of artefacts from the archaeological digs and a model of the settlement reconstructed from early reports and maps. Pathways around the cove lead to the digs and a hilltop where huts for two settler families, nine soldiers and 30 convicts were located.

George Bass and Matthew Flinders had suggested the site in 1798. A 23-year-old naval lieutenant, John Bowen, was given command of the colonising party, which was assembled because Governor King of New South Wales wanted to relieve overcrowding of convicts at Sydney and to pre-empt a possible French claim to Van Diemen's Land. When the colonists arrived, Bowen described Risdon Cove as 'more like a nobleman's park in England than an uncultivated country', and all hands were called to the task of building temporary shelters. The convicts laboured from daybreak till sunset, with an hour off for breakfast and two hours for dinner. Within three months masons had hewn stone from a nearby quarry and completed farm buildings and a store.

But the work was wasted. A senior officer, Colonel David Collins, arrived in February 1804 with his own party of colonists from Port Phillip Bay—now the site of Melbourne. Collins disagreed with the choice of Risdon Cove. The landing place on Risdon Creek was accessible only at certain tides, and the surrounding land was so low that he feared for the safety of stores and buildings. Claims about the fertility of the valley were exaggerated, Collins found. After a short exploration downriver he chose instead Sullivans Cove, on the western shore of the Derwent. Some buildings at Risdon were dismantled for use in the new Hobart Town. Others fell victim to fire and decay, as have the expansive houses, fountains and garden terraces built by later residents of the cove's farming land. Much of the cove itself has silted over since Bowen's party landed, but the low ground around the creek and the gently sloping hills of the valley remain largely unaltered—passed over by the property developers who have crowded the Derwent shores west of Risdon with sprawling suburbs and industrial estates.

Sullivans Cove, a beautiful blend of the old and new

HOBART	Jan	Feb	Mar	Apr	May	Jun	Jul	Aug	Sep	Oct	Nov	Dec
Maximum C°	22	22	20	18	14	12	12	13	15	17	18	20
Minimum C°	12	12	11	9	7	5	5	5	6	8	9	11
Rainfall mm	45	41	44	52	50	57	54	49	53	60	61	56
Humidity %	50	52	51	53	58	60	62	57	51	50	53	53
Rain days	11	9	11	13	14	14	15	15	15	17	15	13
Sunshine hrs	Summer 7 +			Autumn 5 +			Winter 4 +			Spring 6 +		

Beyond the Tasman Bridge soars Mt Wellington, whose pinnacle—1271 metres above sea level—offers one of the finest panoramas in Tasmania

City and Bellerive

Sullivans Cove, a snug haven off the wide estuary of the River Derwent, shelters a bustling port in the heart of Hobart. Liners and freighters berth alongside docks crammed with fishing boats—joined every New Year by yachts finishing races from Sydney and Melbourne. The cove's shape has been greatly altered since its shelter and fresh water prompted Colonel David Collins to site a settlement there in 1804. Landfills and dredging have made small nearshore islands part of the waterfront, and the course of a creek which watered the township has long been diverted and covered by the business district and suburbs which grew behind the port's warehouses. In Salamanca Place, just a short distance from the waterfront, a row of the pitched-roof sandstone buildings which give Hobart its distinctive character remain in good repair. The warehouses and bond stores, built between the 1830s and the 1860s, face a wide, tree-lined thoroughfare; some of them now house restaurants, souvenir shops and art and craft galleries. Clothing, food and bric-a-brac are sold under umbrellas in an open-air market each Saturday morning. The history of the colonial port is well depicted in three museums in the suburb of Battery Point, which flanks the southern wharf of Sullivans Cove and is best explored on foot. The Tasmanian Maritime Museum, at the rear of St Georges Church in Cromwell Street, displays a fine collection of relics from the early days of shipping and whaling around the island. The Van Dieman's Land Folk Museum, in an 1830s mansion, Narryna, exhibits furniture, utensils and clothing used by the Tasmanian pioneers. On Castray Esplanade, near the gardens of Princes Park, the Post Office Museum (closed on Sundays) traces the development of post and telegraph services with documents, photographs and equipment.

To the south of Battery Point, at the northern end of Sandy Bay, moored pleasure craft crowd the nearshore river waters and jetties and slipways line the banks. The 17 storeys of Australia's first casino-hotel tower above the bay on Wrest Point. The 300-bedroom hotel and its three res-

taurants, cabaret room, and four gaming areas hold well over 4000 people during its busiest periods. Farther south the narrow sandy strip of Long Beach curves around Sandy Bay Point, backed by shaded picnic grounds and playing fields. The beach is popular with city sunbathers, though swimmers are more often tempted downriver or across to Bellerive for cleaner waters.

Bellerive and Howrah became increasingly popular with city-dwellers after the completion of the Tasman Bridge in 1964. New housing developments sprang up on the eastern banks of the Derwent. But in 1975 the ore carrier *Lake Illawarra* ploughed into the bridge, destroying two of its support columns and sinking under the weight of rubble. Twelve people were killed. For the two years it took to repair the bridge, eight

ferries including two former Sydney Harbour boats were needed to transport commuters to and from the city. Otherwise they faced a 42 km journey around to the nearest river crossing at Bridgewater. A ferry still runs to the city from Bellerive Quay, frequently during peak traffic hours and intermittently at other times. Shops cluster on the Kangaroo Bay esplanade, near the ferry wharf, and a yacht club and marina dominate the waterfront. Boats can be launched alongside the clubhouse and across the bay at Rosny Park, close to the greens of a bowling club and the fairways of Rosny's public golf course. From the bowling club, generously equipped picnic grounds dotted with pines curve around Rosny Point below a lookout drive atop the parkland of Rosny Hill. From Bellerive Quay around

Kangaroo Bluff, a scenic drive above low cliffs climbs to the Battery Bluff Reserve. Superb views of Mount Wellington and the city skyline rising above the Derwent spread out before the reserve's grassy slopes. Two muzzle-loading cannon are all that remain of the once-powerful battery of guns which were the bluff's fortifications in the late 19th century, when all Australia feared a Russian invasion. To the south the reserve looks out over the popular sandy stretches of Bellerive and Howrah Beaches, both backed by playing fields and with easy access and small areas for parking.

Hobart's docks and yacht clubs on Sandy Bay face beaches on the eastern banks of the River Derwent

Echoes of a pioneer port

HOBART, more than any other Australian seaport, has held onto its original buildings. It was spared the mercantile frenzies that accompanied mainland gold booms and led to willy-nilly redevelopment in other cities. Many structures from the first half of the 19th century survived. Now, though they occupy prime sites by the River Derwent, they are prized.

A stroll between the docks and Battery Point, through the streets that radiate from Sullivans Cove, affords glimpses of the Georgian colonial settlement Hobart once was. The oldest remaining buildings are clustered behind Constitution Dock, between Davey and Macquarie Streets. They include the sandstone Commissariat Store, started in 1808 when the township was only four years old, and a cottage built before 1815. Along with a big brick bond store, dating from 1824, they are used as administrative quarters for the neighbouring Tasmanian Museum.

Parliament House, at the head of Salamanca Place, originated in 1835 as a customs house and gave its name to the nearby Customs House Hotel, first licensed in 1844. Along Salamanca Place itself, handsome sandstone warehouses and bond stores of similar age lead a thriving new existence as boutiques and galleries for tourists. An expansion of the precinct, in progress during 1986, uses traditional sandstone and brick in a style that matches the old buildings.

Westella, in Elizabeth Street, was known in its day as the most splendid private home in Australia. Built for a wool merchant in 1835, it served unofficially as a town hall: Queen Victoria's accession to the throne was proclaimed from its steps in 1837. Other dwellings dating from the Georgian period include a charming group of artisans' cottages on Battery Point and graceful estate houses on former farmland at New Town.

Stoke House at New Town

Salamanca Place: boutiques and galleries from old warehouses

Old Magistrates' Court: stern and sturdy

An artisan's cottage on Battery Point, built perhaps for a shipwright

Old mercantile and port offices flank Franklin wharf

Sunnyside's *inviting entrance, New Town*

How Sunnyside *stablehands were summoned*

Narryna, *now a folk museum*

0 — 5km

TASMAN HIGHWAY

Pitt Water

ARTHUR

to Eaglehawk
Neck

to Hobart

Hobart
Airport

HIGHWAY

Seven Mile Beach

Tiger Head Bay

Dodges Ferry

Carlton

Spectacle Island

Carlton River

Spectacle Head

Carlton
Beach

Carlton Bluff

Primrose
Sands

Primrose
Beach

Gypsy
Bay

Renard Point

Primrose Point

Frederick Henry
Bay

Green Head

Sloping Island

Black Rock
Hill

Cremorne

Pipe Clay
Lagoon

Tasman
Peninsula

Clifton
Beach

Storm Bay

*Shallow Pipe Clay Lagoon, behind Clifton Beach,
almost empties of water at low tide*

Frederick Henry Bay

Spectacle Head shields the deep entrance channel to Pitt Water from the regular lines of ocean waves that push into Frederick Henry Bay

Hobart's two patrolled surfing beaches seem sheltered by the islands and peninsulas off Tasmania's south-east coast. But swells travelling north into Storm Bay and Frederick Henry Bay break with considerable force on the long, uncluttered, sandy shores of Clifton and Carlton Beaches, producing excellent board-riding waves and strong rips which keep lifesavers busy in summer. At the western end of Clifton Beach the cracked faces of limestone rocks slope steeply to the sea from clifftop pastures. The beach's lifesaving club is hidden from the bay by thickly grassed dunes and backed by pine trees contorted by the persistent onshore winds. To the north, a sealed road curves around the shallow tidal inlet of Pipe Clay Lagoon to a boat-launching ramp at Cremorne. The ramp is simply a continuation of the road skirting the lagoon's eastern shores and cars with trailers can park on the hard sand beyond the end of the road. At high water the lagoon provides sheltered swimming and its deeper channel is a safe anchorage. Anglers launching into the lagoon can make for offshore bay waters for fishing.

Facing Cremorne in the north-western corner of Frederick Henry Bay are low dunes backing the long, flat curve of Carlton Beach. The surf clubhouse is the only building on the beach, though holiday cottages and houses are strung out behind the dunes to Dodges Ferry in the north. At the southern end of the beach hard, grey sand spreads out around the mouth of the Carlton River, its narrow channel flowing between the grey rocks of sparsely wooded Carlton Bluff and grassed dunes on the river's west bank. North of Spectacle Head, red clay cliffs drop to smooth beach sands and rusting boatsheds on the waterfront. Immediately offshore the small hump of Spectacle Island breaks the surface of the glittering water, two trees sprouting from its grass-covered knob and a patch of sandy beach lining its northern shores. The boat ramp at Tiger Head Bay, at the mouth of the inlet to Pitt Water, runs to the bay between wooden and corrugated iron shacks. Directly opposite Tiger Head Bay a line of pine trees backs the dunes of Seven Mile Beach, reached along Pitt Water Road, just east of Hobart Airport.

The township of Dodges Ferry, like most of the settlements around Frederick Henry Bay, consisted mainly of weekend cottages until the 1960s, when Hobart commuters began to move in. Modern brick bungalows and tall A-frame timber houses share the town with old, weather-worn shacks. New subdivisions at Bally Park and Primrose Sands have opened the area to greater numbers of Hobart residents. Scattered cottages and the sale signs of an expanding real estate development overlook the long ribbon of Primrose Beach from the slopes behind Renard Point. Roadside lookouts give sweeping views over Frederick Henry Bay and the hills which appear to enclose the sea in every direction. To the south are the naked rock edges of Green Head and Black Rock Hill at the northern end of Tasman Peninsula. A general store, Primrose Sands' sole commercial facility, sits at the eastern end of the beach with playground equipment behind the beach's steep dune ridge. Around Primrose Point, boatsheds with narrow wooden jetties line the pebble shore of Gypsy Bay, where a concrete ramp feeds over the rim of stones.

Subject index